Hitler's War Against the Partisans during the Stalingrad Offensive

DEDICATION

This book is dedicated to
Alexei Anatolyevich Navalny
Rest in peace

Hitler's War Against the Partisans during the Stalingrad Offensive

Spring 1942 to the Spring of 1943

Dr Antonio J. Muñoz

AN IMPRINT OF PEN & SWORD BOOKS LTD
YORKSHIRE – PHILADELPHIA

First published in Great Britain in 2025 by
FRONTLINE BOOKS
an imprint of Pen & Sword Books Ltd
Yorkshire – Philadelphia

ISBN 978-1-03612-531-8

A CIP catalogue record for this book is available from the British Library.

Typeset by Concept, Huddersfield, West Yorkshire, HD4 5JL
Printed on paper from a sustainable source by
CPI Group (UK) Ltd, Croydon CR0 4YY

MIX
Paper | Supporting responsible forestry
FSC® C013604

The Publisher's authorised representative in the EU for product safety is Authorised Rep Compliance Ltd, Ground Floor, 71 Lower Baggot Street, Dublin D02 P593, Ireland – www.arccompliance.com

For a complete list of Pen & Sword titles please contact
PEN & SWORD BOOKS LTD
47 Church Street, Barnsley, South Yorkshire, S70 2AS, England
E-mail: enquiries@pen-and-sword.co.uk
Website: www.pen-and-sword.co.uk
or
PEN & SWORD BOOKS
1950 Lawrence Rd, Havertown, PA 19083, USA
E-mail: uspen-and-sword@casematepublishers.com
Website: www.penandswordbooks.com

Contents

List of plates

Author's Note

A regime, of whatever kind, collapses only under the weight of defeat.
[Benito Mussolini]

History is cyclical

John Gray was one of only a few academics in the world who anticipated, and warned of, the coming economic collapse of 2008. He claims that economic boom periods in the market can be deceptive, given that history is cyclical. The key word we should take note of is 'cyclical', meaning that history is never progressive but recurring. In simple terms, history repeats itself. With regard to history repeating itself, I have observed numerous parallels between Adolf Hitler and Vladimir Putin, proving Dr Gray's analysis of repeating cycles. Back in the 1930s and 1940s it was expansionist dictatorships that threatened the world. Although Benito Mussolini and the Empire of Japan represented a threat to peace, Adolf Hitler and Nazism were the greater dangers. Today Xi Jinping is pushing communist China into a more aggressive stance with regard to the South China Sea and the issue of Taiwan.

Yet it is Vladimir Putin of the Russian Federation who is now the larger danger to world peace. During the past ten years, our world has seen the rise of autocrats all over the planet. Many nations are now run by authoritarian regimes. Examples that immediately come to mind are Kim Jong-un of North Korea, Bashar al-Assad of Syria, Viktor Orbán of Hungary, Recep Tayyip Erdoğan of Turkey, Daniel Ortega of Nicaragua, Nicolas Maduro of Venezuela, Miguel Diaz-Canel of Cuba, Aleksander Lukashenko of Belarus, Ramzan Kadirov of Chechnya and, of course, Vladimir Putin of the Russian Federation. The list of autocrats is much longer. In fact, in the past seventeen years there has been a decline in democracy around the world. Only twenty-five nations have seen improvements in human rights and advances in liberal reforms, while a whopping sixty nations have slipped into authoritarianism.[1]

That is more than double the number of nations who have come closer to democracy. If our twentieth-century history is our guidepost, and if this trend continues, then we will likely see more conflicts brought on by men who call themselves 'General Secretary', 'Chairman', 'Supreme Leader' or even 'President for Life'. In particular, Vladimir Putin has been active in exporting his despotism beyond the borders of the Russian Federation. That is what sets him apart from other despots. While most authoritarian leaders today are content with oppressing their own people, Vladimir Putin has begun 'exporting' his dictatorship to other nations. Of course, I'm referring to the current invasion of Ukraine. The parallels between Hitler and Putin, as we shall see, are there for anyone to observe if they care to notice.

Waiting in the wings, much like Benito Mussolini did from 1939 to 1940, Xi Jinping of China is looking to see if Putin gets away with carving up Ukraine. Like Putin, Xi Jinping has an eye on conquering land outside the current borders of mainland China. In addition to building artificial islands in the South China Sea, then claiming 'territorial waters' around them, the Chinese communist government in Beijing has always claimed that Taiwan is a 'breakaway' province that rightfully belongs to mainland China. Taiwan was established on the island of Formosa after General Chiang Kai Shek and the Nationalist forces lost the Chinese civil war in 1949. If Putin succeeds in taking Ukraine, the Chinese communist leader may feel emboldened to make a similar attempt to grab Taiwan by force, sooner rather than later.

The long Russian authoritarian winter

In 1960 Gerald Reitlinger published a groundbreaking study titled *The House built on Sand: The Conflicts of German Policy in Russia, 1941–1945*. Dr Reitlinger explained how the German attempt at empire-building in the East failed, given the absurd and counterproductive Nazi policies towards the very people whom they wished to rule. This work was released around the height of the Cold War. It was timely then because it showed, among other things, that many of the people who inhabited the Soviet Union had been, and continued to be, unhappy with the communist system. The establishment of the 'Iron Curtain', as Winston Churchill described it in 1946, imprisoned not only those peoples living within the borders of the Union of Soviet Socialist Republics (USSR), but all of eastern Europe as well. The population in these areas chafed at the lack of freedom and inaccessibility to even basic consumer goods that were needed for everyday life. The Soviet system stifled individuality and offered only repression, deprivation and harshness to its citizens.

Vladimir Lenin's Bolshevik state was not that dissimilar to the Czar's rule when it came to repression. In fact, Lenin's government proved to be harsher than the Czars had ever been. Joseph Stalin's rule (1924–1953) was even more severe. Current estimates by Russian scholars as to the number of people who perished as a result of Stalin's regime stand at around 20 million. The only one to beat that record is Adolf Hitler. The communist state that followed under Nikita Khrushchev (beginning in 1953) and Leonid Brezhnev (in 1964) was, in many ways, not as repressive as the Stalinist period, but the system had not altered substantially enough for the population of the Soviet Union to enjoy the benefits that come from living in a free society. In that communist 'utopia', individuals could not question or criticize the state. Doing so was to risk ostracism, alienation or even imprisonment. People also lived in fear that someone would inform on them if they were overheard complaining about the state or said the 'wrong thing'.

Free travel was not permitted and individuals could not enjoy the benefits that come from economic independence, except for high party officials who received rewards that the common Soviet citizen could only dream of. In essence, the autocracy of the Czars and the dictatorship of the Leninist and Stalinist period gave way to the oligarchy of the old guard in the Central Committee of the Communist Party. Throughout the communist period, citizens of the USSR would spend hours standing in bread lines or queueing at the local department store, hoping to be able to purchase provisions or scarce consumer goods. This was because most of the nation's GDP was going to the production of military hardware.

Why did Russia end up as a kleptocracy?

When Brezhnev died in 1982, Yuri Andropov, another old-timer from the Central Committee, was elected General Secretary of the Communist Party. Andropov died in 1984 after serving less than two years, at which point another old-timer, Konstantine Chernenko, was elected. Chernenko lasted an even shorter time than Andropov, dying in 1985, not even a year after assuming office. Members of the Central Committee thereupon chose a candidate significantly younger than most of the old guard who had served up until then. The hope was that this new General Secretary would not have to be replaced in a couple of years. This turned out to be Mikhail Gorbachev. Gorbachev was born in 1931 of a Russian father and Ukrainian mother. Employing what he called *Glasnost* (openness) and *Perestroika* (restructuring), Gorbachev set about trying to reorganize the Soviet economic and political system. The job seemed insurmountable, but Gorbachev began to make slow progress.

However, the changes that he was implementing seemed so progressive and democratic that in 1991 the hardliners in the Communist Party attempted a coup against Gorbachev. The coup ultimately failed, and that failure led directly to the collapse of the USSR and the formation of the Russian Federation under Boris Yeltsin. The establishment of the Russian Federation in 1991 seemed to bring hope that perhaps the long Russian 'authoritarian winter' might break, and democracy could finally take hold. Unfortunately, two things occurred which quickly halted the swing towards democracy. First, instead of trying to support the newly created democratic institutions in Russia, the United States declared victory in the Cold War and set about establishing itself as the sole superpower in the world. Secondly, the appointment of Vladimir Putin as president of the Russian Federation in 1999 eventually condemned Russia's newly born democracy to a slow death.

Putin, a KGB hardliner and a true believer in the Soviet communist system, worked slowly at first, crippling and undermining the newly created democratic institutions in Russia. In this he adopted the old Benito Mussolini adage: 'If you pluck a chicken one feather at a time, no one will notice.' So, following this method, Putin usurped the democratic checks and balances in the country and slowly created the kleptocracy that exists in Russia today. Putin was not alone in this. He had help from people who felt as he did. The Weimar Republic was likewise undermined by officials who resented democracy and longed for a return to the rule of the *Kaiser*. Still others wished for a new authoritarian leader to emerge. These men worked against the republic from within, subverting the government. The parallels here between the failed Weimar Republic and the failed attempt to bring true democracy to Russia are obvious.

Where was the United States?

Following the collapse of the USSR, the United States (US) involved itself in several conflicts, some of which were not of its making, like Saddam Hussein's invasion of Kuwait in 1991 and the 2001 attack on America by Al Qaeda. But in 2003 the US elected to invade Iraq. This was a war of choice that ultimately proved to be costly and debilitating to the US in terms of lives lost, the huge financial expense of the conflict, and the loss of political capital around the world. George Bush Jr opted for a pre-emptive policy that said the US would act if it saw a threat in the making. This unnecessary conflict also helped to destabilize the delicate political balance in the Middle East. While it was true that Al Qaeda was responsible for attacking the US on 11 September 2001, its presence was in Afghanistan, not Iraq. In order to justify the invasion of Iraq, the US government accused Saddam Hussein of having weapons of mass destruction. Hussein was also blamed for conspiring with Al Qaeda, even though those in the US government knew very well that Hussein was a secular tyrant, who would not have allowed a fundamentalist theocratic movement like Al Qaeda into his country.

By 2003 Saddam Hussein was no longer a threat to the US or even to his Arab or Persian neighbours. After his defeat in 1991, he had been content to remain within the borders of Iraq and butcher his own people. However, the neo-conservatives in the George Bush Jr administration saw an opportunity for regime change, under the twin guises of the pre-emptive policy and of fighting Al Qaeda. They felt this change could occur at the point of a gun, and that ousting Hussein would alter the political landscape of the Middle East in favour of the US. The political situation in the Middle East did change after the invasion of Iraq, but it was not the change for which the neo-conservatives had hoped. The nation that in the end benefited most from Saddam Hussein's fall was the Islamic Republic of Iran. Today Iraq has close relations and partners with Iran, while the US has lukewarm relations with Iraq. At great cost in human life and financial expense, the US has inadvertently aided a sworn enemy (Iran).

Hubris, it seemed, had taken the US to a place where it was completely invested in what would become the longest conflict it had ever fought. Initially in Afghanistan, only limited US forces were employed, backed up by local warlords whose allegiance was not guaranteed. The US had used few forces at the start of the Afghan war because it was saving the bulk of the troops for the invasion of Iraq. As a result, the one chance to capture Osama bin Laden early, at Tora Bora, was lost because one of the Afghan 'allies' was bought off and turned a blind eye while Osama bin Laden and his cohorts slipped away. Mistakes were also made in Iraq once the country was occupied.

The first mistake was placing a minority Shiite leader to head the new Iraqi government. After a lifetime of being abused by the Sunni majority, the Shiites were dying for payback. Nouri al-Maliki began to favour the Shiites, while the Sunni were marginalized. Another mistake was the United States government's decision to disband the entire Iraqi Army, using the Coalition Provisional Authority. The Iraqi Army employed hundreds of thousands of Sunnis. The consequences of demobilizing so many Sunni men would prove to be detrimental. These decisions, and others, led directly to further alienation and resentment among the Sunni population. Many former Iraqi soldiers, now out of work and seeing their country led by a Shiite leader bent on weakening the power of the Sunni majority, were easily radicalized. These ex-Iraqi Army soldiers became ready recruits for a new terrorist organization: ISIS. Slowly but steadily, attacks against US troops in Iraq began to increase.

The demise of the fledgling Russian democracy

While the US was distracted with its Iraqi adventure, Russia was struggling to establish its democratic institutions. The period from 1991 to 1999, I would venture to say, was very similar to the period of the Weimar Republic from 1921 to 1933. A nation that was only accustomed to one form of authoritarianism or another (Germany in 1921 and Russia in 1991) was asked to accept democratic institutions and to embrace them willingly. As stated earlier, as in the Weimar Republic, there were people in the new Russian government who opposed democracy. The principal opponent in Russia's bid for liberalism was Vladimir Putin. When he was appointed President of the Russian Federation (after Boris Yeltsin retired), he was in a perfect position to attack that nascent Russian democracy from within. Just as Putin was given the position of President of the Russian Federation in 1999, Hitler was given the position of Chancellor of Germany in 1933, and just like Putin, he began to undermine the Weimar Republic until he obtained the dictatorship that he wanted. Again, the parallels between both men are obvious.

Putin was a child of the communist system and was wholly indoctrinated in the principles that had kept the USSR together. Using patience and the dirty tricks of his former KGB trade, he employed bribery, coercion and blackmail, and even worked with the Russian and Chechen mafia to eliminate or intimidate politicians, industrialists and reporters, forcing them to bend to his will. Those who refused to be subverted were killed. Those critics whom Putin could not reach because they were living outside the Russian Federation were eventually killed as well. It became quite common for Russian dissidents to be poisoned with Polonium-210 by agents of the Russian Federation's Federal Security Service (FSB), many of whom were former KGB members. For example, Russian dissident Alexander Litvinenko was poisoned in 2006. In 2015 another dissident, Boris Nemtsov, was assassinated while taking a walk near the Kremlin. Those who are in the know claim that it was the Chechen mafia who killed Nemtsov, yet the person who benefited most from his murder was Vladimir Putin. While living in the United Kingdom, Sergei Skripal and his daughter were poisoned using Novichok in 2018. In 2020 Alexei Navalny, a brave critic of Putin, was poisoned. He survived, only to be charged with false corruption charges that sent him to jail for thirteen years. Navalny died on 16 February 2024. He was only 47 years old. Many people had warned Navalny not to return to Russia, for fear of what would happen. Nevertheless, this courageous critic of Putin refused to be cowed. Like so many before him, he paid the ultimate price for defending democracy in Russia. Since the start of the Second Chechen War (in 2000), more than 200 Russian politicians and reporters from television and print media have been assassinated in Russia, a number that parallels the number of moderate and left-leaning German politicians and newspaper editors who were killed by right-wing assassins during the period of the Weimar Republic. Slowly, Putin has destroyed or usurped the new democratic institutions in Russia, including a free press. Adolf Hitler did the same thing.

The Russian parliament has become simply a rubber stamp for Putin's wishes and desires in much the same way that members of the *Reichstag* became a rubber stamp for Hitler. Newspaper and TV reporters in Russia must toe the line and only present to the Russian people the version of history and events that Putin wants to show them. This is yet another parallel with Hitler's Third Reich. Once he was certain that his position as President of the Russian Federation was secure for another twenty years, Putin lamented openly that the collapse of the Soviet Union was the greatest calamity to befall the world in the twentieth century. We hear today, as the Russian invasion of Ukraine continues to wreak destruction, pain, misery and death, that the majority of Russians support Putin's war and his version of events. The ludicrous and spurious accusation by Putin that he is eliminating Nazis from the Ukrainian government is simply an excuse for aggression.

Unfortunately, he is believed by the majority of Russians. It's not merely the *babushkas* who believe him, but middle-aged people and even young adults. This is because Vladimir Putin has turned what were independent and impartial Russian news outlets into the political mouthpiece of his regime. Those who are not fooled do not dare to speak openly. The situation has not been helped by the fact that the majority of the Russian people have not experienced true democracy and its advantages for any serious amount of time. Not knowing any better, perhaps some Russians actually prefer the harshness and repression of a police state, simply because it is familiar to them.

Professor Jeffrey Herff, an expert on the history of the Weimar Republic, remarked in 1986 that the Weimar Republic 'was a republic without republicans'. This was echoed by Sebastian Ullrich in a work that was released in 2009.[2] Both claimed that the German people at the time were only accustomed to authoritarian rule, and therefore were less inclined to support a democratic government when it was offered to them, especially when there were anti-democratic agents working from within to undermine that very democracy. This is the same scenario that Russia has experienced since 1999. It is also another reason why democracy was not firmly embedded in Russian society. Granted, there were some in Russia who tried to defend the newly created independent institutions, like a free press. Many who did so were targeted and paid the ultimate price. Putin and his cronies made sure of that, and that democracy would not flower in Russia. Taking all of this into account, we can say that the parallels between the history of the Weimar Republic and the Russian Federation are undeniable.

A forgotten lesson from the past

While the US was spending much human capital and economic effort being the sole superpower of the world, fighting both a war of consequence and a war of choice, what it should have been doing was supporting Russia's young democracy by all means. Frankly, the Americans dropped the ball, forgetting their own history. Back in 1918, when the First World War ended, President Woodrow Wilson wished to aid the newly established democracies of Europe that had been created from the ashes of four former empires. He wanted to do this by sending both money and experts to those new democratic nations in Europe. Two things put a stop to this. First, Wilson had a stroke towards the end of his second term that incapacitated him for about a year. Second, the US Congress refused to allocate any funds towards supporting the new democracies of Europe. Instead, the US became isolationist and ignored Europe altogether.

Within twenty years (by 1938), the only true democracy left in central Europe was Czechoslovakia.[3] In that same year Adolf Hitler's threats yielded appeasement from the West yet again.[4] At Munich, Adolf Hitler was able to acquire the Sudetenland from Czechoslovakia, after he promised Neville Chamberlain and Édouard Daladier that he would make no further territorial demands. The Sudetenland was a stretch of frontier border between Germany and Czechoslovakia that contained a sizeable *volksdeutsch* (ethnic German) population. The Sudetenland also happened to contain the principal mountain defences for Czechoslovakia. At Munich, Édouard Daladier of France and Neville Chamberlain of the United Kingdom didn't even bother inviting the Czechs to the negotiating table. Benito Mussolini, who really had nothing to do with the problem, showed up at the meeting uninvited, but was given a seat, while the Czechs, whose future was being decided, were left out.

When the Germans acquired the Sudetenland, they effectively stripped the country of its defensive fortifications along the Czech-German border. Months later, in March 1939, Hitler's armies quietly marched in and took over what was left of the Czechoslovakian nation. Hitler's troops entered Prague during a heavy snowstorm, which ironically intimated the dark period ahead for the Czech people. Had the US supported the new democracies of Europe after the First World War, events might have had a different outcome. In 1991, instead of declaring victory in the Cold War, the US should have assured that victory over the USSR by supporting democracy in Russia by any and all means possible.

Edmund Burke was right

We can speculate that matters might have been different if the United States in 1991 had concentrated on making sure that democracy would take a firm hold in Russia. Today the nation of Ukraine, and indeed all peaceful nations of the world, are suffering from Russian aggression, directly or indirectly, either at the point of a gun or through rising food and fuel prices, all because for years many nations turned a blind eye to Russia's bullying. Ukrainians are dying by the thousands and people around the world are starving because the war is affecting grain shipments. The world had to suffer the Second World War because Adolf Hitler was appeased from 1934 until 1938, as he became stronger and more dangerous. Vladimir Putin has been emboldened by the apathy and lethargy of the West. Europe in particular has had a large dependence on Russian oil and natural gas. This has led the nations of Europe to ignore Russia's growing belligerence in exchange for a steady energy supply. The Russian Army, long known for its brutality and heartlessness, devastated Grozny, the capital of Chechnya, in 1994. The Russian Army did terrible things in Georgia, when Russian-backed separatists in the South Ossetian *Oblast* declared their independence from Georgia in 2008 and sought Russian 'protection'.[5]

The heinous tactic of targeting civilians, as seen in Ukraine, was perfected by the Russian Army during the Syrian civil war in 2016. Entire cities in Syria were levelled by Russian artillery and air strikes. In particular, hospitals and schools were targeted as a way of demoralizing their opponents. In the twisted logic of tyrants, killing the children of your enemy limits the rise of future soldiers who will oppose you. Even chemical weapons were used against the Syrian civilian population. Although President Obama warned Bashar al-Assad of Syria that employing chemical weapons was a line he should not cross, Assad, who benefited from the protection of the Russian Army, employed those chemical weapons to horrific effect.

The US and others condemned this barbaric act, but in the end nothing was done by any Western leader, just as nothing had been done when the Russians committed war crimes in Chechnya and in Georgia. Employing terror and targeting the civilian population have become part of the *modus operandi* of the Russian Army. That sounds awfully familiar if we think back on the Nazi period with its politicized army, which committed untold war crimes. During the Second World War the Third Reich kidnapped tens of thousands of Nordic-looking children from all across Europe. They did so in order to raise them as Nazis. Today, Putin's regime has admitted to stealing as many as 700,000 Ukrainian children, under the guise of protecting them from the war. The woman in charge of coordinating this massive effort is Maria Lvova-Belova, one of Putin's stooges. Stories are now filtering out of Russia that indicate Putin has ordered the indoctrination of these Ukrainian children in order to raise them as Russians. Again, the parallels between what the Nazis did and what Putin is doing are there for anyone to see.

Empty promises

In 1991, when the Soviet Union collapsed, both the newly created Russian Federation and the US made a promise to Ukraine that if it would give up its nuclear arsenal (there were nuclear missiles stationed in Ukraine), the United States and the Russian Federation would guarantee and protect the territorial integrity of its borders. In February 2014 Vladimir Putin ordered the invasion and occupation of the Crimea and its annexation from Ukraine for the Russian Federation. This was followed up on 6 April 2014 when Russian-backed separatists began a war against the Ukrainian government in the Donbas region of eastern Ukraine. The attempt aimed to wrest control of this eastern Ukrainian province, rich in minerals and industrial capacity, from Ukraine and unite it with Russia. Russia supplied these separatist rebels with an abundance of military equipment, and continues to do so today. It appears then that Ukraine might have done better had it kept its nuclear arsenal as a deterrent to any would-be invader, rather than depending on the empty promises of both the US and the Russian Federation to guarantee its borders.

As with all other acts of Russian aggression, the US and Europe's leading powers employed words of condemnation in 2014, but not much else. This is exactly what happened between 1934 and 1938. Was it a surprise to the US and the European nations that, after years of their turning a blind eye to what Putin was doing, he felt emboldened enough to invade another sovereign nation? In order to find an excuse to swallow up the rest of Ukraine, Putin has made the baseless accusation that the country is being run by Nazis. This is truly a classic case of psychological projection, given that Ukraine's president, Volodymyr Zelensky, happens to be Jewish, and the only person behaving like a Nazi happens to be named Putin. Just as the Western leaders had appeased Hitler for years, culminating in the signing of the infamous Munich Agreement, so has the West appeased Putin by allowing him to run roughshod over his neighbours for years.

With the formal invasion of Ukraine on 24 February 2022, the birds of appeasement and economic pragmatism have come home to roost, and only too late has the West realized that Putin needs to be confronted. Only when Adolf Hitler's forces marched into what was left of Czechoslovakia in March 1939, ending that nation's liberty, did the British Prime Minister Neville Chamberlain and the French Prime Minister Édouard Daladier finally realize that Hitler, like all schoolyard bullies, needed to be opposed. The months between September 1938 and March 1939 have gone down in history as a testament to what happens when democracies fail to confront tyranny. We must now also add February 2014 to this shameful list. Confronting Hitler much earlier might have avoided war, or at least reduced the terrible cost in lives that the Second World War brought. By the same token, opposing Vladimir Putin earlier might have also prevented further Russian aggression. If he were alive today to witness the tragic events unfolding in Ukraine, Edmund Burke, the Irish-born British statesman, would have repeated his famous warning: 'All tyranny needs to gain a foothold is for people of good conscience to remain silent.' Again, the parallels between the Nazi period and now are uncanny.

The same old dream of empire-building

Today we are faced with a Hitler-wanna-be in the guise of the Russian President. Putin's goal is no less than the re-establishment of a Russian empire like the one that existed during the time of the USSR. Realizing that he can't live for ever, and contemplating how Russians will remember him, Putin is attempting to re-establish the territorial boundaries of what used to be the USSR as his legacy. Like all other tyrants before him, his goal will ultimately fail, but not before tens of thousands or even hundreds of thousands of innocent people lose their lives. The only thing that will defeat Vladimir Putin is the will and military support of the West, coupled with the resistance of the brave Ukrainian people. Unfortunately, western support for Ukraine is faltering. The result of the recent US presidential election all but guarantees that in 2025 the US will abandon Ukraine and, as a result, allow Putin to eventually conquer that democratic nation.

At home in Russia there are stirrings of dissent, but Putin's police state is firmly entrenched. In 2017 he created the *Natsional'naya gvardiya* (National Guard), known as the Special Police Force. This organization is a police formation of some 340,000 soldiers, whose members are only answerable and loyal to Putin himself. This paramilitary organization sounds very similar in make-up and allegiance to Hitler's *Sturmabteilung* (SA) Stormtroopers, or even the *Schutzstaffel* (SS). Now, the only way that Putin will fall from power is if military affairs take a further bad turn for Russia. Putin knows that his future as leader of the Russian Federation depends on victory in Ukraine, no matter what that victory might cost. If Putin is thwarted in taking Ukraine, he will lose power and most likely his life. Therefore, he will continue to act ruthlessly and show no mercy. His past track record suggests he will be willing to sacrifice everything, including the lives of Russian people, to obtain that victory. Recently some politicians in the West have been pushing the Ukrainian government to make peace with Russia. What these 'armchair generals' don't realize is that allowing Vladimir Putin to keep what land he has stolen from Ukraine will only encourage him to continue his aggression at a later date. The temporary peace will also give him time to re-equip and retrain the Russian Army. The Ukrainians understand that they cannot compromise or try to reason with a man like Putin. To Putin, compromise is a sign of weakness. The only thing he understands is brute force. In this, he is accompanied by a legion of Russian tyrants who came before him, going all the way back to Ivan the Terrible. Putin is merely the latest Russian tyrant.

Behind the lines, the Ukrainian partisan movement has begun to take a toll on the Russian invader. The war, it seems, will last longer than Putin had expected. Hopefully, Putin's attempt at empire-building will fail. In the meantime, those politicians, generals and rich oligarchs around Putin, who support his kleptocracy, are waiting to see if the Russian Führer suffers more military reversals, or if the West abandons Ukraine. If history is a harbinger, then this war of aggression will decide not only Ukraine's future but also Putin's ultimate place in history. Just as the Nazis failed at building an empire in the East, Putin too, it is hoped, will fail in his attempt to create an empire along the lines of his beloved USSR. Dr John Gray's observation that history is cyclical has to be considered, given the many parallels between the Nazi period and now. If Putin suffers more military reversals on the battlefield, then, as Hitler before him discovered, he may find himself inside a house of cards that is about to collapse on him. Benito Mussolini's famous quote, 'a regime, of whatever kind, collapses only under the weight of defeat', will then have been proven true.

Dr Antonio J. Muñoz

Introduction

A different kind of war

Why was it that Nazi Germany was unable to create an eastern empire that, many historians agree, could have supplied land and resources to keep the Third Reich alive for a thousand years? The answer lies in the nature of the Nazi system itself. During the Second World War Nazi policy regarding the combating of partisans, especially in eastern Europe, including the USSR, involved the tactic of *kollektive gewaltmassnahmen*.[1] This policy punished all for the acts of a few. For example, an attack by guerrilla forces against German units or interests made the local population near that attack as responsible for it as the guerrillas themselves. This and other German policies dealing with civilian and military matters would eventually work to undermine German rule in the East. The idea behind *kollektive gewaltmassnahmen* was the German belief that, fearing reprisals, the local population in an occupied region behind German lines would inform on the partisans before the guerrillas had a chance to launch any attacks against German interests. In addition, several orders created shortly before the start of the Russian campaign, collectively referred to by historians as the *Verbrecherbefehle*, were meant to give an air of 'legality' to such policies as *kollektive gewaltmassnahmen* that were criminal and illegal in wartime. These official announcements would quickly become standard policy in the East. They would also end up costing the lives of many civilians.

With the invasion of the Soviet Union on 22 June 1941, various Nazi ideologies would come together in a deadly cocktail that would shape the German struggle in the East. Anti-Polish and anti-Jewish sentiments were already causing the deaths of thousands in German-occupied Poland. The idea that the Jewish, Romany and eastern European people were inferior to Germans, and natural enemies of Germany, made it easier for the Nazis to prosecute the Russian campaign in a more barbaric manner. In effect, dehumanizing these people made it easier for Germans to kill them. It's an established fact that anti-Semitism was the principal factor in the Nazis' eventual decision to attempt to murder the entire Jewish population of Europe. Christopher Browning states that the society in which Germans lived at the time was imbued with a steady dose of anti-Semitic propaganda, which denigrated and marginalized the Jews to the point where they began to be seen as less than human and, by extension, life unworthy of life (*Lebensunwertes Leben*):

> As *Leutnant* Drucker said with extraordinary understatement, 'Under the influence of the times, my attitude to the Jews was marked by a certain aversion.' The denigration of Jews and the proclamation of Germanic racial superiority was so constant, so pervasive, so relentless, that it must have shaped the general attitudes of masses of people in Germany, including the average reserve policeman.[2]

Just as importantly, however, Christian Streit has described very persuasively how anti-communism was 'a factor of crucial importance' in the process of creating an extermination policy during the period prior to and during the Russian campaign.[3] A perfect example of this is the infamous commissar order, which gave all German troops, irrespective of branch of service or rank, the ability to execute any and all Red Army commissars either right after capture or immediately after interrogation. While the Nazis had behaved, and continued to behave, harshly towards the Polish nation, their cruelty there did not compare to that which they planned to inflict during their campaign in the Soviet Union.[4] That is not to say that Poland would be spared the full brunt of the Nazis' wrath. On the contrary, as soon as the German invasion of the Soviet Union began, Poland would feel the full weight of this war of extermination (*vernichtungskrieg*). Repression begets cruelty, and the Germans would increase their campaign of terror against the Polish nation as the war in the East progressed. In effect, these criminal orders allowed the *Ostheer* to operate under a completely different set of rules from those that had been followed when the Wehrmacht conquered western Europe.[5] In this new form of warfare, simply being a Jew became synonymous with being a partisan. As such, all Jews were subject to execution on sight.

In addition, the Russian military and civilian population would have no legal protection from killings of any kind. Since the USSR had never signed the Geneva Convention on the treatment of captured enemy prisoners, the Nazis considered they had *carte blanche* in treating all captured enemy combatants and civilians in whichever way they wished. This included the use of immediate executions if it was deemed necessary by the local German commander, meaning that the lowest-ranked German soldier (even a lowly corporal) had the right to execute captured prisoners if he deemed it necessary. Nazi ideology, coupled with what was virtually a mandate to kill, fused together in the Russian campaign to create the *Weltanschauungskrieg* (ideological war) against what the Nazis referred to as the 'Judeo-Bolshevist' threat. Given such wide latitude, the struggle in the East would be unprecedented in terms of its intensity, ferocity and brutality. With the Nazi belief that the *lebensunwertes leben* Jewish race was a polluting factor in German life, this idea was now further expanded upon to suit the circumstances of the war in the East. This was accomplished by (as stated earlier) making the killing of Jews synonymous with fighting the partisans. Adolf Hitler even said that the war in the East was an opportunity for the German troops to kill all those they felt opposed them.

The belief that *Jeder Jude ist ein Guerrillakampfer* (every Jew is a guerrilla fighter) was hammered home by officers not only within the SS and *Ordnungspolizei*, but throughout the entire Wehrmacht. As if to reaffirm this view, Wilhelm Keitel issued the following order, dated 16 December 1942, regarding the combating of partisans. The command seemed to reiterate the criminal orders completely, almost a year and a half after the German invasion. A portion of the order reads:

> The troops therefore have the right and the duty to use, in this fight, any means, even against women and children, provided they are conducive to success. Scruples, of any sort whatsoever, are a crime against the German people and against the front-line soldier who bears the consequences of attacks by bands of guerrillas and who cannot understand why any should be shown to them or their associates. These principles must serve as a basis for operations against bands in the East. No German participating in action against bands or their associates is to be held responsible for acts of violence either from a disciplinary or a judicial point of view. Commanders of troops engaged in action against the bands are obliged to see to it that all officers of units under their command be immediately and thoroughly notified of this order, that their legal advisers be immediately acquainted therewith and that no judgments be passed which are in contradiction thereto.[6]

This policy made it easy for regular German army troops to both work side by side with SS units fighting the partisans and assisting the *SS Einsatzgruppen* in eliminating the Jewish population, and commit crimes against the Jewish and non-Jewish population under the guise of combating the guerrillas. Romany were added to the category of *lebensunwertes leben*, so they too would be targeted wherever they were encountered. In many instances these murders were carried out independently of the SS mobile killing units, the Einsatzgruppen. Even rear area army garrison commanders have been shown to have cooperated with the SS and to have undertaken operations against Jews and Romany on their own initiative. The above order, issued by Keitel, stipulated that no soldier was to be punished for any acts which he committed while under the pretext of fighting the guerrillas and keeping order behind the lines. In addition, women and children were specifically mentioned as not being an exception to this rule.

What Keitel meant is clear enough: the killing of women and children in the East would be permitted. Notice also that all of this served, as he put it, as 'a basis for operations in the East', meaning that the war and the tactics which the *Ostheer* was employing in the Soviet Union were unique to this particular front. Was this the case because the Germans saw the eastern Europeans as subhuman and less worthy of life? Was it because Josef Stalin did not ascribe to the Geneva Convention? Was it anti-communist hatred? Was it the brutalization which occurred on the Eastern Front, as Omer Bartov and others have argued, which contributed to the barbarization of the German soldier? Was it anti-Semitism? Was it hatred of the *Zigeuner* (gypsies)? The answer (sadly) is all of the above. All of these representative biases and bigotries were inflamed by Nazi propaganda and indoctrination. The Germans brought these biases to the East, and when coupled together with criminal military orders, permitting brutality and mass murder, they engendered in the *Ostheer* a feeling that immoral conduct would be condoned. A major role in combating the partisans in the USSR was played not only by SS and police forces, but by the *Ostheer*. This included ancillary and volunteer auxiliary units of the German Army. In addition, Keitel's order also reinforced the German Armed Forces High Command directive against communist insurrection in occupied territories, issued on 16 September 1941, and also the infamous 'Reichenau Order' of 10 October 1941 on the conduct of troops in the eastern territories, which partly read as follows:

> The most important objective of this campaign against the Jewish-Bolshevik system is the complete destruction of its sources of power and the extermination of the Asiatic influence in European Civilization ... Therefore, the soldier must have full understanding for the necessity of a severe but just revenge on subhuman Jewry. The Army has to aim at another purpose, i.e., the annihilation of revolts in the hinterland which, as experience proves, have always been caused by the Jews ... This is the only way to fulfill our historic task to liberate the German people once and for ever from the Asiatic-Jewish danger.[7]

In 2004 Ben Shepperd published a work detailing the war guilt of (principally) two such German units: two security divisions as they operated in central Russia from 1941 to 1943.[8] Although his work covered only two security divisions, the author argued that their behaviour proved how National Socialist indoctrination, combined with the brutality of the war in the East, created the conditions that allowed for widespread murders under the guise of combating the Soviet partisans. Shepperd's approach was to build his case from the bottom up, by illustrating a consistent pattern of action within the battalions and regiments of these security divisions. His study is important because it reinforced existing research on the criminal excesses of the Wehrmacht in the East.

The book, however, would have been aided further if Shepperd had been able to cite other cases in similar German rear area and front-line commands, to support the theory that this type of behaviour in the *Ostheer* was widespread and commonplace throughout the entire width and scope of the Eastern Front. By citing examples of atrocities committed by these units, Shepperd showed how, in the region of central Russia and Belarus, the degenerative brutality that National Socialism caused, when combined with the constant and vicious combat of the war in the East, worked to harden the German soldier and accustomed him to murder, even illegal killings.[9] This work will argue that similar criminal behaviours were perpetrated by German rear-area security forces throughout the East, including Poland, and what comprised the USSR at the time.

My research has affirmed what Dr Shepperd and other academics refer to as the brutalization theory. But this is just one piece of the puzzle if we are to understand Nazi *Ost* policy. In this work, I have covered a wider area, citing numerous examples from the occupation of Poland, the Baltic States, Belarus, Ukraine and European Russia. The conclusions provide verifiable evidence of this widespread practice of criminal conduct which even seeped into the Nazi civilian administration in the East. Like Shepperd and other researchers, I have worked from the bottom up, by going through reels of captured German records detailing the history of these rear area forces that operated in the East from 1939 until 1944. Cases also abound of front-line troops behaving criminally during anti-guerrilla sweeps. All that happened in the East was in keeping with a strategy prepared before the invasion. *Generalplan Ost* was a Nazi plan developed as a blueprint for the genocide and democide that would take place in the East as a precursor to German colonization. This plan required the Germans to be brutal and ruthless in the East. Employing the typical German penchant for fulfilling obligations, the *Ostheer* carried out this order to devastating effect.

The debate over German Army criminality in the East

Gerald Reitlinger is one of the earliest, if not the first, historians to have brought up the subject of possible participation of the German military in the heinous murders of the Jewish population of the USSR. Prior to this early work, the only substantive reference to this German Army and Holocaust connection lay in the High Command trials that occurred within the context of the Nuremberg War Crimes Trials of 1946–1948. Reitlinger pointed to this in his ground-breaking 1956 study, *The SS: Alibi of a Nation*.[10] He began there, and others followed after him, with further proof that it wasn't just the

Jewish people who were targeted, but the civilian population as a whole – and the *Ostheer* was knee-deep in it all.

With this work, Reitlinger established a foundation upon which others would follow and contribute, in much the same way that the base of a house is built, and other workers later add the walls and roof. The crux of his argument was that by blaming all the evils committed by the Nazi regime on the SS, the German nation, and therefore the army as a whole, could be exculpated from any guilt. Reitlinger followed that classic work four years later in 1960 with *The House Built on Sand: The Conflicts of German Policy in Russia, 1939–1945*.[11] In it, he detailed how the Nazi leaders and their German Army counterparts had prepared for a different kind of war in the Soviet Union. The criminal orders made the campaign different, in that these orders were a virtual licence to kill. In this he was repeating points already made by Alexander Dallin in *German Rule in Russia, 1941–1945: A Study of Occupation Policies*, in which Dallin described the 'Commissar Decree' among other documents linking the German Army to the Holocaust and the illegal killings of the general population.[12]

Reitlinger pointed to documents written to senior German Army commanders by the Nazi leadership – collectively referred to by historians as the 'criminal orders' – which provided the *Ostheer* with its 'mandate' to allow for the killing of the local population, especially the Jewish population. These orders document how German military courts would not apply to Russian civilians, how the SS and police units were to work outside military commands, and also included the infamous Commissar Order and the Barbarossa Jurisdiction Order, to name a few. The Jurisdiction Order in effect gave a virtual *carte blanche* to any German soldier fighting in the East to shoot or kill anyone who was categorized as either 'agitators', 'partisans', 'partisan helpers', 'saboteurs', 'political commissars' or 'Jews' without fear of prosecution by any German court or tribunal. As stated earlier, the terms 'partisan' and 'Jew' were made synonymous, since treatment of both groups would be the same: execution. While many former German Army officers point to the fact that no order originated from the Wehrmacht which specified that the Jewish population was to be targeted for premeditated murder, historian Yitzhak Arad was correct when he stated that because Jews were included in the list of those persons who could be shot on sight, the effect was the same as if the Wehrmacht itself had written the order for the murder of the Jewish population.[13]

The criminal orders, therefore, directly link the Holocaust in the USSR to the German Army. Reitlinger related that shortly after the start of the Russian campaign, a meeting was held on 16 July 1941 in Angerburg. In attendance were Göring, Keitel, Rosenberg, Lammers, Bormann and Adolf Hitler. The

Führer, Reitlinger explained, 'declared that Stalin had ordered partisan warfare behind the German front'. Hitler also commented that this partisan war gave them the ability to eliminate everyone who opposed them.[14] This, of course, included not only the Jews, but anyone considered by the Nazis as an enemy. As a result, on 22 July 1941 a new expanded order was put forth by Adolf Hitler and added to the Barbarossa Jurisdiction Order, which stated explicitly that where SS and other security forces were not available, the German Army itself was to take all measures necessary, even draconian steps, to control the rear areas and those who populated them. They were also to eliminate the partisan threat or 'other dangers' that placed the German armed forces or the war effort at risk. This, Reitlinger wrote, 'became the German soldier's charter for anti-partisan warfare'.[15]

In spite of these early and impressive starts, the study of the German Army connection to the Holocaust and other illegal murders in the East did not really begin to be considered fully until the mid-1980s. It was then that Professor Omer Bartov published his now-classic work, *The Eastern Front, 1941–45, German Troops and the Barbarization of Warfare*. In it, he proposed that the rigours of the Eastern Front – that is, the very nature of the warfare being fought between the Soviet Union and Nazi Germany, as well as pre-existing Nazi ideology – quickly accustomed the typical German soldier to brutalization, which made it easier for him to kill Jewish and non-Jewish civilians, captured soldiers and partisans with little thought to the legality or morality of his actions. Indeed, as stated decades before by Reitlinger and Dallin, the 'criminal orders' gave the members of the German Army, from high-ranking officer down to the lowliest *landser*,[16] the feeling that any action taken under the pretext of these orders would protect them from punishment by any German Army military tribunal.[17]

Bartov's incisive work was followed up three years later, in 1989, by a study titled *The German Army and Nazi Policies in Occupied Russia* by Professor Theo J. Schulte. Dr Schulte proposed that not only had the German Army been complicit in the Holocaust, but that it was part of a Nazi aim which sought 'the total destruction of another society as a fundamental prerequisite for the refashioning of German society'.[18] Here, Schulte was echoing the thoughts of historian Michael Geyer, who argued that the war of ideologies, the *Weltanschauungskrieg*, was not just fought with mere words, but was practised in the East with physical vigour.[19] Two years later, in 1991, Yitzhak Arad reappraised the various criminal orders and expounded and developed on their implications as part of the Yad Vashem Yearbook Series. This important article added 'cement' to the arguments that authors like Bartov and Schulte were developing. Even when discussing the non-military leadership that ruled the German eastern empire, we see the same ideology and action. Why did it take several decades from the publication of Reitlinger and Dallin's works for them to be followed by further research on the criminality of the Wehrmacht in the East? This is an important question.

It is beyond the scope of this work to go into the personal, social or political reasons why the topic remained relatively dormant for so many years, but in 2007 Professors Ronald Smelser and Edward Davies published a study which proposed several reasons for this apparent 20-year hiatus on the topic.[20] Although this study was fraught with numerous assumptions, the authors did conclude correctly that the Cold War may have played a role in sanitizing the German Army from its complicity in the horrors perpetrated in the East. This was done in order to use the full capacity of a revitalized West German state to help block Soviet aggression and intentions during the Cold War.[21] Throughout this period, Smelser and Davies argue, an entire myth about the valour and chivalry of the Wehrmacht was created by numerous American and European writers. In addition, at the end of the Second World War various powers were scrambling to grab as many Nazi scientists as they could get their hands on. The Americans and Russians were the biggest hoarders of German scientific knowledge. Professor Werner von Braun, the Nazi scientist who worked at Peenemunde perfecting the V-1 and V-2 rockets, and who later helped the Americans to reach the moon, immediately comes to mind. The Cold War was also a time when former Nazis, some involved in the Holocaust, were sought by Western intelligence agencies because of their supposed knowledge of the Soviet Union and its people.

An important study in understanding how it came to pass that 80 million Germans fell sway to Hitler and the Nazis and aided in the destruction of European Jewry came when Christopher R. Browning published his definitive study, *Ordinary Men: Reserve Police Battalion 101 and the Final Solution in Poland*. A few years later, in 1995, German author Paul Kohl published a little-circulated work called *Der Krieg der Deutschen Wehrmacht und der Polizei 1941–1944* ('The War of the German Armed Forces and Police 1941–1944'). In it, he argued that indeed the German Army had followed the *Führerprinzip* (Leader Principle) of the *Weltanschauungskrieg* to its inevitable conclusion.[22]

Following the work by Kohl, Walter Manoschek edited a book in 1996 titled *Die Wehrmacht im Rassenkrieg: Der Vernichtungskrieg Hinter der Front* ('The [German] Armed Forces in the Race War: The War of Annihilation Behind the Front'). The numerous contributors to this significant work, which included such notables as Raul Hilberg, Manfred Messerschmidt, Wolfram Wette, Christian Streit, Hans Safrian, Hannes Heer, Bertrand Perz, Ela Hornung, and Reinhold Gärtner, referenced incidences that occurred in the Soviet Union, but went a step further by describing the political and propaganda preparations and conditioning Germans were subjected to by the

Nazi state before they even set foot on Soviet soil. Walter Manoschek, also managed to document a comparable occurrence of a German Army atrocity in Serbia, thus further cementing the truth of the unlawful activities prevalent in the Nazi-era German Army.[23] Willi Dreßen had also recorded Wehrmacht atrocities in Serbia and Russia in an article published in the 1993 edition of the Yad Vashem Yearbook Series.[24] The numerous eyewitness reports in his book cemented those accounts with apparently indelible ink. That same year Hannes Heer and Klaus Naumann edited and published an extremely important study, *Vernichtungskrieg: Verbrechen der Wehrmacht 1941 bis 1944*,[25] that propelled the topic of German Army complicity in atrocities to a whole new level by attacking the question from the top and bottom – that is, by not only presenting documentary evidence of guilt, but showing in a very lucid and straightforward manner how the very nature of the Nazi regime worked to create the conditions leading to complicity from all corners of the Wehrmacht and civilian apparatus.[26] The book turned out to be so popular and important that in 2000 it was translated into the English language in annotated format.[27] The book proved very successful in the US, but interest was especially high in Germany, where there was a growing awareness of what had been a taboo subject until 1990: German Army complicity in atrocities and sanctioned murder. An exhibit was eventually created. That exhibit toured Germany for many years in the 1990s and was considered extremely controversial.[28]

German military veteran groups protested that this exhibition was negatively painting too broad a picture of the Wehrmacht. A huge, oversized volume was produced in 2002: *Verbrechen der Wehrmacht: Dimensionen des Vernichtungskrieges 1941–1944*.[29] Its 764 pages are chock-full of documents, photographs, reports from diaries, interviews, eyewitness accounts and other documentary evidence about the crimes of the German Army during the Nazi period. The sheer size and scope of this volume attests to the extent of the German Army's participation in these crimes, for surely if today the institute that produced it, the *Hamburger Institut für Sozialforschung*,[30] could have amassed such a work, what other crimes were committed during the Second World War that for lack of evidence we shall never know about? That same year Wolfram Wette, who until then had been a contributing writer to this topic, published his first single and full study on the subject,[31] translated into the English language as *The Wehrmacht: History, Myth, Reality*. In it, Wette studied not only the top generals and middle-management officers but also included reports and testimonials from lowly privates as well. In his closing analysis, he stated:

> In recent years we have gained greater insight into the experience of the 'average Joe' in uniform meaning the many millions of enlisted men and

> noncommissioned officers who participated in the exterminationist campaign on the eastern front. Many of them followed the generals' ideological guidelines reluctantly, while others supported the campaign on the basis of their own convictions. Recent research has revealed a considerable amount of agreement with and support for the regime's goals at the bottom of the military hierarchy. Very few summoned the courage to resist this war – to the extent that it was possible at all. While the Wehrmacht was officially dissolved after the capitulation of May 8, 1945, that did not put an end to its history. Some believe that only after that date did the Wehrmacht achieve its ultimate victory, namely, in its struggle to preserve its image as an army with 'clean hands' in the eyes of the public both at home and abroad. The myth of the Wehrmacht lived on. The policy of apology evident in the memoirs of former generals – in concert with like-minded people in West Germany – worked successfully for decades.[32]

Wette reached the conclusion that perhaps by 2002 (the year when his work was published and several years after the *Hamburger Institut* exhibit) Germany was now ready to admit that the legend of the Wehrmacht's 'clean hands' could finally belong to the past.[33] However, old habits are hard to break. During the mid-1990s an American political scientist would reopen the old wounds caused by German war guilt that perhaps the travelling exhibit on Wehrmacht crimes had merely scratched. So heated and controversial were this author's assertions that the national media both in the US and in Europe picked up on it and carried the story for months. That author's name was Daniel J. Goldhagen, and the debate about the German Army's war guilt was about to expand to the whole German nation's war guilt. By the early 1990s the question over the extent of German Army complicity in *ha Shoah* (the Holocaust) almost certainly helped to partly inspire Goldhagen's work, *Hitler's Willing Executioners: Ordinary Germans and the Holocaust*.[34]

Goldhagen's book sold over 80,000 copies in its first print run, catching the attention not only of academics but of the general public. American and European media covered the story about the controversy that the book produced. It also stirred up a hornets' nest of arguments among academics for and against the theory which Goldhagen proposed. In the book he argued that the majority of Germans were willing participants in the Holocaust because of their predisposed negative conditioning towards Jewry. Accusations and counterarguments appeared from every corner of academia. Julius H. Schoeps edited the first work which appeared in Germany to counter Goldhagen's argument: *Ein Volk von Mordern? Die Dokumentation zur Goldhagen-Kontroverse um die Rolle der Deutschen im Holocaust*.[35] Not all of the rebuttals to Goldhagen's book came from Germany. Domestic scholars like

Fritz Stern, a German-Jewish refugee who, at the time Goldhagen's work was released, was teaching at Columbia University, had some tough criticism to dish out as well. Stern's counterargument seemed persuasive, as did the strength of his words:

> Goldhagen singles out those murderers who were 'ordinary Germans' and who, he insists, were motivated solely by their 'cognitive model' of the Jew. He then moves from specific and harrowing examples to a grotesque extrapolation: having examined the acts of some hundreds or perhaps even thousands of people, he insists that almost all Germans were moved by the same hatred, approved the killing, and would have acted in like fashion if chance had so decreed. As he writes, '... the institutions treated here ... should permit the motivations of the perpetrators in those particular institutions to be uncovered, and also allow for generalizing both to the perpetrators as a group and to the second target group of this study, the German people.' The leap from individual cases to the German people at large is unpersuasive, but necessary for his indictment of his 'second target group'.[36]

That was but a taste of the argument that all Germans were willing participants in the Holocaust, based on several hundred or several thousand Germans who did take part. Dr Stern was pointing out the fact that you cannot assume that 80 million Germans were willing participants, based on thousands who did play a leading role in the Holocaust. This argument was reinforced when further research about the complicity of German Army units in the Holocaust began to be studied in greater detail (a process which began in the mid-1980s). It only affirms the continued importance of researching this topic even today. The implication of Goldhagen's work is clear: all Germans bear responsibility for the deaths of 6 million Jews. Thus, Goldhagen stirred many passions which have very real personal, social and political implications. Geoffrey P. Megargee's work *War of Annihilation: Combat and Genocide on the Eastern Front, 1941* is perhaps one of the better studies to be released, and referred to what Goldhagen was claiming. In it, Megargee merges some of the theories expounded by Goldhagen, arguing that Germans in general were predisposed to the kind of annihilation war waged in Russia. Most academics, however, have only proven the guilt of the Wehrmacht during the war. In his conclusions, Megargee states, according to his premise, the crux of German Army guilt:

> In order to ensure their victory, the generals also helped lay the plans for Hitler's vision of an exterminationist war. Later they would claim that the SS was solely responsible for the crimes in the east, but in fact the military's role was crucial. At the most basic level, the crimes could never

> have taken place if the Wehrmacht had not conquered the ground, but the generals' culpability extends well beyond that fact. They encouraged their soldiers in an attitude that placed little or no value on the life of Soviet civilians, in fact, they ordered their men to use the harshest conceivable means to establish German dominance. They planned for the deliberate starvation of millions of people and for forced labor by millions more. They laid the groundwork for the fatal neglect of Soviet prisoners of war, whose care was their responsibility by international law. And they played a key role in planning for the elimination of the Communist leadership and intelligentsia, including those in uniform, as well as anyone who resisted German rule. That last goal provided the perfect cover for the SS Einsatzgruppen and other killing units to murder anyone whom they saw as a threat, including hundreds of thousands of Jewish men, women and children. Since most of the military's leaders believed that Jews were fundamentally hostile and dangerous, they were able to persuade themselves, with little apparent difficulty, that killing all the Jews was necessary to secure the conquered territories.[37]

The only drawback to Megargee's book is that he only used published works and as a result could only come to conclusions from the observations and assessments of other authors. However, he laid out exactly what the Wehrmacht generals did which stained their escutcheon of honour for ever. Another important work regarding German attitudes and decisions made in the East was published a year earlier, in 2005. It was titled *Abgehort: Deutsche Generale in britischer Kriegsgefangenschaft 1942–1945* ('Monitored: German Generals in British War Captivity 1942–1945'). This work, edited by Sönke Neitzel, is a massive compilation of secret conversations taped by British intelligence of German officers held in British prisoner-of-war (POW) camps from 1942 to 1945. The book was thought important enough to be translated into the English language in 2008. The importance of this study is that in many of these secret conversations, German officers talked openly of the annihilation war in the East. Not knowing that they were being recorded, they showed emotions ranging from arrogant joy to total indifference. One such example from the book describes a conversation secretly recorded in a POW camp by the British on 6 May 1945, between *Generalleutnant* Maximilian Siry, the former commander of the German *347. Infanterie Division*, and *Generalstabsintendant* Pauer of the *Oberkommandos des Heeres*.[38] Pauer just listened while Siry expounded on how he would have handled the massive POW problem which the *Ostheer* had to deal with during the Russian campaign:

> *Siry*: One mustn't admit it openly, but we were far too soft. All these horrors have landed us in the soup now. But if we'd carried them through to the hilt, made the people disappear completely – no one would say a

> thing. These half measures are always wrong. In the East I suggested once to the *Korps* [command] – thousands of POWs were coming back, without anyone guarding them, because there were no people there to do it. It went quite well in France, because the Frenchman is so degenerate that if you said to him: 'You will report to the POW collecting point in the rear' the stupid idiot really did go along there. But in Russia there was a space of 50–80km [30–50 miles], that is to say, a 2 to 3 days' march, between the armoured spearheads and the following close formations. No Russians went to the rear, they lagged behind and then took to the woods left and right, where they could live all right. So, I said: 'That's no good, we must simply cut off one of their legs, or break a leg, or the right forearm, so that they won't be able to fight in the next four weeks and so that we can round them up.' There was an outcry when I said one must simply smash their legs with a club. At the time, of course, I didn't really condone it either, but now I think it's quite right. We've seen that we cannot conduct a war because we're not hard enough, not barbaric enough. The Russians are that all right.[39]

This outlook did not just arise out of the blue. The Nazis had nine years (1933–1941) to imbue the German nation with a hatred of Jewry and the Slavic people in the East. This hatred was nurtured, fed and finally legalized by a series of orders that, when combined with anti-Semitic and anti-communist ideology, worked to create conditions that caused criminality on a grand scale. However, we must admit that there existed in the German nation (and indeed in most European countries) a base level of antipathy by the gentile community towards the Jewish people. Religious anti-Semitism had existed in Europe for hundreds of years. What made the Nazi period different was that racial anti-Semitism was now added, in much the same way that one adds more kindling to a fire. The Nazis were able to exponentially increase that basic anti-Semitic sentiment to the point of madness. There is no doubt now that the German Army bears a good portion of the guilt for the horrors that occurred in the East. The outcome of the debate as to the degree of that war guilt on the part of the Wehrmacht is still incomplete. This work will hopefully add additional bricks and mortar to the studies mentioned in this introduction, but more precisely it provides additional documentation to Dr Timothy Snyder's magnum opus *Bloodlands: Europe Between Hitler and Stalin*[40] and Mark Mazower's equally important study *Hitler's Empire: How the Nazis Ruled Europe*.[41] The documentation herein affirms a cruel and extremely genocidal comportment on the part of the Germans that was particular to these regions of eastern Europe. This comportment was led by an ideology of exclusion and genocide. It was also the very reason why ultimately Germany was not able to establish an eastern empire as envisaged in *Mein Kampf*.

Fall Blau

In the spring of 1942 the *Ostheer* was attempting to gain its footing after four months of a Soviet winter counteroffensive that not only pushed back the German Army in Russia with serious casualties, but forced it to employ a large number of rear area and security forces as front-line units for lack of sufficient conventional forces. The Red Army winter offensive which began on 5 December 1941 also had repercussions behind the German lines, where the nascent Soviet partisan movement was attempting to grow and gain a foothold. By the spring of 1942 those early partisan units were ready to expand. The Germans, aware of the military situation both on the front lines and in the rear of their armies, also prepared to counter the growing partisan threat. As the German military planned to continue the Russian campaign into the summer of 1942, new security forces were gathered together and sent to the Soviet Union, and a new headquarters, specifically intended to fight the guerrilla menace, was established. In 1942 the *Ostheer*, acting on Adolf Hitler's orders, launched *Fall Blau* (Case Blue), the 1942 summer offensive which was aimed at capturing the Caucasus Mountains and the Russian oil fields that lay there. As the German southern armies began to advance further into southern Russia, the German anti-partisan effort behind the lines of Army Group South grew. When the Wehrmacht eventually reached the Don river bend, where the city of Stalingrad (today's Volgograd) was located, one part of the southern army group veered towards Stalingrad, while the bulk of the German forces moved south, into the Caucasus Mountains.

Meanwhile, during the spring and summer of 1942 a strong guerrilla presence coalesced in Belarusia, central and northern Russia. This was a force composed of former Red Army soldiers, Communist Party functionaries, Komsomol members, university students and ordinary citizens who took up arms and were now threatening the very lifeblood of the German *Ostheer*. The war in the East was as spectacular in 1942 as it had been in 1941. This time, however, the focus of the German assault was southern Russia. The *Ostheer* could no longer wage a full-scale attack along the entire width and breadth of the Russian Front. It was incapable of doing what it had done in the summer and autumn of 1941. In the spring of 1942 Adolf Hitler was faced with a momentous decision. Should the German Army strike towards Leningrad, and link up with the Finnish Army? Should it take Moscow, and thus capture the political and all-important communications hub of the Soviet Union? Should Sevastopol be conquered so that the Crimea could finally be taken? Or should the Germans strike towards the Caucasus Mountains and the vast oil fields that lay there? This decision would have far-reaching consequences for the outcome of the war in the East.

In the end, the Führer attempted to capture three of the four objectives, but in incremental steps. He would first capture Sevastopol with the 11th Army and clear the Crimea of Russian forces. Then he sent half of the 11th Army to the Leningrad sector while the other half remained to take part in the German drive on the Caucasus Mountains. Dividing the 11th Army was a mistake, and the plan began to go wrong as the forces sent to the Leningrad sector proved insufficient for the task of capturing that city. The German summer offensive in the region of Army Group South had envisioned numerous envelopment operations, where Red Army forces would be encircled by the panzer divisions and then finished off by the advancing infantry. Instead, the Soviets opted for an orderly withdrawal eastward, thus avoiding the large encirclements and husbanding their forces by trading space for time – time in which they would reinforce the south and evaluate the enemy's intentions, and plan a counter-stroke that would deal the Axis invaders a fatal wound. By August 1942 it was clear that Hitler was again dividing his forces because he wanted more than one objective. While the German 6th Army was tasked with capturing the city named after the communist leader, more and more German forces were sent into the bloody fight. Before October 1942 a good part of the German 4th Panzer Army was also drawn to Stalingrad, while the 3rd Romanian Army, the German 17th Army, the 1st Panzer Army and parts of the 4th Panzer Army headed for Ploesti and Tiflis in the Caucasus Mountains.

The 6th Army and the adjacent Axis armies would have been a sufficient force to act as a mobile left flank screen for the Axis advance on the Caucasus Mountains. There was no need to capture Stalingrad. Had the entire 4th Panzer Army been available, both Grozny and Tiflis could have been taken, and the Wehrmacht would have been set for the rest of the war as far as petrol was concerned, while the Red Army would begin to suffer shortages. That, however, was not to be. Hitler wanted to boast that he had taken the city named after his opponent, so he ordered the 6th Army to capture Stalingrad. That decision handed the Germans defeat in their 1942 summer campaign and resulted in the loss of almost five entire armies (the 6th Army and half of the 4th Panzer Army, and three crushed Axis armies). The defeat at Stalingrad and the withdrawal from the Caucasus also brought the realization that after 1942 Germany could not defeat the Soviet Union. The defeat of Operation Zitadelle, conducted seven months later (July 1943), guaranteed that Germany would lose the war in the East. All of this occurred because Hitler attempted to gain too many objectives in 1942 with insufficient forces. The consequences of his military decisions, such as deciding to capture Stalingrad, turned the war against the Germans. Behind the lines, the war also began to change in favour of the defender. The year 1941 saw the nascent partisan army sprouting small branches from a small bud. The year 1942 saw its growth to proportions that required more and more German security forces behind the front lines. This is when the story of the partisan and anti-partisan war became intense, and this is where we pick up the story of that bitter conflict.

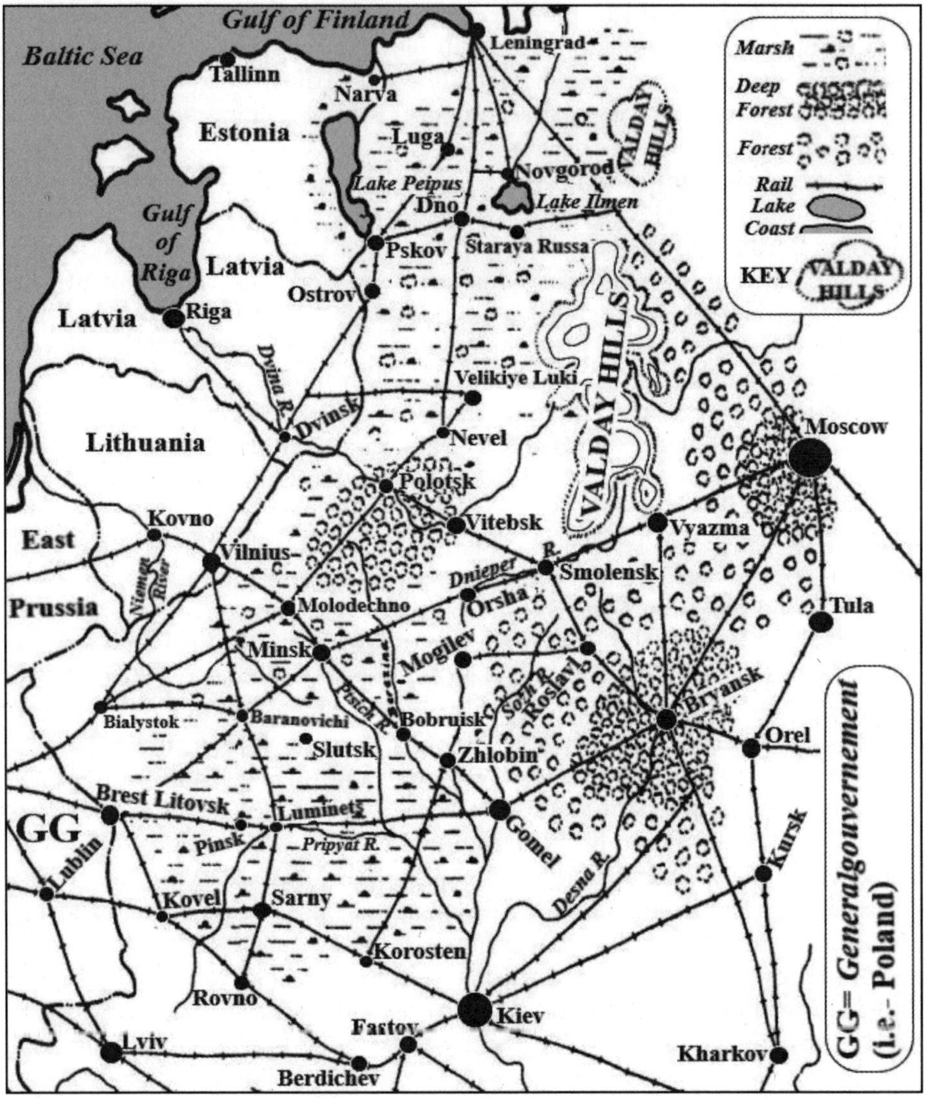

Map 1. Principal rail lines in north and central Russia. The map also depicts the major topographical features of this region of eastern Europe.

Chapter 1

Police reinforcements and the war behind the lines

Police reinforcements

As 1941 turned into 1942 the German Army in Russia was reeling from the Red Army winter counteroffensive. Everywhere along the front lines German forces had been either pushed back, severely depleted, surrounded or destroyed. As a result of these Red Army operations, several German pockets had been created, like the one at Cholm. The Demyansk pocket was a thin salient surrounded on three sides by Soviet forces. It took everything they had for the Germans to prevent Cholm from falling and the Demyansk pocket from being completely cut off. As spring approached, however, help was on the way. Inside Germany, new army formations – including rear area security forces – were being mobilized. One such rear area unit was the 18th Police Mountain Infantry Regiment. The very fact that at the beginning of 1942 a special police mountain regiment was ordered to be formed indicates just how engaged in the fighting behind the lines the German police forces were, and how intense it was becoming. This new mountain regiment was also to contain an artillery battalion and an armoured car company for support.[1] The current police battalions and regiments in the USSR were split up as follows: nine battalions were serving with the security divisions, one in the SD, one in the *Organization Todt*, and three battalions and two companies in the Eastland region, while three battalions and one cavalry battalion were located in Ukraine. The large numbers of SS, police, army and auxiliary volunteer forces actually began to grow in the summer of 1942. The police regiments and battalions listed in Table 1.1 were organized for employment in Russia and elsewhere in 1942.

In the spring of 1942, a new SS headquarters staff was created to help fight the growing partisan menace in the USSR. Himmler was made the titular head of fighting the guerrillas but for actual operations in the field, he chose SS Lieutenant-General Erich von dem Bach-Zelewski, who was currently the head of the Higher SS and Police Leader White Russia (Belarus) command. He was appointed to head this new anti-partisan office titled *Bandenbekämpfung Verbände Hauptquartier* (Headquarters for Units Fighting Gangs). This

Table 1.1. German police units in the East, 1942.

Regiment	Region of Russia in 1942 (by sequence)	Police Battalions	Comments
1	NR, BR, CR, UK, SR	2, 3, 10	I. Battalion of Police Regiment 1 was sent to Army Group North, while the companies under II. Battalion of Police Regiment 1 were employed individually by the SD in Russia.
2	BR, CR	11, 13, 22	Included I. Police Artillery Battalion
3	n/a	66, 68, 105	Formed and used in Holland in 1942–1943. The 105th Police Battalion had previously served as III. Battalion of Police Regiment 12.
4	n/a	316, 323	Formed and employed in France in 1942. III. Battalion was added when the 62nd Organization Todt Battalion was redesignated *en masse*, as the III. Battalion of Police Regiment 4.
5	n/a	64, 322	Formed and employed in Serbia in 1942. The I. Battalion of Police Regiment 3 was added to Police Regiment 5 at the beginning of 1943.
6	UK, SR	82, 311, 318	Destroyed in January 1943 in front-line fighting.
7	n/a	123, 309, 317	Formed in Germany and sent to Norway in January 1943.
8	BR, CR, SR	91, 111, 134	Sent to Army Group South and destroyed there in January 1943.
9	NR	61, 112, 132	Destroyed in July 1944.
10	UK, SR	45, 303, 314	Police Regiment 10 was created by simply redesignating Police Regiment South. The regiment survived to withdraw to the Adriatic Coast in 1944.
11	UK, SR	304, 315, 320	Police Regiment 11 was simply a redesignation of the Police Regiment for Special Employment in June 1942.
12	n/a	103, 104, 105	Formed in Holland, later dispersed to Italy and Hungary in 1943 and 1944.
13	BR, CR	6, 85, 301	Formed by a redesignation of Police Regiment Centre.

14	BR, CR, UK	51, 122, 313	Employed behind Army Group Centre from July until mid-December 1942. Destroyed near Kharkov in January 1943. According to Werner Regenberg, the 313th Order Police Battalion was replaced by a battalion of Ukrainian auxiliary policemen, which became the new III. Battalion of Police Regiment 14 in the summer of 1942. The 313th Police Battalion then became the III. Battalion of Police Regiment 28 Todt.
15	NR, UK, SR	305, 306, 310	I. Battalion was located in Ukraine, while the II. and III. Battalions were sent to North Russia. The I. Battalion was destroyed on 29 January 1943.
16	NR	56, 102, 121	The II. and III. Battalions of Police Regiment 15 (ex-102nd and 121st Police Battalions) were attached temporarily from 1942 to 1943.
17	NR	42, 74, 69	Some battalions were used to form other regiments in 1943.
18	n/a	302, 312, 325	This regiment was employed in Upper Krajina, Slovenia, in 1942, then in Finland (1942–1943) and Greece (1943–1944). This police mountain infantry regiment also had a three-battery police artillery battalion attached, as well as a tank company made up of captured Italian vehicles. The tank company was added in 1943.
19	n/a	72, 171, 181	Upper and Lower Krajina, Slovenia, from 1942 to 1943, then France in 1944.
20	n/a	I, II, III	Formed and employed in the Czech areas by taking three battalions from the six-battalion strong Police Regiment Bohemia, formed in 1938.
21	n/a	I, II, III	Formed and employed in the Czech areas by taking three battalions from the six-battalion strong Police Regiment Bohemia, formed in 1938.
22	n/a, then BR	41, 53, III	The III. Battalion was formed by grouping together the individual police companies stationed in Zamosz, Lublin and Cracow. The regiment was formed in Warsaw, Poland, and sent to Belarusia in July 1944.
23	n/a	307, II, III	The II. and III. Battalions were formed by grouping together the individual police companies stationed in Cracow (Krakau), Rzeszow (Reichshof), L'viv (Lemberg) and Radom. The regiment was formed and served in Cracow from 1942 to 1944.
24	n/a, then BR	83, 93, 153	I. and II. Battalions were sent to Belarusia in 1943, while the III. Battalion was sent to Krajina in Slovenia, then to France in 1944.

Regiment	Region of Russia in 1942 (by sequence)	Police Battalions	Comments
25	n/a	65, 67, 101	The regiment was formed in Lublin, Warsaw. The I. Battalion was sent to Ljubljana, Slovenia, in August 1944.
26	n/a, then BR, UK, and NR	251, 255, 256	This regiment was formed in Trondheim, Norway, then reformed in Belarus in March 1943 and employed there during the summer of 1943. The III. Battalion was used in Ukraine in October 1943. By December 1943 the regiment was in the region of Army Group North under SS Battlegroup Jeckeln.
27	n/a	9, 44, 319, 321	Formed in Oslo, Norway, using four police battalions instead of three.
28	n/a, then NR, UK	62, 69, 313	This regiment was formed in November 1942 in France. It contained the honorary title 'Todt'. The I. Battalion remained in France, while the II. Battalion was sent to Riga in Latvia and the III. Battalion to Poltava in southern Russia.

Battalion	Region in 1942	Company or Squadron	Comments
TN 1	NR	1–3 Companies	TN 1 was employed by the Higher SS and Police Command there.
TN 2	BR, CR	1–3 Companies	TN 2 was employed by the Higher SS and Police Command there.
TN 3	UK, SR	1–3 Companies	TN 3 was employed by the Higher SS and Police Command there.
GB 1	P (created June 1942)	1–3 Companies	
GB 2	n/a, then P	1–3 Companies	Formed in Lublin, Poland, in February 1943.
RB 1	UK, SR	1–2 Squadron	First employed in January 1942. It comprised two cavalry squadrons.
RB 2	UK, SR	1–3 Squadrons	First employed in September 1942. It comprised three cavalry squadrons.
RB 3	P	1–3 Squadrons	Formed in Posen.

KEY:BR = Belarusia, CR = Central Russia, NR = North Russia and Baltic Region, SR = Southern Russia, UK = Ukraine, P= Poland, C = Caucasus, (N) = Formerly Police Regiment North; (C) = Formerly Police Regiment Centre, (S) = Formerly Police Regiment South. TN = *Technische Nothilfe Bataillon* (Emergency Technical Battalion), RB = *Reiter Bataillon* (Police Cavalry Battalion), made up primarily of ethnic-Germans who were Ukrainians. *Schwadron* (Squadron). GB = *Gendarmerie* Battalion (motorized).

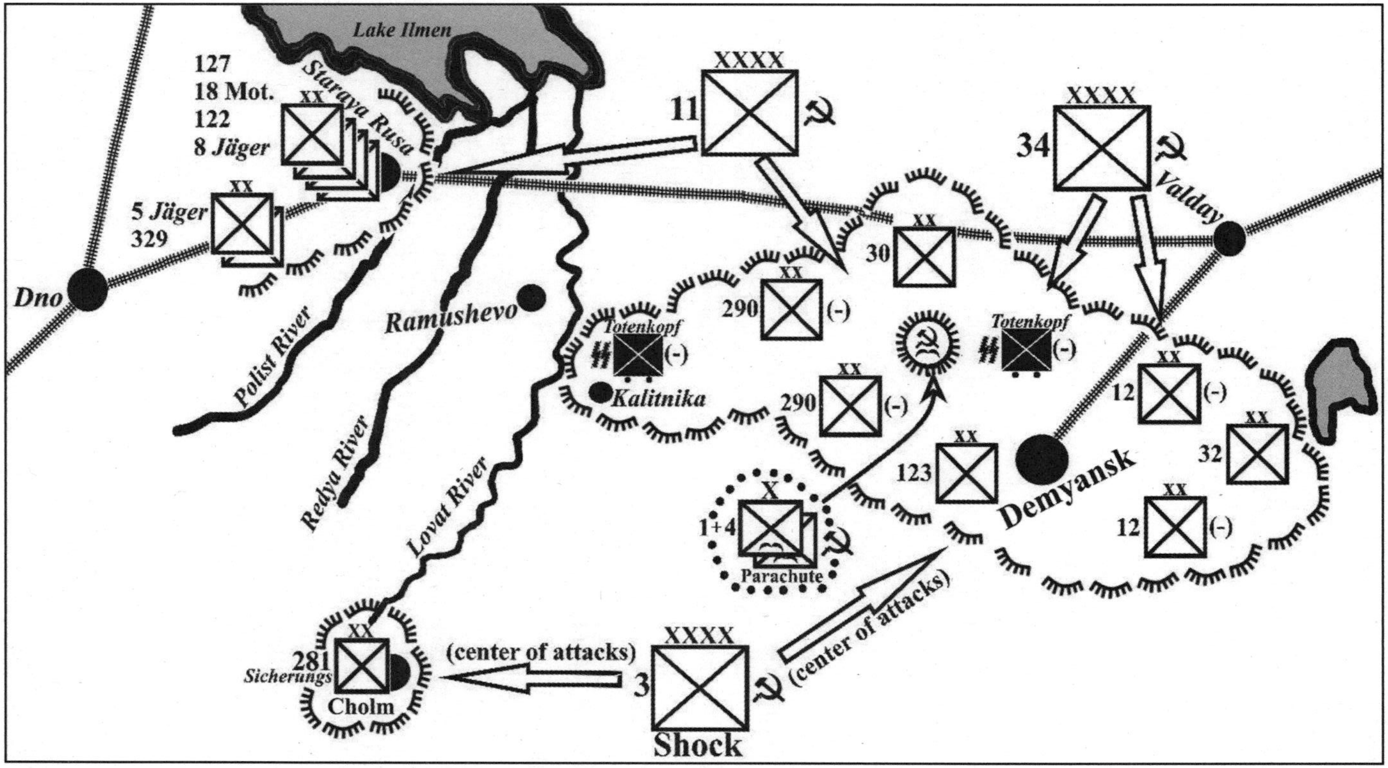

Map 2. The Soviet winter offensive of 1941–1942 mauled the German Army in the East, managing to trap several divisions in temporary pockets. The largest was the Demyansk Pocket and the smallest was the Cholm pocket. Eventually German forces were able to break through to the beleaguered troops holding Demyansk. In February 1943 the Demyansk salient, which jutted out from the German front lines, had to be abandoned. By forsaking the salient, the Germans were able to significantly shorten their front lines.

command would organize all the major anti-partisan drives and would help to gather, assign and coordinate the operations. To this end the National Leader of the SS Heinrich Himmler began to bring in additional SS and police forces into the USSR. The German Army also assisted by transferring from the Reich several security divisions, training and replacement units and field training formations that would in theory help secure the rear of the German Army in the East. In September 1942 Himmler published a booklet entitled *Bandenbekämpfung* (Combating Gangs) which was a guide on how to fight the guerrillas and how German anti-partisan forces were to conduct themselves.

The SS and police reinforcements for Belarusia became so numerous that by 1 October 1942 the *Kommandeur der Ordnungspolizei* (Commander of the Order Police) in the capital Minsk stated that his available forces included 1,394 German policemen, 8,374 Belarusian volunteers in the *Ordnungs Einzeldienst* (auxiliary police) and 1,456 volunteers in the Belarusian *Schutzmannschaft* (self-defence) battalions.[2] At the beginning of 1942 the strength of the *Schutzmannschaft Einzeldienst* (Self-Defence Auxiliary Police) stood at around 30,000 men. By the autumn of 1942, however, author Martin Dean states that number had increased to 170,000 men.[3] Many of these units were specialized formations. They were employed in central Russia and Belarus (White Russia) in 1941 and 1942, with various results. As the war behind the German lines intensified, so did the gravity of German reprisals against the local civilian populations. One such example was *Unternehmen Greif* (Operation Griffin).

Unternehmen Greif (Operation Griffin): 14–20 August 1942

This anti-guerrilla drive took place between 14 and 20 August 1942 in the area where the German 213th Security Division was operating and was aimed at guerrilla forces between Orsha and Vitebsk. It was a precursor to *Unternehmen Sumpffieber* (Operation Swamp Fever), launched in late August 1942. German forces employed in the action included the 406th Security Regiment of the 213th Security Division, plus the 244th, 324th, 373rd, 573rd and 583rd Security Battalions. On 9 July 1942 the 307th Police Battalion, which had been serving as the I. Battalion of Police Regiment Centre, was redesignated as the I. Battalion of Police Regiment 23. This police battalion was also used in Griffin, covering the northern sector of the operation.

Operation Griffin cost 1,390 lives, mostly civilians living in the area's villages and hamlets who were charged with aiding the guerrillas.[4] Only about 120 of those killed were actual partisan fighters. Apparently, it did not matter to the Germans if the assistance the villagers gave the guerrillas was willing or unwilling. The 427th Regional Defence Battalion and the 627th Eastern Battalion were used to create an easterly blocking force, in case of a possible escape attempt by the partisans.

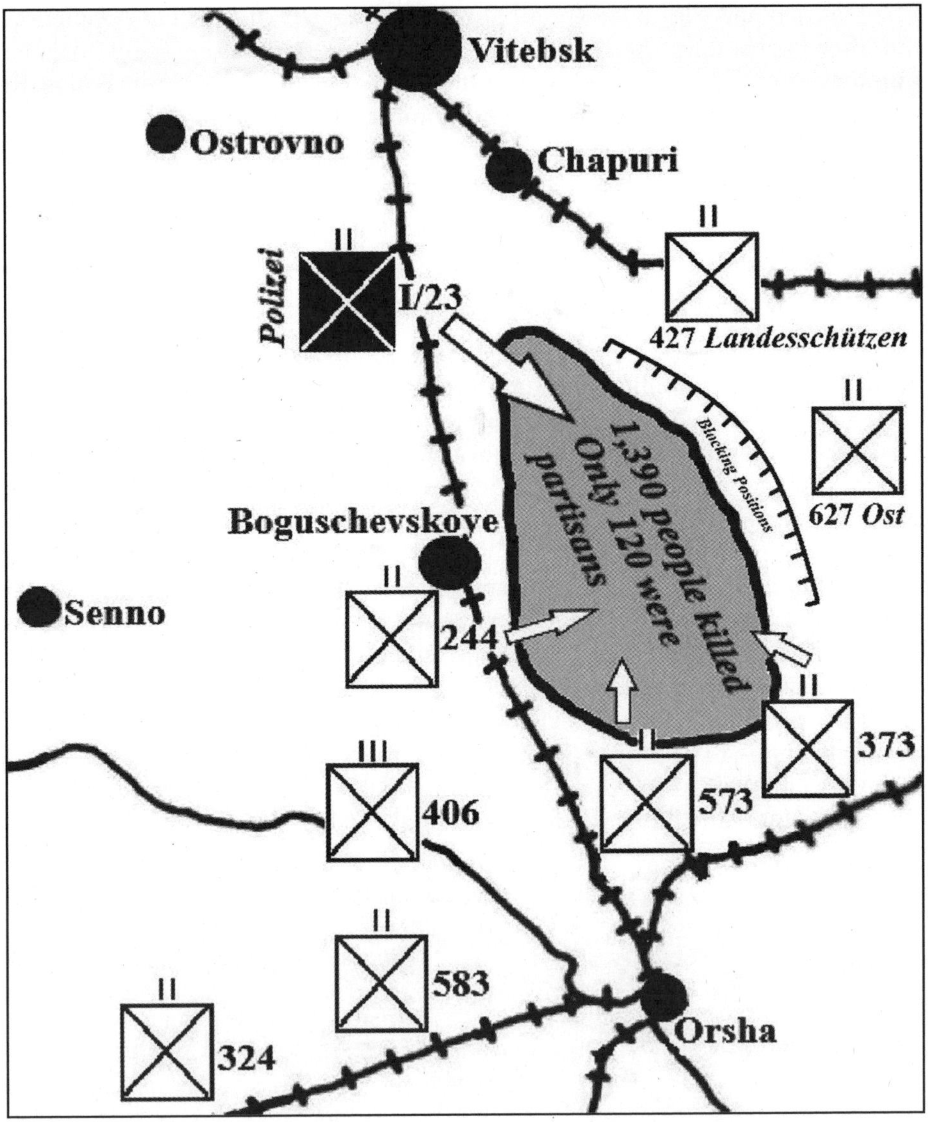

Map 3. German units employed during Operation Griffin and the general location of forces.

Unternehmen Bamberg (Operation Bamberg): 26 March–6 April 1942

This early anti-partisan drive took place in the area of Glusk, Paritschi and Oktyabrski, just south of the town of Bobruisk (in the eastern Polesie region). German units here included the 707th Security Division, the 203rd Security Brigade, the 102nd Slovak Infantry Regiment and the 315th Police Battalion.

The German and Slovakian forces purposely targeted the civilian population and after twelve days the body count stood at approximately 5,000 civilians who were shot dead or burned alive. Of the 5,000 people killed, only 650 were positively identified as guerrillas, and some 200 were Jews. The Germans captured only forty-seven weapons. German losses were seven killed and eight wounded. Slovakian losses are unknown. Of the estimated 1,500–2,000 partisans in the region, somewhere between 850 and 1,350 guerrillas managed to escape the trap.

Unternehmen München (Operation Munich): 19–29 March 1942

In the area east of Smolensk, which included the cities of Yelnya, Dorogobuzh and Yartsevo, Soviet Lieutenant General Belov had created a partisan 'republic' containing about 20,000 Soviet fighters. From the German perspective, this large force, led by Belov himself, was composed of both regular and irregular fighters. It was the largest partisan concentration in the rear of the German front to date. The republic was even connected to the Soviet side by the establishment and use of several crude airfields. The scale of the problems Belov caused the Wehrmacht can be seen from the fact that it took three large military operations, codenamed Munich, Hannover I and Hannover II, and employing rear area as well as regular army divisions, to fully destroy this partisan concentration. The existence of this republic indicated how large and well supplied the Soviet partisans were becoming by the spring of 1942, as did the fact that it took the Germans nearly two months to clear the Yelna-Dorogobuzh area of guerrilla forces.

Map 4. Operation Munich, 19–29 March 1942.

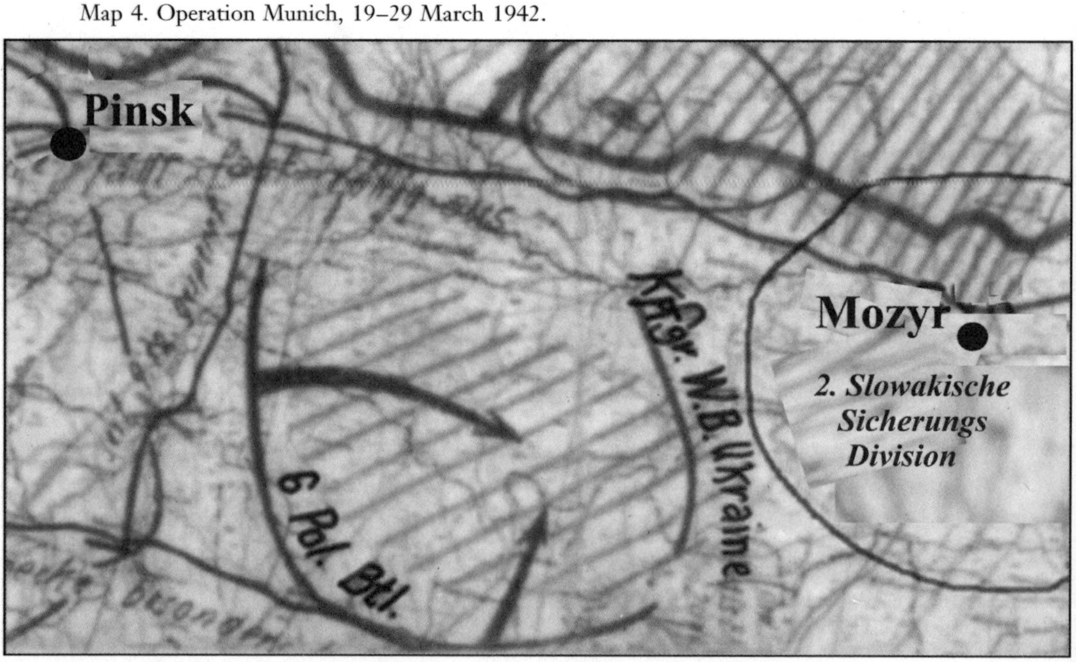

The 221st Security Division had to withdraw all of its units from the front and relocate them to the rear army area of Army Group Centre. There, after a general overhaul of the division, the unit took part in all three of the anti-partisan operations: Operation Munich (19–29 March), Hannover I (24–30 May) and Hannover II (3–11 June). The Munich operation involved three German divisions, controlled by a corps headquarters command, and had Luftwaffe support. The action was led mainly by the 350th Infantry Regiment of the 221st Security Division.[5] This drive was launched against especially numerous and well-trained guerrillas, most of whom were former Red Army soldiers now turned partisan.

> The operations encompassed mobile encircling movements over wide areas, and the [221st] division, now consisting almost entirely of second-rate Landesschützen Bataillone, suffered heavily from appalling weather, lack of fuel and low fighting power. It was also plagued by spirited Soviet counterattacks, bitter fighting and heavy casualties.[6]

Unternehmen München (Operation Munich): 15 March–12 May 1942

Note: This operation was separate from another undertaking launched on the border region between Ukraine and Belarusia, also codenamed 'Munich'.

This operation was an anti-partisan drive launched under the command of the *Wehrmacht Befehlshaber Ukraine* (Armed Forces Military Commander Ukraine). The operation was centred on the area inside the Pinsk-Ovruch-Mozyr triangle, and the forces employed were substantial:

- Cossack Infantry Battalion Mozyr (6 companies)
- 2nd Slovak Infantry Regiment
- 4th Security Regiment
- 252nd Self-Defence Battalion
- 45th Police Battalion
- 303rd Police Battalion
- 313th Police Battalion
- 1st Police Cavalry Battalion
- 33rd Reserve Police Battalion[7]
- 82nd Police Battalion
- Elements of the 105th Hungarian Light Division
- 82nd Police Signals Company
- 302nd Police Signals Company
- 3rd Technical Emergency Battalion
- 4th Technical Emergency Battalion

The operation resulted in some 4,000–5,000 people murdered, of whom fewer than 200 were verifiable partisans. Unfortunately, as for the other Operation

Munich, no additional data on this operation has been forthcoming. Between the Bamberg and Munich drives, around 7,000–8,000 people were murdered.[8]

Unternehmen Hannover I and *II* (Operation Hannover I and II): 24–30 May and 3–11 June 1942

Operation Hannover combined both front-line units and rear area security forces in an attempt to clear the region bordering Spas Demensk-Yelnya-Dorogobuzh-Vyazma of a large partisan force that also included units of the Red Army's 1st Cavalry Corps and the 4th Parachute Corps. The region lay immediately behind the front lines of the German 4th Army. The drive took place in two steps, the first 24–30 May, and the second 3–11 June 1942. The whole operation netted 4,000 enemy killed and 6,000 taken prisoner. German losses were 200 missing in action and 468 killed. The Germans combed through roughly 480 towns, villages and hamlets, but it seems the civilian population was mostly left untouched, because this was principally an operation employing front-line units.

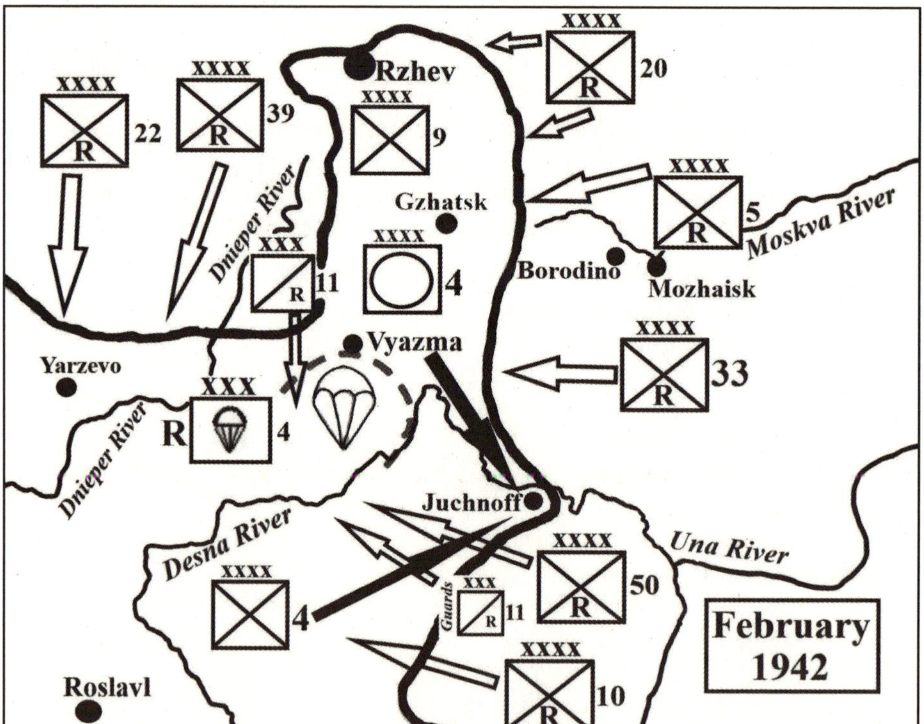

Map 5. Soviet advances in the winter of 1941/1942 would lead to the insertion of Red Army forces deep behind the German lines in and around Rzhev. *Unternehmen Hannover* was the German plan to eliminate these Soviet units.

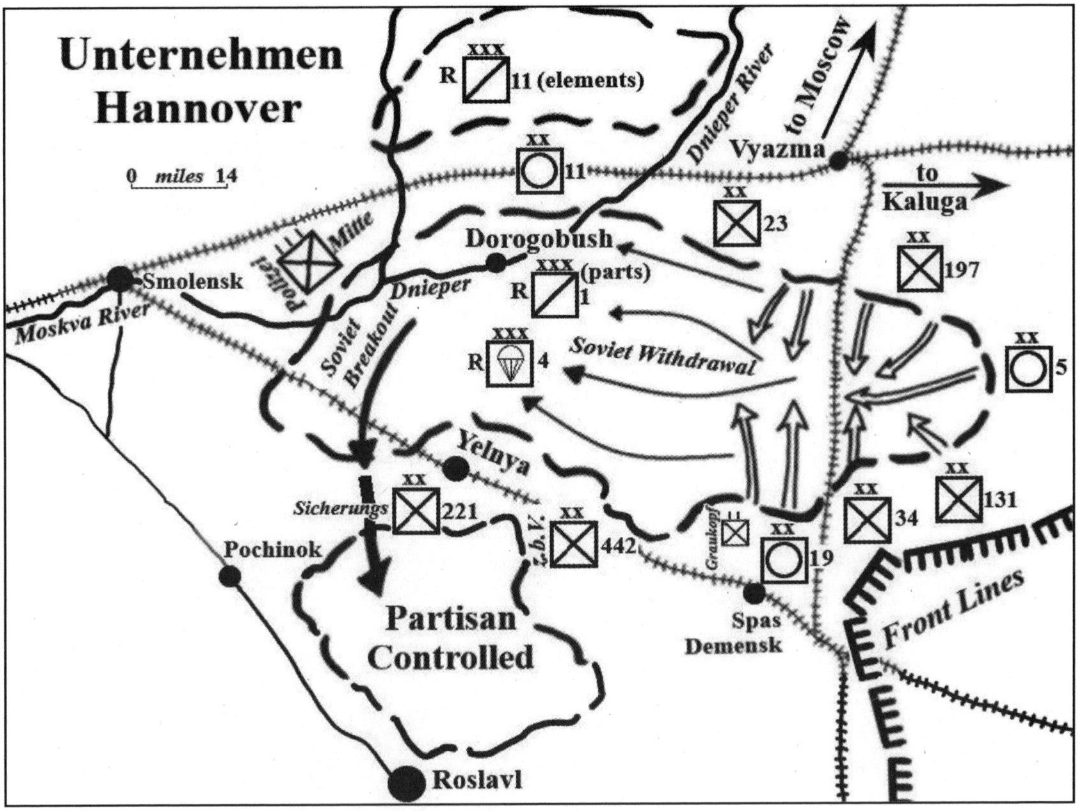

Map 6. *Unternehmen Hannover*, 24 May–11 June 1942.

Unternehmen Sumpffieber (Operation Swamp Fever): 25 August–2 September 1942

This operation encompassed a good part of Belarusia, from Slonim to Brod and from Schodino, Borisov and Brodnya to Lake Snudy. The major driving force was the 1st SS Motorized Brigade (minus the 10th SS Motorized Regiment), with some 2,300 men. The secondary driving force was Police Regiment Barkhold, which included the I. Battalion of Police Regiment 24 (i.e. the old 65th Reserve Police Battalion), plus the 24th Latvian Self-Defence Battalion.[9] The blocking force in the south included units of the 339th Static Infantry Division, situated in and around Slutsk.

In the north, located just south of Vileika and Lake Vilyia, was Police Regiment Binz, which comprised the I. Battalion of Police Regiment 23 (i.e. the old 307th Police Battalion), plus the 3rd Lithuanian Self-Defence Battalion. Finally, the 18th Latvian Self-Defence Battalion held positions at Schodino, waiting for the advance of both the 1st SS Motorized Brigade and Police Regiment Barkhold.

The 1st SS Motorized Brigade was led by SS Brigadier General and Major General of the Waffen SS Karl Freiherr von Fischer-Treuenfeld, while SS Oberführer and Colonel of the Gendarmerie Walter Schimana controlled

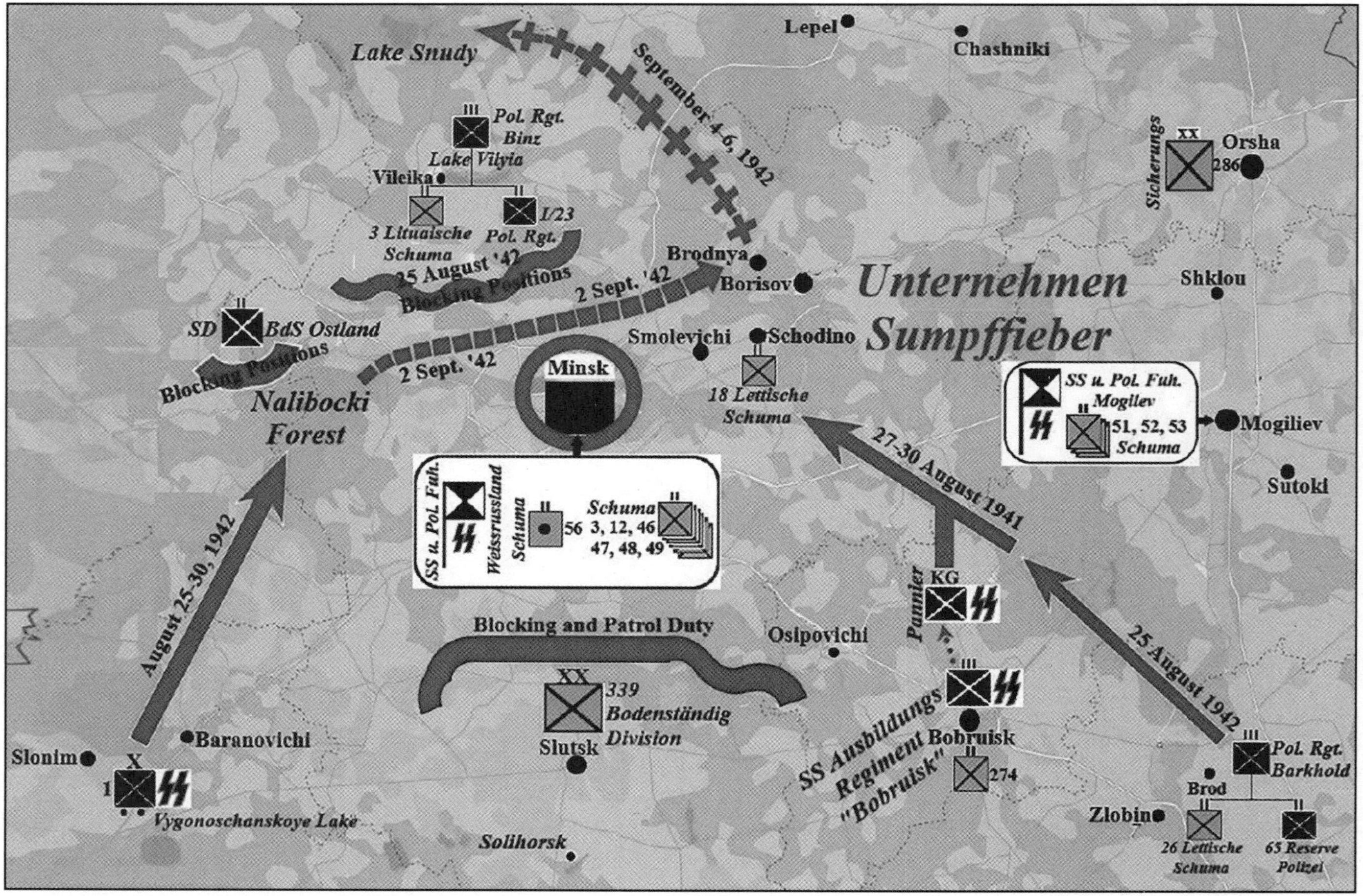

Map 7. Operation Swamp Fever, 25 August–2 September 1942.

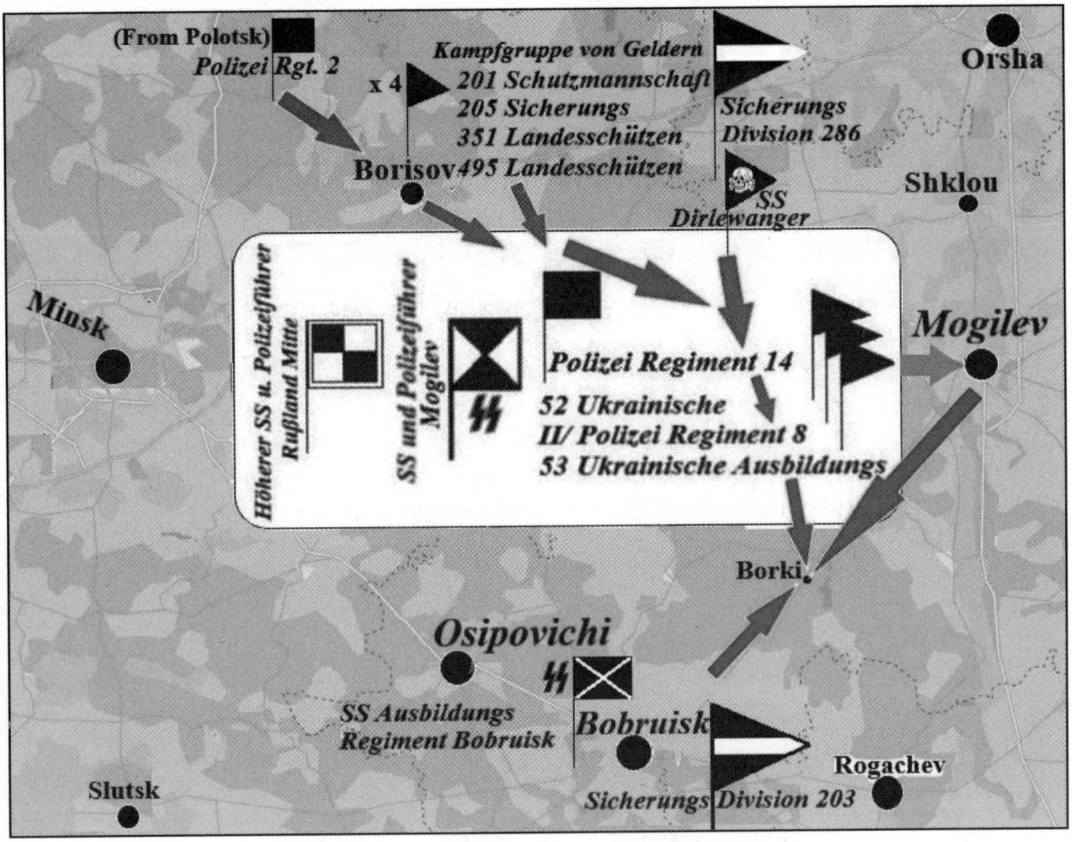

Map 8. The final phase of Operation Swamp Fever.

Police Regiment Binz and Police Regiment Barkhold. Reserve forces located in Minsk included the 15th Lithuanian Self-Defence Battalion, two companies of the Latvian 266-E *Schutzmannschaft* Battalion and a Self-Defence Training Company, which was a training company for *Schuma* personnel. In total, Schimana could count on 3,750 men. The operation therefore had a total of 6,050 men (not including the roughly 4,000 men of the 339th Static Division). In addition, SS Brigadier General and Major General of the Police Heinz Jost, who was Commander of the Security Police and Security Service in the Eastland, supplied additional men by way of a reinforced security service battalion containing 24 German officers and 244 NCOs and enlisted personnel, plus 350 Latvian and 100 Russian volunteers (718 officers, NCOs and enlisted men in total). During the operation 8,350 Jews were murdered. Approximately 6,000 were killed in Baranovichi alone. Some 1,217 additional people were deported to work in Germany, while only 389 actual partisans were killed.

Operation Polar Bear I, II and III: January 1943

This operation was launched south of Bryansk, mainly between Dimitriyev and Mikhailovka. The purpose of the operation was to eliminate any partisan forces that still remained in the area after Operation Triangle and Quadrangle in late September 1942. During that drive the Germans had hoped to completely destroy the Panchenko Partisan Brigade. This new drive would still not accomplish the partisan brigade's destruction, but the unit's actions and combat effectiveness were so impressive that it caught the attention of the head of the German Secret Field Police, General Wilhelm Krichbaum:

> An investigation of partisan activities in Mikhailovka Rayon (south-southeast of Dimitrovsk) which was started in July 1942 led to the uncovering of the Panchenko band. Several actions to break up this band failed, and the investigation, under the direction of a chief informant and conducted on a stepped-up scale in connection with 'Operation Polar Bear' in January 1943, resulted in an entirely new evaluation of this group. The analysis and comparison of the extensive results of the

Map 9. Operation Polar Bear I, II and III. This map also shows the area of operations and units that took part in Operation Triangle and Quadrangle (17 September–2 October 1942).

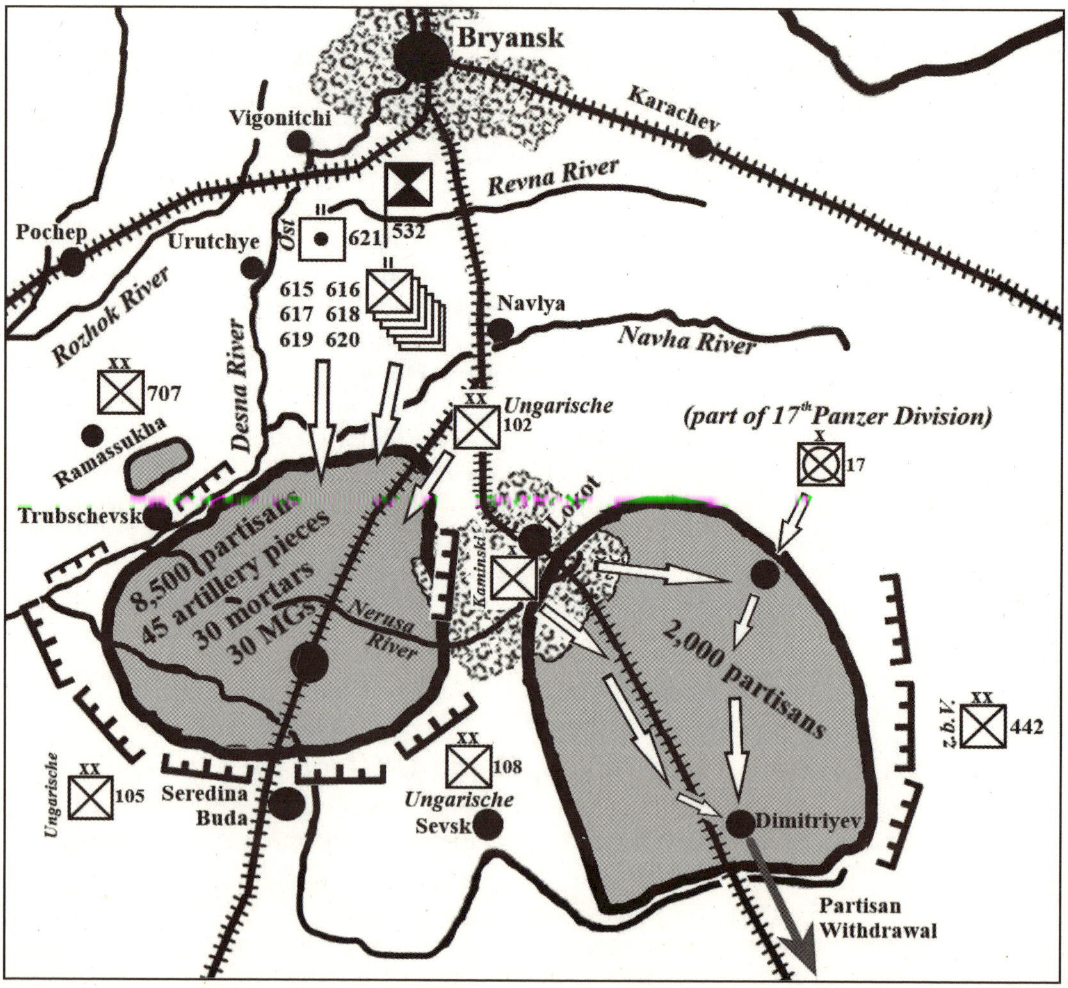

> investigation available so far indicate that the Panchenko band must be credited with an importance which goes far beyond the previously known or recognized scope of partisan activity.[10]

The new drive against these partisan forces south of Bryansk was split up into three separate parts, numbered I, II and III. Soviet partisan strength in the region of Bryansk-Orel amounted to about 14,600 guerrillas.[11] Of that number, approximately 10,500 were located south of Bryansk. The forces involved in this operation employed indigenous forces under Korück 532, and the Kaminski Brigade stationed in Lokot. In the spring of 1943 Korück 532 could count on 11,058 volunteers in the various eastern battalions, while the Kaminski Brigade had a strength of 6,519 men. In addition, fourteen so-called 'people's defence battalions' numbering some 8,191 men were also on hand.[12] Hungarian forces employed included the 102nd and 108th Hungarian Security Divisions, as well as part of the 105th Hungarian Security Division led by Seredina Buda. German troops included Oberst Rübsam's 17. Panzergrenadier Brigade, who was the former commander of the 17. *Kavallerie Regiment*.[13]

Colonel Karl Rübsam was a highly decorated Army officer. He had been awarded the German Cross in Gold on 20 March 1942 while leading the 63rd Rifle Regiment of the 17th Panzer Division.[14] The 11th *Jäger Bataillon* was operating under Group Rübsam, while the 10th *Jäger Bataillon* was operating with the Russian volunteer battalions of Korück 532. The 17th Armoured Infantry Brigade had been formed on 5 July 1942 and was an integral part of the 17th Panzer Division.[15] Other German troops used during the drive included Lieutenant General Karl Bornemann's 442nd Division for Special Employment, which was used as the headquarters staff to control such diverse units as the 102nd Hungarian Security Division and the 17th Armoured Infantry Brigade.[16]

Operation Harvest Festival II: 30 January–9 February 1943

Three days after the end of Harvest Festival I, Harvest Festival II began. It involved a sweep of the rail line between Slutsk and Brest (Litovsk), as well as the rail line between Minsk and Ivieniec.[17] Three battle groups were organized, named 'Worm', 'Binz' and 'Griep' after their respective commanders: Police Colonel Paul Worm, commander of Police Regiment 13, SS Major and Police Major Siegfried Binz, the commander of I. Battalion of Police Regiment 23, and Police Lieutenant Colonel Hans Griep, commander of Police Regiment 2.[18] In January 1943 the Druzhina SS Brigade was already operating as part of SS Brigadier General Kurt von Gottberg's SS Battlegroup.[19] Battlegroup Binz comprised SS Sonderkommando Dirlewanger, as well as a battalion from the Druzhina SS Brigade[20] and what was referred to as the Rodionov Battalion.[21] Obviously only one battalion from the Druzhina SS Brigade, led by Vladimir Gil himself (aka Rodionov), was taking part in the operation. The attack along the two railway lines netted a small number of guerrillas.

At this time SS Major Franz Magill was temporarily leading SS Sonderkommando Dirlewanger while its commander was away from his post.[22] Oskar Dirlewanger returned to assume command of the SS penal unit on 20 February 1943. Worm's Police Regiment 13 had been recently attached to the 9th Army, its I. and III. Battalions having served under this higher command from 1 November 1942 until 20 January 1943. During this period its II. Battalion had been a part of the Smolensk garrison.[23] Harvest Festival II netted a total of 2,400 'partisans' killed and another 2,300 'partisan helpers' and 'partisan suspects' shot after being apprehended. Total losses between 9 January and 8 February 1943 numbered 3,200 people categorized as partisans and listed as killed in battle, with another 2,300 apprehended and later shot.[24] The tally for both operations, extrapolating for overlapping dates, was 7,660 people. Records show that of this number, 144 were shot by SS Sonderkommando Dirlewanger during Operation Harvest Festival II.[25]

Operation Ankara I and II: 19 December 1942–21 January 1943

Ankara I (19–24 December 1942) was launched in the region of Khotimsk-Nivnoye-Shurbin-Balynkovichi with: the staff of the 36th Security Regiment, the 1st Battalion of Police Regiment 8, the 3rd Battalion of the 638th Infantry Regiment (French volunteers), the 604th Eastern Battalion 'Pripjet' and the 3rd Company of the 791st Security Battalion. Ankara II (18–20 January 1943) took place in the area of Chotimsk-Shirkovka-Katolin-Nivnoye with the staff of the 36th Security Regiment as the headquarters controlling:

- *southern attack group*: the 3rd Battalion (minus its 1st Company) of the 638th Infantry Regiment (French volunteers);
- *central attack group*: the 2nd Company of the 791st Security Battalion, 1st Battalion of Police Regiment 8 (without its 1st Company), Artillery Battery 'Uhse', the 1st Company of 3rd Battalion of the 638th Infantry Regiment (French volunteers); and
- *northern attack group*: the 604th Eastern Battalion 'Pripjet' (minus its 1st Company), the 1st Company of the 1st Battalion of Police Regiment 8, Group Fischer (part of the 45th Security Regiment), and the 1st Company of the 604th Eastern Battalion 'Pripjet'.

During this second drive, the 930th Grenadier Regiment was to provide security troops in the towns of Mglin and Novnoye Khotismsky.

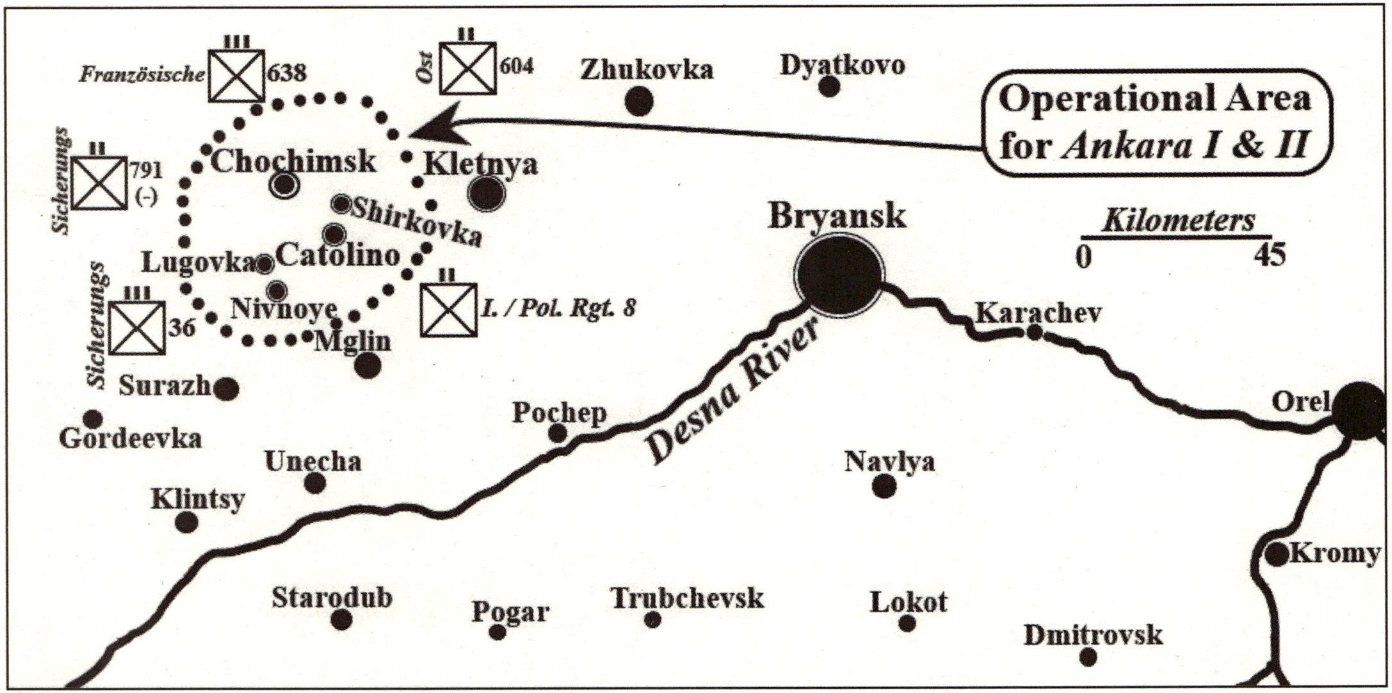

Map 10. The area of operations for Ankara I and Ankara II in relation to the city of Bryansk.

The order of battle for the 221st Security Division was as follows:

CO: Major General Karl Freiherr von Lersner
Ia: Lieutenant Colonel Helmuth Kreidel (July 1942–September 1943)

350th Infantry Regiment (reinforced)

I. Battalion:

1. Company	3. Company
2. Company	4. (MG) Company

II. Battalion:

5. Company	7. Company
6. Company	8. (MG) Company

III. Battalion:

9. Company	11. Company
10. Company	12. (MG) Company

I. Battalion of the 221st Artillery Regiment

1. Battery	3. Battery
2. Battery	

701st Guard Battalion (renamed 791st Security Battalion on 28 June 1942)

1. Company	3. Company
2. Company	4. Company

824th Signals Battalion

I. Battalion of Police Regiment 8:

1. Company	3. Company
2. Company	4. Company

1st and 2nd Cavalry Squadrons of the 221st Cavalry Battalion

45th Regional Defence Regiment

I. Battalion:

1. Company	3. Company
2. Company	4. Company

II. Battalion:

5. Company	7. Company
6. Company	8. Company

III. Battalion:

9. Company	11. Company	13. Company[26]
10. Company	12. Company	14. Company[27]

***221st Supply Forces* (350th Divisional Supply Leader)**
Eastern Troops in the division (as of 5 September 1943):
45th Eastern Security Company, 221st Eastern Company, 221st Eastern Cavalry Squadron, 350th Eastern Supply Company, 930th Eastern Security Company, 930th Eastern Security Squadron.

Eastern Troops in the division (as of 22 November 1943):
45th Eastern Security Company, 221st Eastern Company, 350th Eastern Supply Company, 930th Eastern Security Company, 930th Eastern Security Squadron.

The major unit that took part in Ankara I and II was the 221st Security Division, supported by the 36th Security Regiment of the 286th Security Division. The 36th Security Regiment had been established in June 1942 using the 642nd, 555th and 794th Security Battalions.[28] The attention of the 221st Security Division in December 1942 seemed to be focused on where the partisan problem seemed worst, particularly the northeastern Mamayevka Forest sector, while Ankara I and II both targeted the localities of Nivnoye, Lugovka, Catolino, Zhirkovka (Shirkovka) and Khotimsky (Chochimsk):[29]

> The 221st Security Division's view of the Ankara operations, conducted in the northeastern sector of the division's jurisdiction primarily by the 36th Security Regiment, was that the operations' purpose was to pacify the area, not plunder it. The regiment ordered that quota levels be strictly observed in the requisitioning of livestock, horses and produce, so as to ensure that the subsistence level be maintained. The 221st itself was even more unequivocal; there was to be no unbridled exploitation, even in those villages which had not achieved the necessary quota. For Ankara II, requisitioning was in most cases restricted, again, to collecting quotas from inhabited villages; only in the case of abandoned villages was the requisitioning to be more thorough and all-encompassing. Much of the livestock and foodstuffs procured in Ankara II, it seems, was not plundered from villages, but was in fact picked up when the partisans abandoned it. Moreover, the division imposed a total ban on the burning of villages for the duration of Ankara II. This may well have been a direct response to excesses committed during Ankara, for which the division had allowed the burning of villages 'under certain circumstances'.[30]

Operation Shooting Star: 23 January–12 February 1943

Operation Shooting Star was aimed at partisan units located in the forested region west of the Dubrovno-Vladimirskoye highway.[31] The German forces employed were strictly SS and police units. This anti-partisan drive was launched against guerrillas in the region west of the town of Dubrovno, where main rail and road links led to Moscow. This region was the principal supply line for the entire Army Group Centre. Beginning in November 1942, the Soviet partisans had been making an effort to cut off that supply line, and their efforts continued through July 1943. The Soviet plan to liberate all of Belarus by the summer of 1943 called on the partisan units in this region to cut the German supply line. In the end, Belarus was not conquered by the Red

Army until the summer of 1944. No other information has been forthcoming on this operation.

Unternehmen Klette I (Operation Burdock I): 12–25 October 1942

In the forested area around Mamayevka, southeast of the town of Kletnya in the Bryansk region,[32] the partisans had amassed a force of some 6,000 guerrilla fighters. The area of the Bryansk Oblast would suffer terrible damage as a result of the partisan and anti-partisan war. No records exist for how many villages and towns were attacked and destroyed by the partisans, but we do know the extent of the damage done by the Germans. During the occupation the Wehrmacht in the Bryansk Oblast purportedly destroyed 1,016 towns and villages and killed around 76,100 civilians.[33] Forces under Korück 532, led by *Generalleutnant* Friedrich-Gustav Bernhard, took part in this drive.[34] Those forces included the 615th–620th Eastern Battalions, the 621st Eastern Artillery Battalion and the 787th Security Battalion. A recently

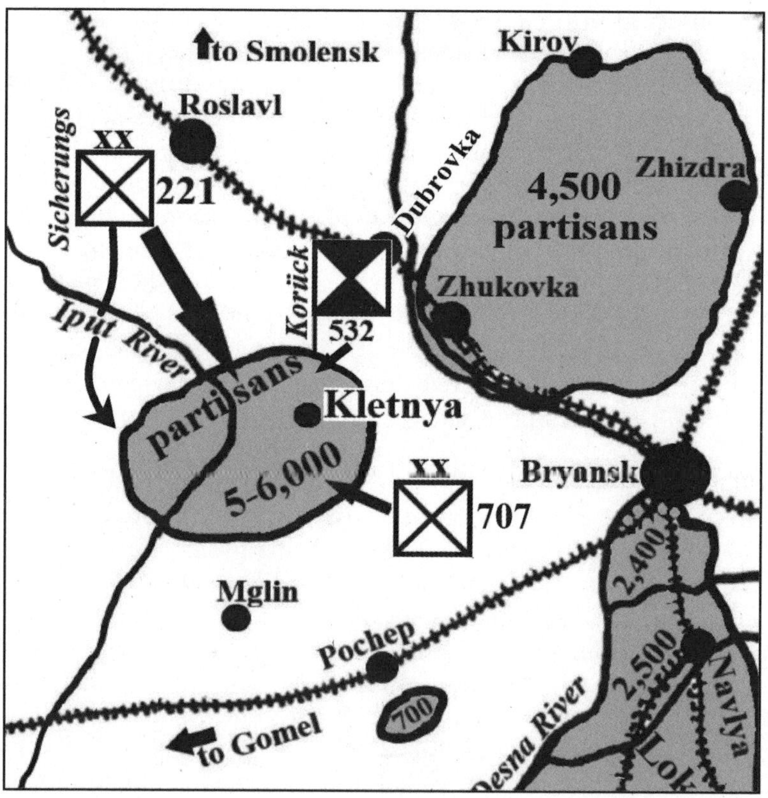

Map 11. *Unternehmen Klette I*: 12–25 October 1942.

established eastern unit, the 627th Volga-Tartar Eastern Battalion, was in ready reserve. The 707th Infantry Division employed one regiment, the 727th Infantry Regiment, for the operation.

Unternehmen Klette II (Operation Burdock II): 15 January–9 February 1943

Since the autumn of 1942 the Germans had wished to rid themselves of a partisan region centred in the area north of Kletnya and the heavily wooded Mamayevka forest region west of Bryansk. The operation was strictly an Army affair and no SS or police units were involved. An earlier operation, launched in the autumn of 1942, had pitted 1,600 Germans against an estimated 4,000 guerrillas and had proved an utter failure. Only 43 partisans had been killed and 2 captured, while the remainder withdrew easily. By the end of the year the number of guerrillas operating in this region of the Bryansk front stood at around 6,000 men. For Burdock II, the Germans employed a larger force against the partisans. The principal German unit was the 707th Infantry Division (static). Units from Korück 532 also assisted, as did a regiment from the 102nd Hungarian Security Division. The forest was covered by snow and the Germans also had to contend with a snow storm during the operation, but they still managed to kill about 745 guerrillas.

This was a small tactical victory but the partisans won an operational victory by escaping the German noose and avoiding destruction. By May 1943 this

Map 12. Area of operations for *Unternehmen Klette I and II* (Burdock I and II).

region contained around 8,000 guerrillas and would require another German anti-partisan drive.[35] For Burdock II, elements of the 221st Security Division were brought in behind the lines of the 2nd Panzer Army. Burdock II took place in January–February 1943. Units employed included the 791st Security Battalion, the I. Battalion of SS Police Regiment 8, the III. Battalion of the 638th French Infantry Regiment (reinforced) and the 604th Eastern Battalion. All these units had been sent to take part in Burdock II without any rest, after fighting on the front lines.[36] This second operation netted fifty-three small arms captured and 149 partisans killed.[37] The small number of guerrillas killed and the paltry number of weapons captured meant that the partisans had once again managed to evade the brunt of the German anti-partisan drive.

Chapter 2

Partisan warfare in the region of Army Group North

Increasing partisan threat

By July 1942 the number of partisan detachments in the Leningrad region had increased to fifty-eight units totalling 5,024 men.[1] Most of these guerrilla units operated in small groups of 50–100 men. Two notable exceptions during the spring and summer of 1942 were the 2nd and 3rd Partisan Brigades, which together accounted for 2,000 out of the 5,000-plus guerrillas in the area. The 2nd Partisan Brigade operated around Dno, while the 3rd operated south of Opochka. The most important guerrilla developments in the region of Army Group North during the winter of 1941/42 included the capture and establishment, by the 2nd Partisan Brigade, of a 'partisan region' (*krai*) bounded by the towns Dno-Staraya-Russa-Bezhanitsy-Cholm.[2] Several German attempts to reduce the partisan region in July–August 1941, principally with SS and police units, only managed to arouse anger and resentment which manifested itself by way of new partisan recruits.[3] In December 1941 a combined SD, Police and Baltic auxiliary police force was launched against the partisan region closest to the city of Leningrad, between Tosno and Siverskaya.

By the end of July 1942, the principal partisan areas in the region of Army Group North were as follows:[4]

- the marshy region southeast of Dno;
- the eastern part of the Kudova District;
- the region south of Opotschka;
- the regions surrounding the Krasny–Sebesh and Opotschka–Novorchev roads;
- the regions south and west of Puschkinskiye Gery;
- the wooded region east of Gdov, mostly east of the Piyussa river, as well as south and north of Gdov;
- the wooded region east of Pleskau (Pskov); and
- the wooded region south of the log road between Maramorka and Okonevo.

The estimated number of guerrillas in these areas in June 1942 was around 4,000–5,000 men, and growing. This was a force that the German command

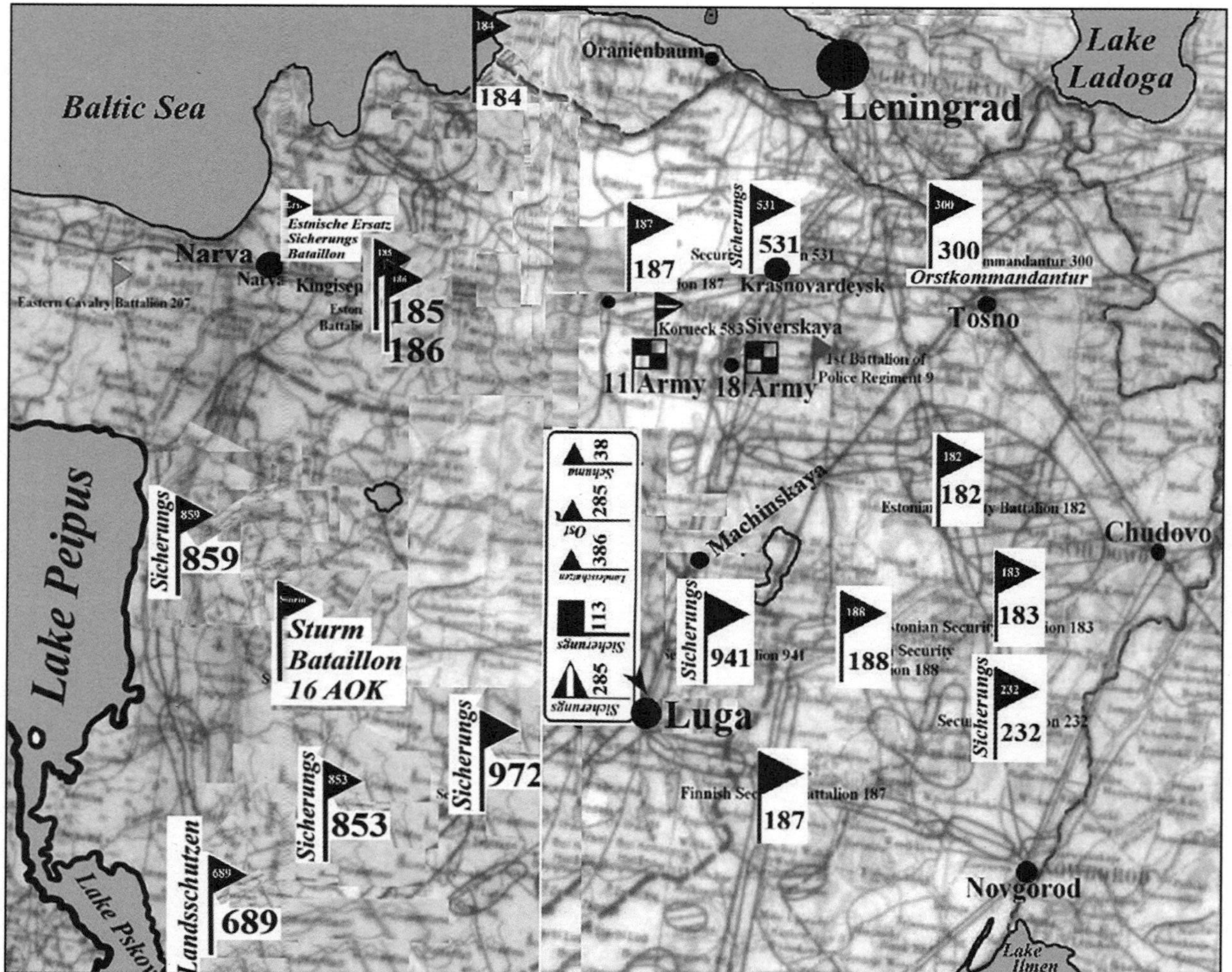

Map 13. German and Baltic anti-partisan forces in the rear of Army Group North, 1–12 September 1942.

needed to deal with, and the high number of partisans in this region of the front explains why so many battlegroups had to be formed to combat the Soviet guerrillas.

By the beginning of the autumn of 1942 the number of guerrillas in that same region had increased to four partisan brigades and thirty weak detachments. The increase in partisan activity in the region of Army Group North from 1942 forced the Germans to employ more forces there to guard the rear areas. The map above shows the location of part of the 388th Field Training Division, which made its appearance in October 1942. The 388th Field Training Division was formed on 9 September 1942 for service behind the lines of Army Group North. The staff came from Military District I, while the cadres were taken from military units in Military Districts II and VIII. The division was filled out using personnel from the *Reichsarbeitsdienst* (RAD, Reich National Labour Service). It initially comprised two regiments: the 639th and 640th Infantry (Field Training) Regiments. On 15 March 1944 the 391st Field Training Division, which comprised four regiments, handed over one regiment, the 391st Infantry (Field Training) Regiment, to the control of the 388th Field Training Division. On 19 May 1944 the 388th Field Training Division was renamed Field Training Division North.

The region north of the Polotsk lowlands and west of Velikiye Luki was an area of intense guerrilla activity with numerous partisan detachments and brigades. For the fight against these partisans, and others in the region of Army Group North, the principal headquarters command responsible for controlling the rear areas was known as the Rear Area Army Commander, abbreviated to Korück. Korück 583 operated behind the 18th Army and Korück 584 behind the 16th Army. These were the equivalent to divisional headquarters commands and led a conglomerate of battalions and regiments. For example, on 29 July 1943 Korück 584 had the following forces at its disposal:[5]

820th Field Command
Assault Battalion of the 16th Army
5th Latvian Self-Defence Battalion
13th Latvian Self-Defence Battalion
267th Latvian Self-Defence Battalion
561st Military Field Police Battalion (motorized)
I. Battalion of the 113th Security Regiment
II. Battalion of the 113th Security Regiment
653rd Eastern Battalion
668th Eastern Battalion
669th Eastern Battalion
868th Security Battalion

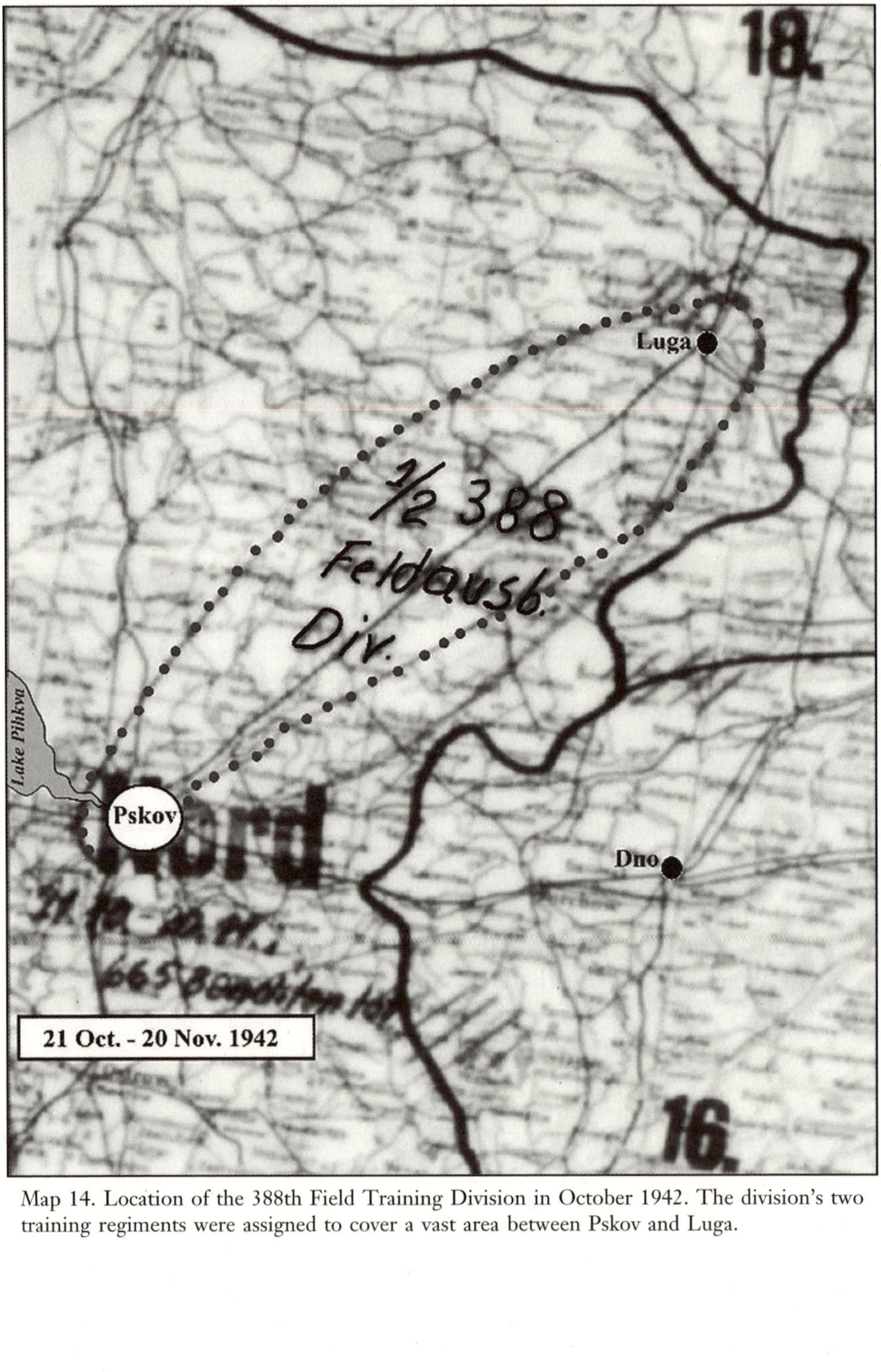

Map 14. Location of the 388th Field Training Division in October 1942. The division's two training regiments were assigned to cover a vast area between Pskov and Luga.

869th Security Battalion
671st Eastern Supply Company
Field Training Battalion of the 18th Army

The German *Feldkommandantur* (Field Command) headquarters held the equivalent staff of a regiment and were part of the military government which ran the countryside in the regions where Nazi civilian administration was not established. This was usually the region between the front lines and the rear areas already under Nazi civilian control, although they could also be located within the civilian region. The Field Command headquarters controlled lower administrative staffs that were called Local Commands. These were basically Army garrison or city administrative headquarters staffs, which were the equivalent to battalion staffs. The Field Command headquarters and Local Command headquarters comprised the German Army's rear area administrative organization within the various German army groups from 1941 to 1944. For Army Group North, they included the following headquarters and staff:

18th Army – Korück 583 – Siverskaya
579 Higher Field Command – Luga: 1941
312th Field Command – Krasnovardeysk: 1941–March 1943
  255th Local Command – Tosno: 1941–1944
  305th Local Command – Krasnovardeysk: 1942–1944
  322nd Local Command – Krasnoye Selo: 1941–1944
  341st Local Command – Siverskaya: 1942–1944
190th Field Command – Luga: 1941–January 1942
569th Field Command – Luga: 1941–1944
  315th Local Command – Yatchera: 1942–1944
  351st Local Command – Vyritsa: 1942–1944
  299th Local Command – Ljuban: 1942–1944
  331st Local Command – Chudovo: 1942
  574th Local Command – Volosovo: 1941–1944
  858th Local Command – Voloshovo: 1942
  859th Local Command – Voloshovo: 1942
182nd Field Command – Batetskaya: 1941–1943
819th Field Command – Oredesh: 1942–1943
  276th Local Command – Oredesh: 1941–1944
  361st Local Command – Batetskaya: 1942–1944
  864th Local Command – Utorgosch: 1941–1944
238th Field Command Narva – Narva[6]: 1944
247th Field Command – Narva: 1941–1943
819th Field Command – Narva: 1943–1944
  257th Local Command – Narva: 1942
  852nd Local Command – Narva: 1943–1944

371st Local Command – Kingisepp: 1942
362nd Local Command – Kotly: 1944
820th Field Command – Staraya Russa:[7] 1943–1944

16th Army – Korück 584 – Dno
241st Field Command – Pskov: 1941–1944[8]
820th Field Command – Staraya Russa: 1941–1942
311th Local Command – Pazherevitsy: 1942–1945
360th Local Command – Staraya Russa: 1942–1944
865th Local Command – Volot: 1941–1943
820th Field Command – Schimsk: 1943
257th Local Command – Dulovo: 1942–1944
329th Local Command – Loknia: 1943–1944
321st Local Command – Bezhanitsy: 1941–1944
565th Local Command – Schimsk: 1941–1944
526th Local Command – Soltsy: 1941–1944
822nd Field Command – Ostrov: 1941–1943
534th Local Command – Ostrov: 1941–1944
862nd Local Command – Porchov: 1942
186th Field Command – Opochka: 1941–1944
342nd Local Command – Opochka: 1944
293rd Local Command – Novosalniki: 1942
247th Field Command – Idritza: 1942
701st Local Command – Idritza: 1942
912th Local Command – Dedovichi: 1941–1944
528th Field Command – Sebezh: 1941–1942
359th Local Command – Sebezh: 1942

In addition to the headquarters of the Field Commands, the Local Commands, the Korück commands and the divisional headquarters of the three security divisions assigned to the region, the Germans also employed an SS and police battlegroup almost from the start of the campaign. This was SS Battlegroup Jeckeln, named after its commander, SS Lieutenant General and Lieutenant General of the Police Friedrich Jeckeln. Other SS officers also created battlegroups as the need arose, or as anti-partisan operations were planned and conducted. One such group was SS Battlegroup Knecht, named after Police Colonel Max Knecht, who employed four entire Latvian police battalions in early February 1943 against partisan forces along the Latvian–Belarus border.[9] Jeckeln's battlegroup varied in strength from time to time, but in July 1942, while stationed in Krasnovardeisk, in the Leningrad area, it comprised the 19th, 21st, 29th and 33rd Self-Defence Battalions. It was almost continually committed to fighting the guerrilla forces in the Eastland and in the region of Army Group North from early 1942 until December 1943.[10]

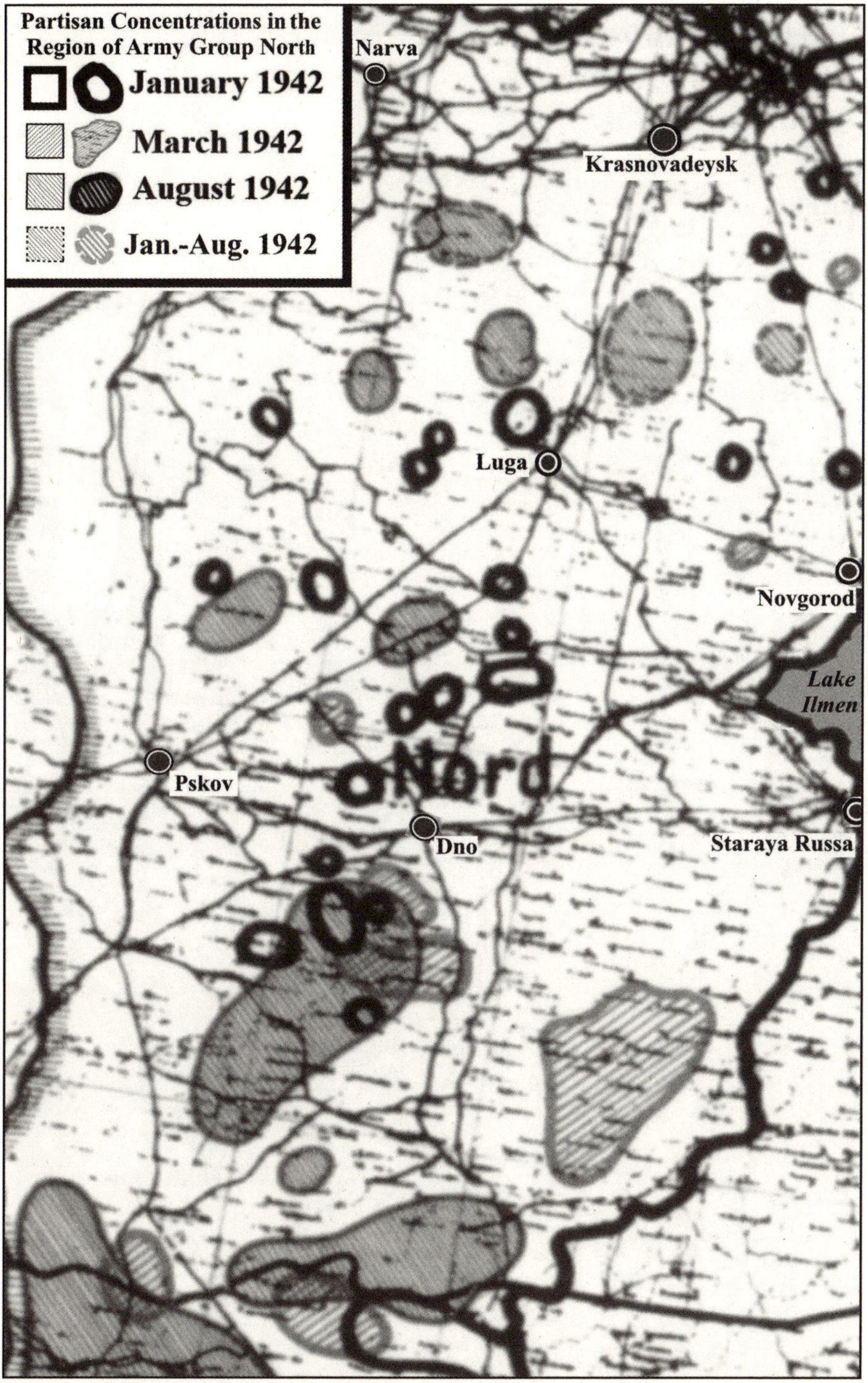

Map 15. Partisan concentrations in the region of Army Group North, 1942.

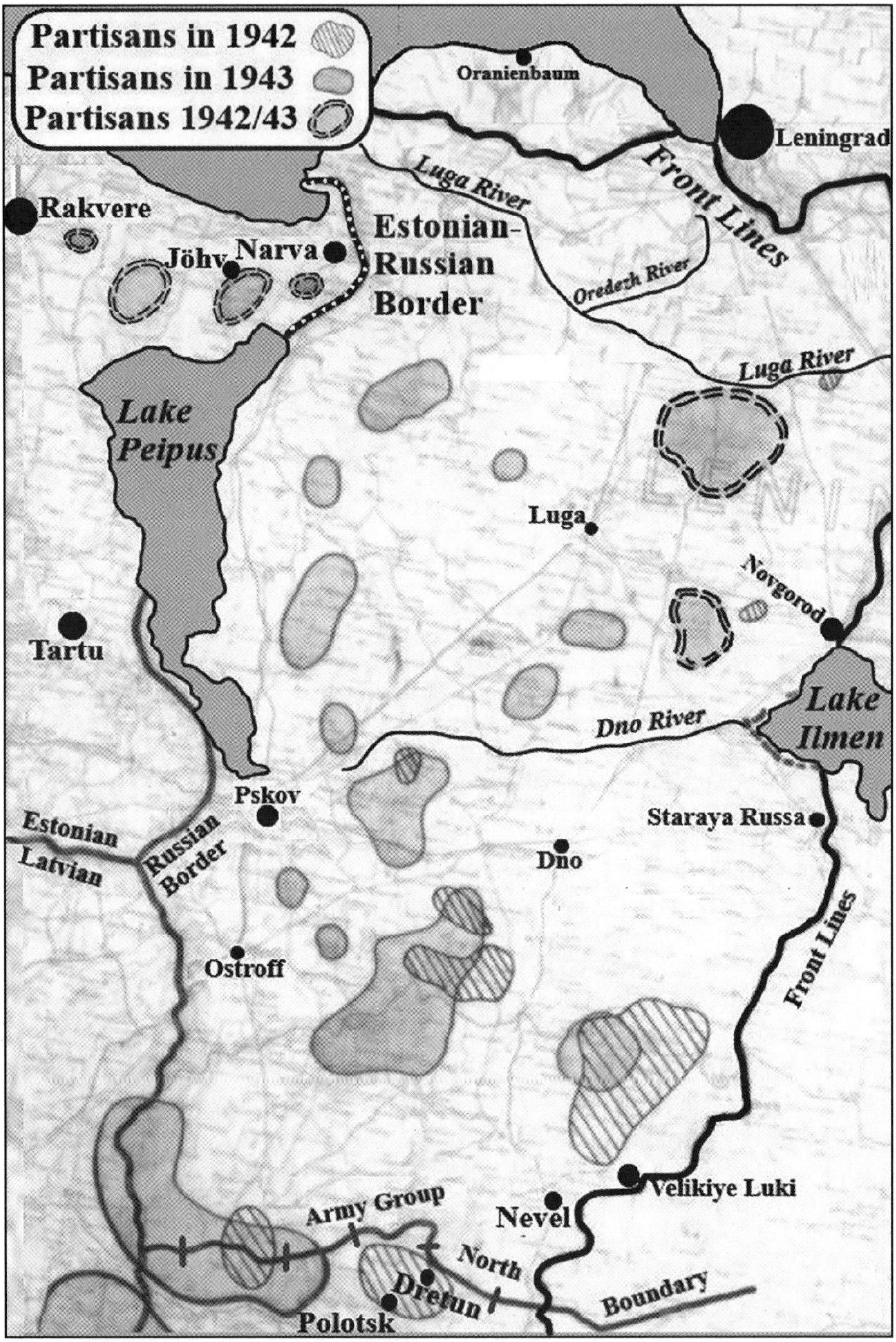

Map 16. Partisan concentrations, August 1943. Areas shaded with diagonal lines indicate partisan concentrations in 1942, while fully shaded areas show partisan concentrations in 1943. Areas with broken outlines indicate partisan concentrations in both 1942 and 1943.

Operation Snow Hare: 24 January–12 February 1943

By the beginning of the second week of January 1943 Field Marshal Günther von Kluge had moved his 3rd Panzer Army headquarters to the western rim of the Toropets bulge, where the Soviet 3rd Shock Army was pressing hard towards Nevel after having encircled German forces at Velikiye Luki.[11] On 15 January 1943 an attempt to relieve the trapped German garrison at Velikiye Luki failed. At this time an estimated 20,000 partisans were roaming the rear of 3rd Panzer Army, adding to the predicament of German forces trying to relieve the garrison at Velikiye Luki while holding off further Red Army attacks. In order to relieve this pressure from the rear, Operation Snow Hare was devised. An anti-partisan drive, it was to be performed primarily by the 201st Security Division, which was the only Army unit available in Army Group Centre for the mission. The SS contributed the II. Battalion of SS Field Recruit Depot Bobruisk for the operation.[12] This recruit depot contained three recruit training battalions and supplied units to fight the partisans in Belarus. The Bobruisk depot has often been confused with a Waffen SS replacement unit stationed in Bereza-Kartuska, but the only SS recruit or replacement formation located in Bereza-Kartuska during the war was the 18th SS Armoured Infantry Training Battalion. The only other SS unit to be stationed in Bereza-Kartuska was the 501st SS Jäger Battalion, which was established on 10 July 1943 by simply renaming the I. Battalion of SS Field Recruit Depot Bobruisk and shifting it from Bobruisk to Bereza-Kartuska.

The Bobruisk recruit depot was organized as follows:

Regimental staff: 169 officers, NCOs and men.
Commander: SS Colonel Rudolf Pannier.

I. Battalion – 898 officers, NCOs and men. Redesignated as the 501st SS Jäger Battalion on 10 July 1943. The battalion was disbanded in October 1944. Commander: SS Major Armin Beilhack (fell 23 August 1943), then SS Major Aleksander Sukkau.

II. Battalion – 599 officers, NCOs and men. Redesignated as the 500th SS Jäger Battalion on 10 July 1943. The battalion was disbanded in October 1944. Commander: SS Major Alexander Sukkau (until 23 August 1943), then SS Captain Rudolf Bachmann.

III. Battalion – 454 officers, NCOs and men. The battalion was disbanded in June 1944 and its men sent to reinforce the 500th and 501st SS Jäger Battalions. Commander: SS Major Heinrich Beyerlein.

The regiment was composed of about 50% Reich Germans, 30% ethnic-Germans from Romania and 20% ethnic-Germans from the Soviet Union.[13] The strength of the regiment on 31 July 1943 was 11 officers, 102 NCOs and 2,007 men.[14] In addition to the I. Battalion of SS Field Recruit Depot

Bobruisk, one German document clearly indicated that SS and police forces under SS Lieutenant General and General of the Police Friedrich Jeckeln were also to be employed in the operation:

> 21.1.43 13.00 Telegram
> From: Commander of Ostland Troops To: Army Group 'Centre'
> Operations Section No. 36/43
>
> SS-Obergruppenführer Jeckeln, the SS representative discussing the 'Snow Hare' operation on January 19, 1943 in Polotsk was informed that the 'Snow Hare' operation would be conducted from the east up to the Polotsk–Idritsa railway line and should be completed approximately by February 13, 1943. SS Obergruppenführer Jeckeln will start operations in the Lake Osveya area at the beginning of February. As information at hand shows that the main partisan district is to the east of the Polotsk–Idritsa railway line, it is desirable to continue the 'Snow Hare' operation to the west of the mentioned railway line and namely that the 'Snow Hare' operation and the Jeckeln operation be combined. These actions in clearing the area are of great importance for introducing law and order in the rear of the Third Tank Army. Please inform your point of view.
>
> Commander of Ostland Troops
> Operations Section No. 36/43
> Strictly Confidential[15]

Another report dated 25 January 1943 stated that troops for the operation were to be gathered by 27 January so that the drive could begin on 28 January 1943. This date contradicts other sources which give the start date as 24 January 1943. Further, the document also stressed that all agricultural products that might be acquired from the partisans and local populace by the troops were to be handed over to specialized collection groups which were to accompany the anti-partisan forces.[16] It appears that before the operation started, elements of the 281st Security Division were also earmarked for it, as the document specifically mentions that the northern flank of the drive was to be covered by one battalion from the 281st Security Division. This division was also to provide special units for blocking the southern boundary of the rear area of Army Group North. The document also affirmed the agreement between the commander of SS forces in the region of Army Group North (SS General Jeckeln) and the Chief of Rear Area Forces, Army Group Centre, about the need to extend the operation under Jeckeln's command in the region of Lake Osveya to the Polotsk-Idritsa railway line. However, the document ended with somewhat vague intentions:[17]

> It has not been clarified as yet whether the Chief of the SS and Police Forces of Army Group North has at his disposal forces sufficient for that

Map 17. The region where *Unternehmen Schneehase* (Operation Snow Hare) took place.

> and whether he really intends to advance further east. Operation Snow Hare will be carried out irrespective of this.[18]

A look at the *Bandenlagekarte* (anti-partisan map) for Operation Snow Hare clearly shows that at the conclusion of the drive, the Germans claimed over 1,000 partisans killed. Unfortunately, no figures were available for civilians in the region who might have been captured or drafted for work in Germany. The German forces arrayed against the partisans were organized in small battlegroups that were thus more mobile. The units that took part in Operation Snow Hare included the following:[19]

Group Perling: Police Major Walter Perling
II. and III. Battalions of the 9th Police Regiment[20]
3. Squadron of the 3rd Cavalry Regiment[21]
One platoon from the 6th Company of the 3rd Cavalry Regiment
20th Cavalry Platoon of the 281st Eastern Cavalry Battalion
One Signals squad from the 822nd Signals Battalion
Destination on 5 January 1943: Ossinowik-Sassliny-Saborowje

Gruppe Bünemann: Police Captain Bünemann
6th Company of the 9th Police Regiment

3rd Company of the 606th Reserve Grenadier Regiment
8th Company of the 113th Rifle Regiment
Flak Platoon Number 2 (Lieutenant Hutter)
15th Cavalry Platoon of the 281st Eastern Cavalry Battalion
A radio squad from the 822nd Communications Battalion
Destination on 5 January 1943: Petkowa-Gorhuschino-Listvenka

Group Nortmann: Police Major Nortmann
Three companies from the 40th Estonian Self-Defence Battalion
15th Cavalry Platoon of the 281st Eastern Cavalry Battalion
One Signals squad from the 822nd Signals Battalion
Destination on 5 January 1943: Borowie-Goruschka-Ladygino

Notice the sprinkling of non-German volunteers serving with these groups. In this case, two Estonian Schuma battalions were involved, as well as the 281st Eastern Cavalry Battalion, which was composed of Russian volunteers.

One typical report, this one from the 281st Security Division three days into the operation, read as follows:

> Operation *Schneehase*: The Gallas group occupied the restricted line north and northeast of Lake Jasno, 40 kilometres [25 miles] southeast of Idriza. Several gun battles with smaller gang groups during the advance into the restricted line. We counted eleven enemy dead, five of our own wounded. Strong gangs in the Zapolje area have been confirmed. They were reported moving 20 kilometres [12 miles] southeast of Kudewer, travelling in a general southerly and southeasterly direction. Perling staff: 1. Kompanie / Polizeiregiment 9 and one platoon of 2. Kompanie Polizeiregiment 9, attacked by a strong band in Borbowez. Major Perling and the squad doctor of I. Bataillon / Polizeiregiment 9 were seriously wounded. The battle lasted seven hours. Own losses: 7 dead, 18 wounded. Enemy losses could not be determined, since the enemy carried away their dead and wounded, but are believed to be not insignificant. The following daily targets are ordered for 28 January: Group Perling, 2. and 3. Kompanie / Polizeiregiment 9 and 2. and 5. Kompanie / Estnische Schutzmannschaft Bataillon 39 to the line running through Saenjutino-Monino 3 kilometres [2 miles] east-northeast, 5 kilometres [3 miles] west-northwest, through Skokowo. To the north, Gruppe Ringel: 1. Kompanie / Feldausbildungs Regiment 40, 1. Kompanie / Estnische Schutzmannschaft Bataillon 40, 1. Kompanie / Estnische Schutzmannschaft Bataillon 39 to a line Monino-Kashkova-Dvorenevo. To the northeast and north: 2. and 3. Kompanie / Estnische Schutzmannschaft Bataillon 40, to a line Rotschkowo-Kolossovo-Wassileva, front to O. Gr. Paschke (Korück 584) for the 28th and 29th the

> Feldkommandantur 186, subordinate to Generalmajor Bruno Scultecus. Group Northmaa (Estnische Schutzmannschaft Bataillon 40) had contact with a band scouting squad. Enemy casualties: 2 dead. The Gallas group captured the area north and northeast of Lake Jasno, forming a barrier for Schneehase. A group of gangs [partisans] were reported on the march along the southern shore of Lake Jasno and received machine gun and anti-aircraft fire. We killed 40 bandits, identified properly using binoculars. Own losses: one seriously wounded.[22]

The partisan war in the Baltic States, 1942–1943

Between 17 February and 13 August 1942 SS Battlegroup Jeckeln fought between Leningrad and Staraya Russa in northern Russia. Throughout 1942 the battlegroup was under the direct operational control of the 50th Army Corps of the 18th German Army. The greatest concentration of guerrilla forces in the Baltic States during the Second World War proved to be along the border region between Lithuania and Belarusia. This region was the centre of guerrilla activity for many reasons. Firstly, the geographic features of the area, with its numerous forests, rivers and bogs, afforded any guerrilla unit the ability to hide. Secondly, there was a relatively larger number of possible partisan recruits in this region due to the larger numbers of Jews living in Lithuania before the war than in Latvia and Estonia, and the fact that White Russian recruits were also accessible to recruitment by the partisan forces. This was important because the Soviet partisan commanders could not rely on the active recruitment of Lithuanian, Latvian or Estonian volunteers since the Stalinist occupation of these Baltic countries had left few willing anti-German recruits for the Soviet partisan forces. In Estonia alone, the number of people who had been executed or deported to Siberia numbered 60,000 by the summer of 1941.[23] Of that number, 11,000 were transported east in June 1941 as the Germans were advancing into the Baltic States and Russia.

Also in June the Soviet NKVD (People's Commissariat for Internal Affairs) apparatus deported 16,000 Latvians as well.[24] It was with this in mind that great stress was placed by the Soviet command on establishing a guerrilla movement in this region.[25] In fact, as the security divisions were making their way through Estonia in 1941 on their way towards northern Russia, they encountered a company of 140 Soviet paratroopers. Dropped near the Estonian town of Hungerberg (German spelling), these men were most likely sent in order to help organize guerrilla units in that northernmost Baltic state. The Soviet parachutists were dealt with by recently organized Estonian police units and the security divisions continued on their drive.[26] In fact, between September 1941 and June 1942 Einsatzgruppe A encountered 122 men who were suspected of being agent-parachutists in Latvia alone.[27] By far the greatest number of guerrillas operating in the Baltic States in 1941 and 1942 were Jews who had escaped the ghettos and were seeking to survive the war and exact revenge on their tormentors. One of the earliest examples was a Jewish fighter group headed by Meier Blit, which headed for the woods near Kovel with just fifteen men on 15 July 1941. This small group of Jewish fighters laid the groundwork for a partisan unit which later joined the Laginov Partisan Division.[28] This group was one of many which were established throughout 1941 and 1942, although no serious guerrilla formation of significant size and capability showed itself in the Baltic States in 1941. This all changed in early 1942, especially after the Soviet winter counteroffensive against the Germans which lasted from 7 December 1941 until early April 1942. This was largely because the Soviet Partisan Command was determined to improve and enlarge the guerrilla forces operating behind the German lines, especially in the Baltic States. This involved a massive recruitment campaign, and the insertion of trained functionaries with specialized radio and sabotage equipment. Russian author Leonid Grenkevich described this important period in the history of the Soviet partisan movement:

> After the Soviet victory in the battle for Moscow, the Soviet High Command attempted to introduce strict military organization in the entire partisan movement. To do so, it sent regular army officers to serve as instructors, advisers, and members of the commands and staffs of partisan forces. Partisan forces grew in strength as a steady flow of NKVD and Party representatives worked in the countryside to recruit new guerrilla formations. Growing confidence in Soviet power, as well as fear on the part of the local population that inevitable retribution would accompany the return of the Red Army, played a significant role in the dramatic increase in partisan power.[29]

In fact, the early Soviet invention of creating and leaving behind destruction battalions as the Red Army withdrew in the summer and autumn months of 1941 indicated the importance the Soviet High Command placed on guerrilla warfare:

> Special destruction battalions formed for this purpose ostensibly were to fight against [German] saboteurs and traitors; hence their official name of 'People's Defence' units. The formation of these battalions in Estonia began on 27 June 1941. Officially, these units were voluntary; in actuality, many people were forcibly recruited. A large number of characters with a shady past, a criminal record, or a streak of Communist fanaticism joined the destruction battalions voluntarily. Thanks to the broad mandate given to the destruction battalion troops, including the right to execute summarily any 'suspicious' person, they unleashed a massacre in

> Estonia. They burned dozens of villages, schools and public buildings to the ground and blew up factories.[30]

This tactic was attempted in the Baltic States, as it was throughout the depth and breadth of the Eastern Front, but in the Baltic States these 'destruction battalions' were often thwarted by locally raised Lithuanian, Latvian or Estonian partisan forces that were opposed to the Soviet occupation of their country:

> They repeatedly ambushed destruction battalion transport columns. In Tartumaa County on 6 July 1941, the Forest Brothers[31] blew up a stretch of railway track and derailed a destruction battalion train.[32]

Jewish resistance

It is clear, then, that in 1941 the Soviet guerrilla movement in the Baltic States could only count on very few, if any, partisan units. By far the greatest number of guerrillas turned out to be either isolated or bypassed Red Army units, most of which were soon caught, or Jews who had managed to escape the round-ups and mass murders that were occurring in the towns and cities as Einsatzgruppe A wound its way north through the Baltic States. Jewish participation in the guerrilla movement in this region, therefore, would prove critical to the early survival of the partisan movement there:

> On 25 November 1941, three Jewish youths, Isaac Einbinder, Ida Galperstein and Yakob Alperowitz, fled from Kurenitz (about 5 miles from the town of Vileika in the Vilnius territory) to the neighbouring forests. They gathered together a group of escaped Soviet war captives and organized the partisan detail 'Borba' (Fight). In 1942, Einbinder was selected to be sent to a school for guerrilla warfare in Moscow. He returned with three hundred other men in a daring breakthrough across the German frontier.[33]

By far the greatest number of Jewish recruits came from the larger ghettos established in the cities of Kaunas (Kovno) and Vilnius (Vilna), both in Lithuania, and Riga in Latvia. Resistance cells in these Jewish ghettos soon also took hold. For the Jews, the Nazis had given them no choice. They could remain in the ghettos, waiting for their turn to be executed, or they could run away to the forest and resist. By far the most effective and the most famous of these Jewish guerrilla groups was the Bielski Otriad, which was established by the Bielski brothers in the autumn of 1941 and began serious partisan operations in the spring of 1942. During the war the Bielski partisan unit contained around 1,200 Jews. Not all of them, however, were capable of fighting, as there were children and elderly people in the Otriad who had been taken in by the Bielski brothers for protection. After the war the Bielski brothers migrated to New York City, where they established a successful construction business. Their exploits only came to light when a book was written about them in 2008 by researcher Dr Nechama Tec from the University of Connecticut.

Another resistance organization was created in the Vilnius ghetto between November 1941 and January 1942.[34] When the Germans began their second wave *Aktion*, aimed at liquidating the Jewish population of the ghettos, in 1942, these organized Jewish groups began to fight back. Although their impact was more symbolic than effective, since they were poorly armed, they nevertheless forced the Germans to change their tactics in eliminating the Jewish ghettos.[35] The Germans were now forced to employ larger forces against the Jewish population that was selected for extermination, although the Jewish populations of the forty-two ghettos had few arms.[36] In the Polesie district of Poland a total of 520 Jewish fighters in eight ghettos resisted the German efforts at Jewish liquidation. In the Vilnius District of Lithuania some 600 Jewish guerrillas were dispersed into fourteen ghettos. But even as the ghettos in the Baltic States were being liquidated in the summer and autumn of 1943, more Jewish fighters would filter out of the cities to try to make their way to the forest camps, which sometimes lay as far as 60 miles away. Many fighters were caught and killed by German or collaborationist patrols, but the exodus of those who were willing to join the guerrilla struggle continued. Survival and revenge were the two driving forces. Table 2.1 shows the type and quantities of arms available to Jewish fighters in the various ghettos.[37]

By 1943 there were two principal partisan brigades operating in the Lithuanian–Belarusian border region. One was led by Tadeusz Szumauskas, whose *nom-de-guerre* was Kazimir, and the other was led by a Jewish commander named Henoch Ziman, who called himself 'Yurgis'.[38] One of the more active, all-Jewish partisan battalions within Kazimir's brigade was the 500-man Vengeance Battalion.

Table 2.1. Arms controlled by Jewish ghetto fighters in 1942.

District	Pistols	Rifles	Sub-Machine Guns	Heavy Machine Guns	Grenades
Vilnius (Lithuania) – 5 ghettos	15	30	1	1	?
Polesie (Poland) – 6 ghettos	20	105	2	2	YES
Novogrudok – 14 ghettos[39]	70	211	13	27	YES
17 other ghettos in Belarus	45	154	20	5	YES
Total	150	500	36	35	200+

Armed Forces Commander Eastland

The *Wehrmacht Befehlshaber Ostland* (Armed Forces Commander Eastland) was in overall charge of all military formations, except for the SS and police, within the region designated as the Eastland. This region included the Baltic states – that is, the former independent states of Latvia, Estonia and Lithuania – and the Belarusian Soviet Socialist Republic (also referred to as White Russia or White Ruthenia).[40] The command therefore was the one that allotted army units for operations in that region, principally in the Baltic states. The Command's first commanding officer was General of the Cavalry Walter Brämer (1 June 1943–30 April 1944), followed by General of Armoured Troops Franz Werner Kempf (1 May–31 August 1944) and General of the Infantry Anton Grasser (1–25 September 1944). Grasser used the staff of the Armed Forces Commander Eastland and incorporated this command with *Armeeabteilung Narwa* (Army Detachment Narva), which was created on 2 February 1944 using the headquarters staff of LIV. Army Corps. This occurred when Grasser assumed command of the Narva Army Detachment.

SS and police operating in the Baltic states and the region of Army Group North

The battlegroup had been created on an emergency basis in the autumn of 1941. Throughout its existence, it employed a wide array of units at varying intervals of time. For example, in May 1942 the 538th Infantry Regiment was added to SS Battlegroup Jeckeln, which was holding a good chunk of the front lines around the Oranienbaum pocket. This regiment was actually part of the 385th Infantry Division, which was sent to southern Russia and later perished with the Italian 8th Army along the Don river bend in February 1943. On 14 February 1944 the 321st Latvian Self-Defence Battalion was likewise assigned to SS Battlegroup Jeckeln. From 19 July to 3 August 1944 Jeckeln's combat group was composed of the following units:

SS Battlegroup Jeckeln
SS Police Regiment 9 (reserve)
SS Battlegroup Krukenberg
- 2nd Latvian Volunteer Police Regiment
- 3rd Latvian Volunteer Police Regiment
- 5th Latvian Frontier Guard Regiment
- 37th Estonian Police Battalion
- 38th Estonian Police Battalion
- 321st Latvian Self-Defence Battalion

SS Battlegroup Knappe
- 2nd Latvian Frontier Guard Regiment
- 4th Latvian Frontier Guard Regiment

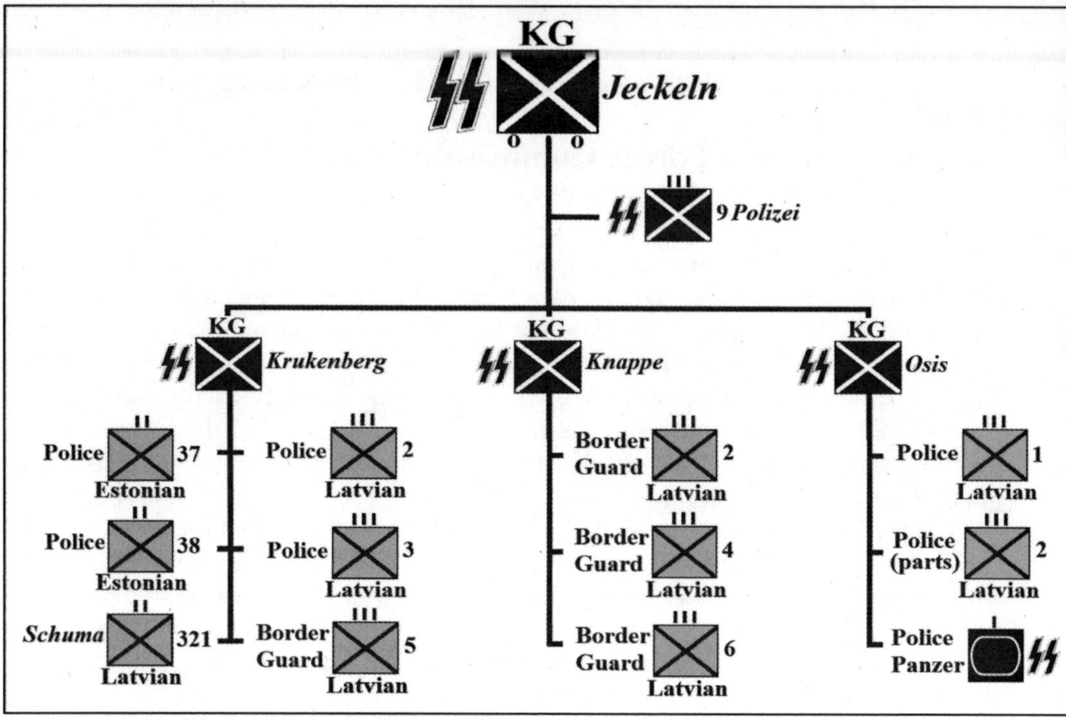

Figure 1. SS Battlegroup Jeckeln, July–August 1944.

- 6th Latvian Frontier Guard Regiment

SS Battlegroup Osis

- 1st Latvian Volunteer Police Regiment Riga
- 2nd Latvian Volunteer Police Regiment (parts)
- German Police Panzer Company

Police Battlegroup Knecht

Police Battlegroup Knecht was an anti-guerrilla force that was initially organized for emergency action along the Latvian–Russian border in November 1941. In early February 1943 it was reconstituted and placed under the same commander, Police Colonel Max Knecht.[41] This combat group was raised in conjunction with Battlegroup Schroeder[42] and was to perform operations against the growing partisan menace on the Latvian–Russian frontier. The battlegroups operated independently of one another, but coordinated their drives. The initial units of Police Battlegroup Knecht are listed below, with their location in February 1943 when they began their anti-partisan sweep:

- 276th Latvian Self-Defence Battalion – Pustina
- 277th Latvian Self-Defence Battalion – Pustina, Asune and Pizani
- 278th Latvian Self-Defence Battalion – between Asune and Pizani
- 279th Latvian Self-Defence Battalion – in and around the southwest region of Redkevice, Veterovice and Vorzowa
- Signals Platoon Lewinski – held in reserve in Pustina

- Flak Platoon Hatje – held in reserve in Pustina
- 10th Gendarmerie Platoon (motorized) – held in reserve in Pustina

German and Latvian language sources regarding the history of the 275th Latvian Self-Defence Battalion concur that the men from this company-sized 'battalion' ended up being absorbed into the 1st Latvian Police Regiment.[43] Indeed, records state that both the 276th and 278th *Schuma* Battalions were also absorbed into the 1st Latvian Police Regiment when it was formed in August 1943. Police Battlegroup Knecht operated as early as the autumn of 1941 in the Eastland region. Its second employment was in the spring of 1943 when it operated along the Lithuanian–Latvian–Belarusian border. Its third employment was in November 1943 when it again took part in anti-partisan operations along the Latvian–Russian border region.

Unternehmen Zeithen: 1 February–19 March 1943

This operation was a local anti-partisan drive that was launched in the region of Demyansk by elements of the 123rd Infantry Division.[44] The operation was to coincide with the evacuation of Demyansk by the Germans (see map overleaf). Some of the partisans targeted were Red Army paratroopers who had been parachuted behind the German lines in an attempt to cut off the Germans at Demyansk. The guerrillas were blocking part of the withdrawal route for the Germans and needed to be dealt with. Forces from the local field command headquarters were also employed (about two battalions). The result netted thirty-two partisans killed and four captured. The captured guerrillas were shot after interrogation. The German withdrawal from Demyansk took place after the operation was concluded and by 1 March 1943 the Russians had taken the town. During January 1943 the 123rd Infantry Division was under the control of II Army Corps.

Unternehmen Zeithen involved large-scale sweeps by the 123rd Infantry Division, as well as elements of the 58th and 254th Infantry Division. These troops were to eliminate or disrupt the partisan presence. The Germans were concerned that the local partisans would interfere with their withdrawal plans from the Demyansk pocket, and complicate the logistics of getting their troops and supplies out in a timely and safe manner. The partisans had been harassing German forces in the area for months, and any potential disruption to the withdrawal could lead to catastrophic losses.

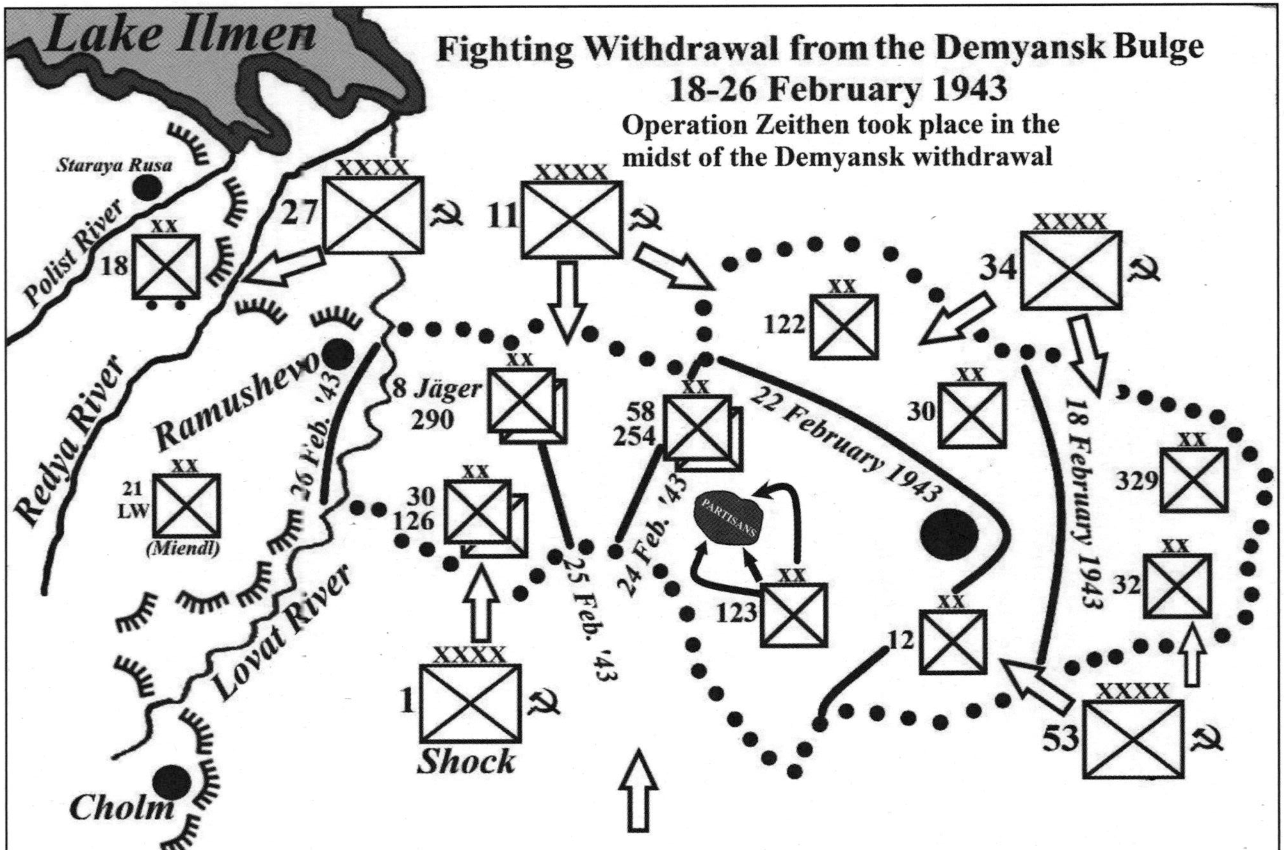

Map 18. Operation Zeithen took place in the midst of the German withdrawal from the Demyansk bulge.

Chapter 3

The war against the Jews and partisans in Belarus, 1942

We should thank the Germans for their policies which have enabled us to fan the flames of the guerrilla movement.

[Alexander Shcherbakov, Politburo member, 1942]

The war against the Jews continued early in 1942. On 21 January the few remaining Jews in the Vilnius ghetto, who had established a resistance cell in order to fight back against the Germans, were rounded up or shot by the local security police command led by SS Colonel Karl Jäger.[1] Author Shalom Cholawsky estimated that about 210,000 Jews remained in Belarusia at the beginning of 1942.[2] According to the above listed numbers, about 175,000 Jews had been killed in White Russia in 1942. This figure is higher than Martin Dean's estimate of 75,000–125,000 Jews killed in Belarusia in 1942–1943.[3] If the figure of about 175,000 Jews killed in White Russia in 1942 alone is correct, then the number of Jews remaining within Belarusian territory by the beginning of 1943 should have been about 30,000–35,000. According to Wilhelm Kube, the number of Jews in Belarusia stood at about 30,000 by the end of 1942.[4] It appears, then, that the estimate of around 175,000 Jews killed in 1942 in Belarus is close to the correct number. If we add the number of Jews killed in Belarusia in 1941 (199,257) to those killed in 1942 (176,496), we come up with a figure of 375,753 killed. Since the pre-war population of Jews in Belarusia stood at around 375,000, it appears that by the end of 1942 the Germans had been able to completely eliminate the entire Belarusian Jewish population.

However, it should not be overlooked that during the war years parts of northeastern Poland were added to White Russia and were counted as Belarusia. This concerned principally the Novogrudok area, where another 83,000 Jews lived. Thus, if we count the 375,000 White Russian Jews and add the 83,000 Jews of the Novogrudok region we get a figure of 458,000 Jewish lives. From this number must be subtracted the White Russian Jews who managed to escape the clutches of the Nazi killing machine, a figure estimated at around 60,000. Of this number, about 39,000 withdrew eastwards and avoided being captured in 1941, while about 21,000 fled the ghettos in 1942 to hide in the Belarusian woods. Thus, if we take the figure of 458,000 pre-war Jews and deduct those Jews who managed to escape, we get an initial number of about 398,000. From this figure we must deduct the Jewish losses for both 1941 (199,257) and 1942 (176,496) before we arrive at a final figure of 22,247 Jews left alive and under German control in Belarus – almost exactly the figure for Jews remaining within the Regional Commissariat for White Ruthenia which Wilhelm Kube mentioned at the end of 1942. To further corroborate this number, another source stated that by the spring of 1943 only 22,000 Jews remained under German control in Belarusia.[5] In 1943 the Germans would conclude their programme of eliminating the Jewish ghettos, but it is clear from these figures that by the end of 1942 White Russia could be considered *Judenfrei* (free of Jews). The following Order Police, *Schuma* and Einsatzgruppen units have been linked to these specific killings in Belarusia in 1942:

Forces under Army command: Commander of the Rear Army Area 102 – about 10,000 Jews from January to July 1942 (in the eastern, militarized part of Belarusia)[6]

- SS Battlegroup Jeckeln – 8,350 Jews in February 1942 (Miczajewice).
- Commander of the Security Police in Minsk, plus Ukrainian and Belarusian militia – 3,412 Jews on 2 March 1942 (Minsk).
- Commander of the Security Police in Baranavichy, plus Ukrainian militia – 2,000–3,000 Jews on 4 March 1942 (Baranavichy).
- Subcommand from Einsatzkommando 9 – 2,653 Jews on 29 May 1942 (Dokshitsy, Glebokie region).
- 2nd Company, Waffen SS Battalion for Special Employment – 1,000 Jews on 15 June 1942 (Minsk).
- Gendarmerie plus auxiliary police personnel – 2,000 Jews on 15 June 1942 (Dzisna).
- 2nd Company, Waffen SS Battalion for Special Employment – 4,000 Jews on 27 June 1942 (Slonim).
- Commander of the Security Police in Minsk[7] and Slonim, plus security service personnel – 8,000–10,000 Jews on 29 June 1942 (Slonim).
- 2nd Company, Waffen SS Battalion for Special Employment – 1,000 Jews on 28 July 1942 (Minsk)
- 322nd Police Battalion – 9,000 Jews on 28–30 July 1942 (Minsk)
- 18th Latvian Self-Defence Battalion, plus local Belarusian police and German Gendarmerie – 750 Jews on 23 September 1942 (Stolpce, Baranovichi district)
- Police Regiment 15 – 289 Jews at the end of September 1942 (Zablotye, Pinsk district)

- Police Regiment 15, Commander of the Security Police in Pinsk, Gendarmerie, Ukrainian self-defence units – 10,000 Jews from 28 October to 1 November 1942 (Pinsk)
- 2nd Company, Waffen SS Battalion for Special Employment – 1,000 Jews on 5 November 1942 (Minsk).[8]

One of the main causes for the Axis defeat in the Soviet Union was their failure to win over the majority of the Soviet population to their cause. The opportunity to do so presented itself to the Nazis in 1941, and even as late as the summer and autumn of 1942. The German response was to treat its eastern volunteers with arrogance and contempt, while placing their jack-boots on the necks of the population. What is amazing is that in spite of their arrogance, their racial bigotry and their anti-Slavic policies, the Germans still managed to rally around a million men to their side. Had their guiding principles been more lenient and their treatment of the Soviet peoples more even-handed, the Third Reich might have won millions more Soviet citizens to their side. This, in turn, might have had an effect on the outcome of the war in the Soviet Union. However, such far-sighted and benevolent policies were not part of the Nazi ideology or psyche. By the autumn of 1942 the few enlightened German soldiers serving on the Russian front could see that their 'untermensch' policy was leading the German campaign into disaster. Hans Becker, a former grenadier with the 20th Panzer Division, experienced the Russian campaign from 1941 until his capture in 1943. He described the Russian attitude towards the Germans in 1942, after a year of German occupation:

> The only serious threat to my peace of mind came from the partisans. They were known to be working in the district in very large numbers, around the towns and in the forests and smaller villages. Germans suffered frequent ambushes, but luckily nothing happened to me. The local villagers, on the other hand, behaved in a remarkably friendly fashion. I often drank Samahonka and Vodka with them and, as far as I could judge, they were most kindly people, though oppressed with famine and all the other miseries of war. When they would see me, they would call out cheerfully from a distance, 'Zdrastvite, Pan', which I came to recognize as the Russian for 'Good day, sir'. Hardly being able to speak a word of Russian yet, I had to rely completely on my interpreter, who came from Czechoslovakia. 'Tell me', I said to him one day, 'Why are these people so friendly?' 'I am sorry if it upsets you,' he replied, 'but they are behaving like this because they are scared stiff.' My dealings with the local [Secret] Field Police [GFP] should have led me to realize this earlier, but we all want to be liked and I had hoped that the villagers had recognized me for a different type of person.[9]

A perfect example of why the villagers so feared the Germans was given by a member of the Belarusian *Ordnungsdienst* (the OD, or Order Service), the collaborationist indigenous police force. A volunteer from the OD was so appalled by what he had seen while he accompanied an SS unit in the field during one anti-partisan drive that he wrote the following report in May 1943 describing what transpired:

> We entered the village (I believe in the Smolensk region) at mid-day and called for the mayor. The SS officer treated this man abysmally, even though he seemed to be a friend. He was ordered to gather all the people in the square, even the babies, and to take steps to round up all those who might be working in the fields. Guards were posted. By 14:00 all were assembled. The SS men had meanwhile filled in their time by walking around the village and doing precisely as they pleased. There was at least one rape, and nothing was done about it. To the assembled people, the SS officer, through me, told them that their area was bandit infested, that they must have collaborated with those bandits, and that disciplinary action would be taken against them. There were twenty-three men in the square. Half of them were separated, irrespective of age and health, and taken down a side alley. The SS men seemed to know exactly what to do. Without one word of an order from the officer, automatic fire began, and then the SS men returned, without the peasants. The women became hysterical and had to be beaten into submission. Then the huts were set on fire, and all food that was found was destroyed. As the flames began to engulf the final row of huts, a man who had obviously been hiding ran out, his clothing partially alight. The SS men, clearly expecting something of the sort, shot him dead before he had taken five paces. This was the signal for further brutality. The SS officer rounded on the mayor, telling him that he was not merely a [partisan] collaborator, but a full bandit. He was therefore to die like a bandit. First, he would admit where the bandit camp was. The mayor refused, quite probably because he did not know. The SS officer then had one of the young girls brought before them, and told the SS Scharführer to 'perform'. I find the following incident impossible to recount. The result was that the girl, stripped naked, had one of her breasts cut off. The mayor still refused to talk. The girl was then shot in front of him, and the SS officer fired a few indiscriminate rounds into the group of women, felling two or three. The final refusal to provide information caused the execution of the mayor by slow strangulation and the death by shooting of the rest of the inhabitants. The SS men left, leaving some seventy dead peasants of all ages behind them. I cannot believe that this is either humane or sensible. Action to stop this must be taken.[10]

This type of treatment was not forgotten by those who survived to describe such atrocities. The people who ultimately benefited from this type of barbarity were the guerrillas themselves, whose ranks were swelled by the addition of new recruits motivated by the one of the strongest of human feelings: hatred. Others simply took to the forests and swamps to avoid being killed by the Germans. On their farms and in their villages they were prey to the whims of both Germans and partisans alike; at least in the forests living as guerrillas they only had to avoid the Germans. Their options were limited. If they joined the local Order Service, there was always the chance that they would be assassinated by the guerrillas, or come home to find out that their entire family had been executed for collaboration and their family farm burned to the ground.[11] It was a terrible time for Soviet citizenry. Refugees also lived in these forest camps, especially those few Jews who had escaped the mass killings of 1941. In the forest region outside Novogrudok in western Belarusia was one such camp, which was home to the largest armed Jewish partisan unit during the entire war. Tobias Bielski and fifty Jews escaped the Novogrudok ghetto in October 1942 and formed what would become the Bielski Partisan *Otriad*.[12] What transpired in the Bielski camp on 6 June 1944, during a very hot summer's day in Belarusia, was typical of the punishment meted out to any German unfortunate enough to be caught by the partisans:

> Those in the Bielski Otriad who had no opportunity to chase after the Germans felt left out. They were disappointed. Then one day, the Bielski partisans brought back three SS men. When word about the arrival of these deserters got around, the entire Otriad, more than a thousand people, descended on headquarters. The crowd was agitated and the few guards had trouble keeping order. When the situation threatened to deteriorate into complete chaos, Tuvia emerged and addressed the people: 'Comrades, partisans, we have three SS murderers. At the moment, we are interrogating them. Soon we will have a verdict. The bloody dogs will get their just punishment. We have lived to avenge ourselves. Be quiet. Do not disturb us in our work.' Tuvia went back inside quickly. One of the few partisans admitted inside the headquarters recalls that 'I will never forget it, how on their knees the SS men were begging for their lives. They pleaded for mercy because they had children and wives at home. They swore that they were not to blame for anything that had happened to the Jews.' Outside, the crowd was impatient. People seemed to be grinding their teeth. Tense yet quiet, they stood, waiting. Then two partisans came out leading a tall blond German, his hands tied behind his back. The mass of people darted toward the prisoner, shoving each other, stepping over one another. The first to reach the SS man was Pupko, the oldest man in the Otriad, described by some as 75 years old, by others

> as 80. With knife in hand, Pupko screamed, 'God, my grandfather was not a murderer, my father was not a murderer, but I will be a murderer.' Something in the old man's voice stopped the crowd's advance. The people halted with their eyes glued to Pupko's knife. As if in a trance, this main actor began the job of cutting up the SS man. A murmur of approval escaped from the mass of people. This wordless conversation urged Pupko to continue, to finish the job. In a few intense, highly charged moments, the SS man was unrecognizable and dead. The two other prisoners were shot.[13]

Based on this testimony, and the location of the SS Penal Regiment Dirlewanger at this time,[14] it is most probable that these three SS men belonged to the infamous Dirlewanger SS penal unit. The unit was composed of poachers, criminals and convicted SS men, as well as felons, and also had a large contingent of political prisoners in its ranks, most of whom were ex-German Communist Party members. There is no mention that they claimed to be communists or political prisoners. Most likely, even if these men had claimed this, they were not likely to be spared, for they would not have been believed. There is no way to substantiate whether these three deserters were from the Dirlewanger SS unit, or were former political prisoners given the chance for freedom if they served in the SS, but the possibility is there – especially given the fact that they were indeed deserters. Throughout the history of the Dirlewanger SS formation, desertions by political prisoners were common.

German strength in Belarus in the autumn of 1942

The strength of the German Order Police and self-defence forces in Belarus on 1 October 1942 stood as follows:

- German order policemen: 1,394
- Police in regular uniform: 8,378
- Men in the self-defence battalions: 1,456.[15]

There were also specialized volunteer formations, such as the Druzhina SS Brigade. The initial use of the Druzhina SS unit had been at Nevel during the crisis winter of 1941/1942. The formation was withdrawn from the front in late February 1942 and by 10 March the strength of the unit was just over 1,000 men. It was during March that the formation was shifted to Glebokie for rest and refitting. By the time the Druzhina SS Brigade reached Glebokie, it was the size of a small regiment. At Glebokie it was relegated to the control of General of the Infantry Max von Schenckendorff for anti-partisan duty. Schenckendorff led Army Group Centre Rear Area Command 102 and as such was responsible for neutralizing the partisan menace behind the army group's front lines. Schenckendorff would be replaced by General of Mountain Troops, Ludwig Kübler, on 22 July 1943.[16]

From March 1942 the Druzhina SS unit was permanently attached to the German rear area command for employment against the guerrillas. It was still a part of the SS security service, but for operational purposes it had been loaned to the German Army and thus came to be assigned to the German 286th Security Division, which had its headquarters just southeast of Glebokie in Orsha.[17] The Druzhina SS formation continued to receive reinforcements while operating as part of the 286th Security Division,[18] and remained at its base in Glebokie between March and June 1942.

In the same year the 201st Security Division also became operational in the area behind Army Group Centre. It began operations in the summer, launching small but numerous anti-guerrilla drives. The headquarters of the 201st Security Division was at Polotsk, just northeast of Glebokie.[19] In July 1942 the Druzhina SS unit was transferred to the control of the 201st Security Division and moved to Stary Bykov. The minor operations conducted by this security division throughout the summer of 1942, and in which the men of the Druzhina took part from July onwards, were eventually stopped by an order from the German High Command so that the 201st Division's forces could concentrate on protecting the railway network in their region from partisan attacks.[20] By September 1942 the Druzhina unit was employed in guarding the Molodechno–Glebokie–Polotsk railway line. One battalion of the Druzhina was said to be located at Kolitchenko at this time.

The month of October 1942 would prove eventful with regard to the entire course of the German anti-partisan campaign. On the 7th National Leader of the SS Heinrich Himmler met with all his SS, SS security service and police leaders in Russia. On the agenda was the conduct of the anti-guerrilla war.[21] One of the results of the meeting was that a single German commander was appointed to lead the counterinsurgency war. Another by-product of the discussion was the supremacy given to the SS/police command to conduct the course of the anti-partisan campaign, with no further hindrance or competition from the Army. In effect, the SS was taking over the running of the war behind the lines. The Army could be used if the SS command needed forces, but any such troops would be under SS control.[22] One further immediate result was the channelling of more SS and police forces into the anti-guerrilla war. For example, a three-company motorized *Gendarmerie* battalion,[23] stationed in reserve in Berlin, was immediately dispatched to Belarusia and placed under the control of SS General Erich von dem Bach-Zelewski.[24] Bach-Zelewski, who had been the Higher SS and Police Leader for Central Russia since 24 May 1941, was now in overall charge of the entire German anti-partisan war in the USSR.[25] His appointment had been announced on 23 October 1942, just sixteen days after Himmler's fateful meeting.[26]

Henceforth, from November 1942, the Druzhina unit would be employed entirely under SS control, not only for administrative and supply purposes, but for operational direction as well. The unit would now be involved in numerous SS-sponsored anti-partisan drives, most of which would prove quite barbaric. The men of the Druzhina SS would get to see first-hand the worst excesses of the Nazi SS. The effect on the morale of the men in the Druzhina formation, upon witnessing how the Germans conducted these drives, could not be a positive one. Later that month the Druzhina SS formation was directed south to the area around Mogilev and ordered to take on the Nichiporovich partisan detachment. The report of the operation states that 500 men (a battalion) of the Druzhina SS took part.[27] To make matters worse for the Druzhina men, the unit would soon be attached to the infamous Dirlewanger SS Penal Battalion,[28] a formation notorious for laying waste to any region in which it operated. Its tactics were not only barbaric but sadistic.[29]

The Dirlewanger SS penal unit had been sent to Belarusia on 29 January 1942 and had immediately begun its campaign of terror. Between January and May 1942, it launched several small but punitive expeditions around Mogilev.[30] The first large operation in which it participated in conjunction with other major SS and police units was *Unternehmen Adler* (Operation Eagle), which began on 20 June and ran through to 7 August 1942. This guerrilla sweep was launched by the German 286th Security Division, to which the Dirlewanger SS unit had been temporarily attached. It was launched with the intention of clearing the Mogilev–Berezina–Bobruisk highway. Other units that took part in this operation included Battlegroup Buchmann, led by SS Colonel and Lieutenant Colonel of the Police Erich Buchmann, which included the I. and II. Battalions of Police Regiment 2, as well as some SD Kommandos of company size. Other units included a battalion of security troops under Major Kopf (203rd Security Division), as well as Battlegroup von Geldern (286th Security Division). In this drive the Germans lost 25 dead, 64 wounded and 2 missing. Partisan losses stood at 1,381 killed and 428 taken prisoner.[31] The Germans captured 13 mortars, 5 flak guns, 9 anti-tank guns, 4 field pieces and 8 howitzers.[32] The culmination of the murder-spree by SS Sonderkommando Dirlewanger occurred on 15 June 1942 when the unit murdered over 2,000 inhabitants of the town of Borki, just west of Lake Chachevichy.[33] On 6 August 1942, a day before the end of Operation Eagle, Heinrich Himmler flew to Mogilev to meet SS generals Bach-Zelewski and Walter Schimana.[34] Part of the reason for the visit was to assess the current operation against the guerrillas. They spoke for two hours, then Himmler flew on to Zhitomir, ending his on-the-spot observation of the operation.

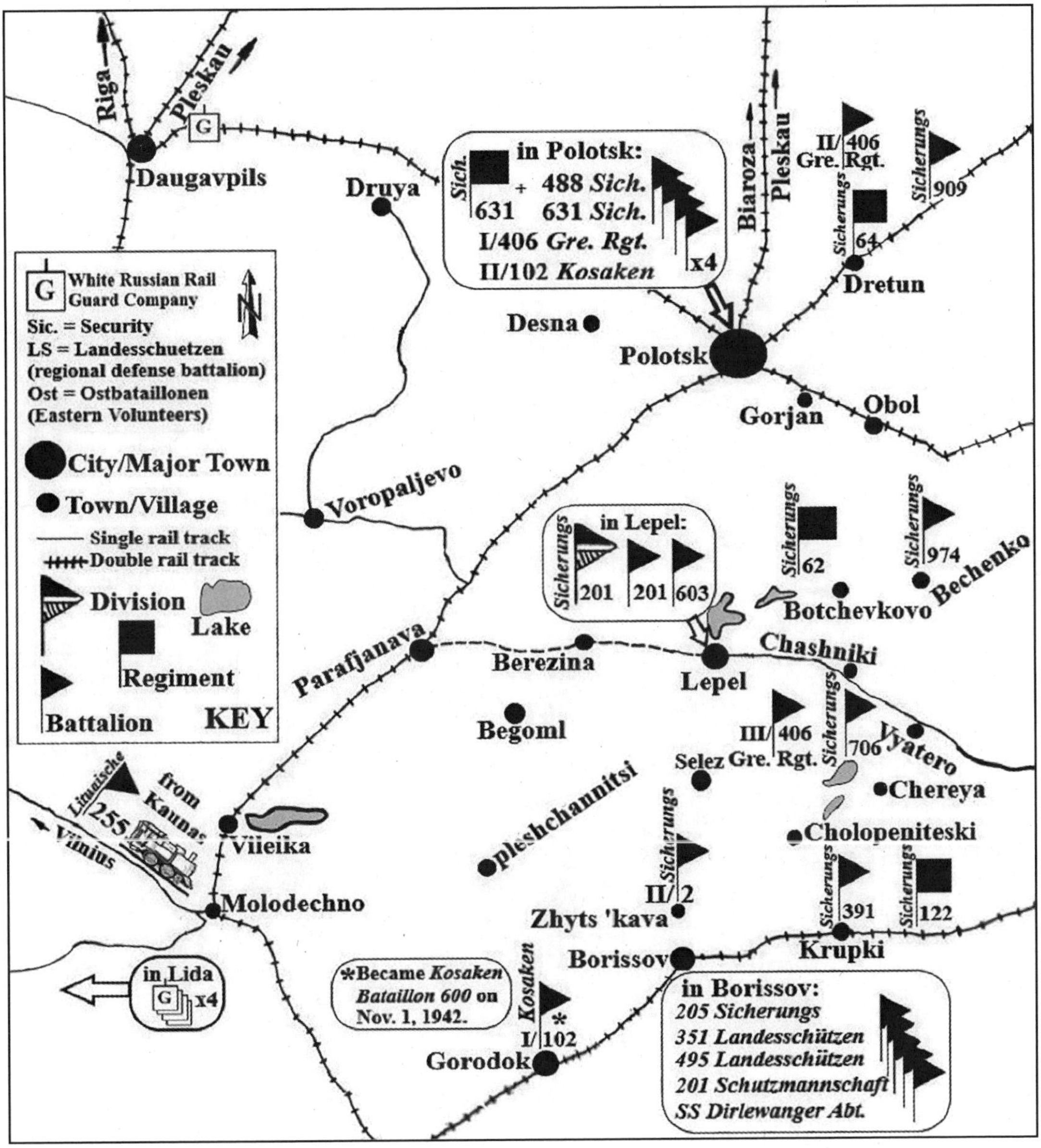

Map 19. German and auxiliary volunteer forces in White Russia, October 1942.

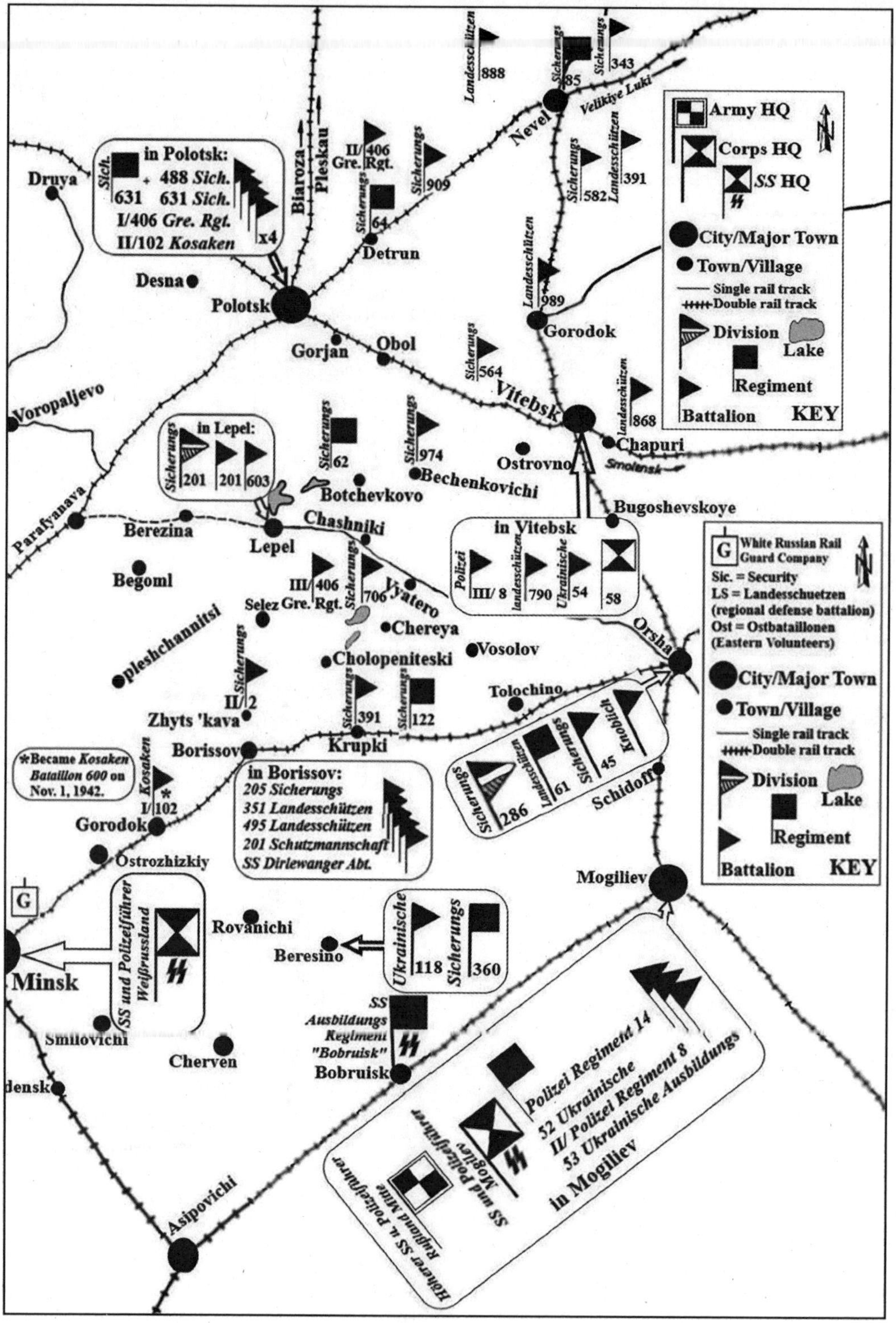

Map 20. German and auxiliary volunteer forces in White Russia, October 1942.

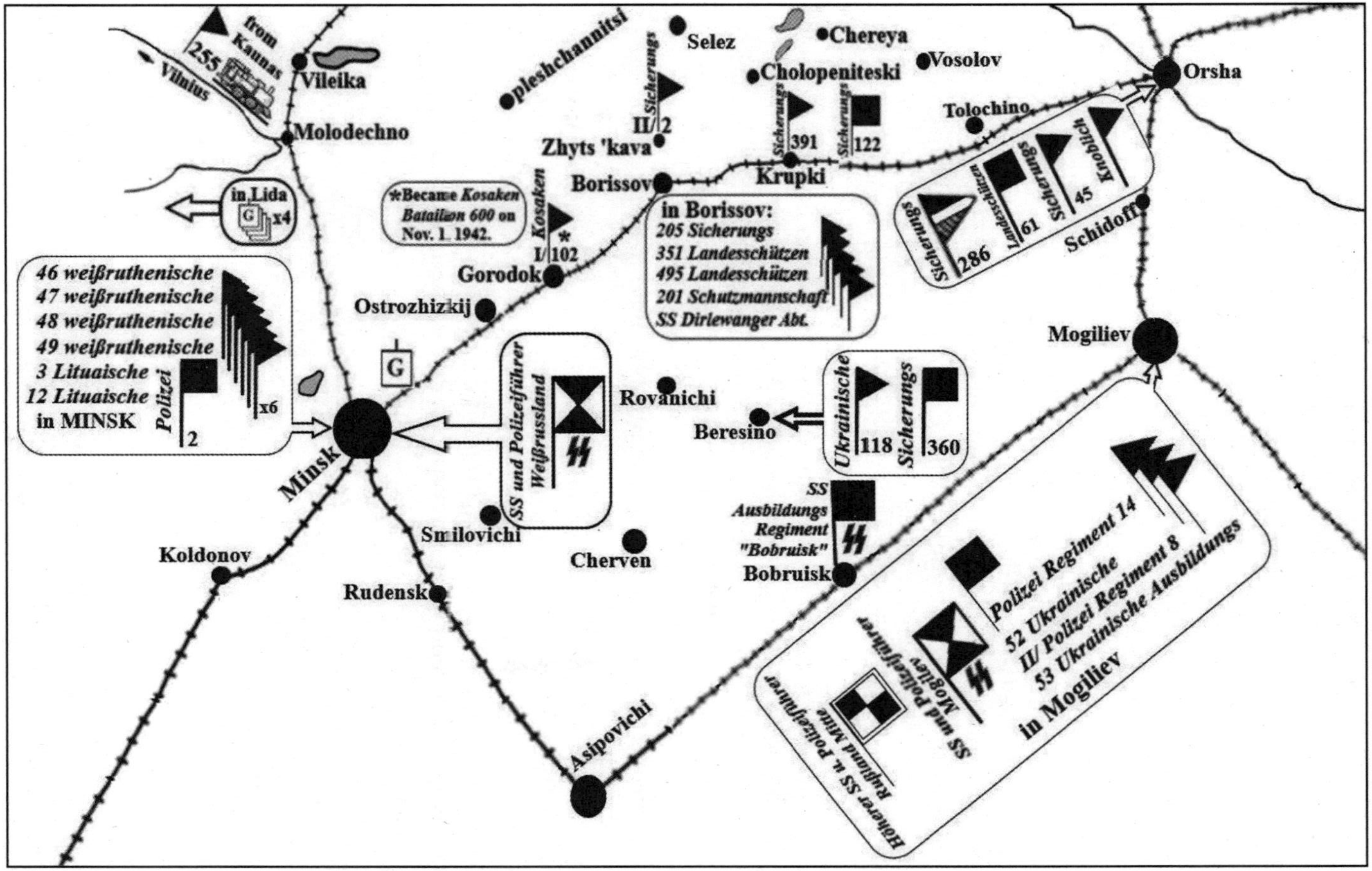

Map 21. German and auxiliary volunteer forces in White Russia, October 1942.

The Secret Field Police in the region of Army Group Centre

For the campaign in the Soviet Union the new position of Chief of the Secret Field Police East was created and was initially assigned to Senior Field Police Director and SS Major Ernst Erich Viktor Rassow. He was responsible to Cuno Schmidt, who held the post of Field Police Chief of the Army.[35] Rassow held the post from 22 June 1941 until January 1942.[36] From January 1942 until July 1944 the position of Chief of the Secret Field Police East was held by Senior Field Police Director Max Häuberer.[37] The deputy commander under Rassow and Häuberer was Field Police Director Joachim Kaintzik. Subordinate to the Chief of the Secret Field Police East were the secret field police staffs in charge of certain regions of the Russian Front, which was divided into three main groups: North, Centre and South. The secret field police posts were similarly divided into Senior Field Police Director at the Commander of the Northern Army Area, Senior Field Police Director at the Commander of the Central Army Area and Senior Field Police Director at the Commander of Army Area South. For Army Group South, the senior secret field police official, from March 1943, was Hans Stephainski. In February 1943 the position of Senior Field Police Director at the Commander of the Central Army Area was held by Bernhard Niggemeyer, while in the region of Army Group North the position of Senior Field Police Director at the Commander of the Northern Army Area was held by Senior Field Police Director Zugnig.

The region of Army Group Centre would see the deployment of the largest number of Secret Field Police units, most likely because the region with the greatest number of Soviet guerrillas was located in the area of Belarusia and the central region of the Russian Front. The principal Secret Field Police groups assigned to central Russia were: GFP- 570, 580, 612, 639, 703, 706,

Table 3.1. Secret Field Police Units in the Region of Army Group Centre.

Secret Field Police Group	Commander Rear Army Area Centre 102
GFP-707, GFP-718, GFP-729	221st Security Division
GFP-709,[38] GFP-716, GFP-723	286th Security Division
GFP-706, GFP-710, GFP-717, GFP-724	403rd Security Division[39]
GFP-709	339th Static Infantry Division[40]
GFP-639	Panzergruppe 2
GFP-703	Panzergruppe 3
GFP-704	Panzer Group 4[41]
GFP-580	9th Army
GFP-612	2nd Army
GFP-570	4th Army

Map 22. Location of collaborationist battalions in the region of the Baltic States, Bialystok District, North Russia and Belarus, July 1942.

707, 709, 710, 716,[42] 717, 718, 723, 724 and 729.[43] As the guerrilla war intensified, the demand for the employment of the Secret Field Police would increase and therefore the number of Secret Field Police units would only grow as the campaign in the East dragged on. By April 1944 there were 3,142 members of the Wehrmacht serving in Secret Field Police units operating in the region of Army Group Centre alone. This number did not include the 25–30 or so additional *östlichen Freiwilligen* (eastern volunteers) attached to each of these units. In July 1944 the number of Germans assigned to the entire Secret Field Police organization stood at around 16,000 men.

From 22 June 1941 until the end of November 1941 Secret Field Police units in the East were responsible for taking into custody some 5,193 people and shooting 737 of them outright. Of those taken into custody, the overwhelming majority were not released, but were instead handed over to the SS security service for what was termed *sonderbehandlung* ('special treatment' – i.e., elimination). The Secret Field Police in the area of Army Group Centre were initially employed under the headquarters listed in Table 3.1.

Vladimir Gil and the Druzhina SS Brigade

By the spring of 1943 there were entire regions behind the German lines where German forces had no presence or control. The German defeat at Stalingrad and the failure of their 1942 summer offensive into southern Russia, and specifically the Caucasus Mountains, had shown the world that Germany could be defeated. This knowledge in turn emboldened those who were still sitting on the fence to join the partisans so they would be on the winning side when this dance of death finally ended. Those who had sided with the Germans were now nervous and having second thoughts. Buyer's remorse was also setting in, as two years of German rule had shown exactly who the Nazis were. One of those disaffected Russian volunteers was Vladimir Vladimirovich Gil, whose *nom de guerre* was I.G. Rodionov. At the start of the Russo-German war Gil was a lieutenant colonel on the staff of the Red Army's 229th Rifle Division.[44] He and others from his division were taken prisoner on 16 July 1941 and sent to a German prisoner of war camp. In the autumn of 1941, Gil was approached by SS Major Hans Shindowski, an SD officer who wanted to employ Gil and other ex-Red Army officers in a special anti-communist unit. By 1 May 1942 the strength of this unit was 100 men, most of them officers. After spending a month in Germany, taking lessons on operating behind the lines, the men were sent to Parczew and Lublin for more training. Further recruitment yielded a strength of a small brigade by the summer of 1942, which became the Druzhina Brigade. In August 1942 the Druzhina Brigade was also sent to Smolensk, where its members took part in their first anti-partisan drive a month later in the region of Bykhaw, near Mogilev.

Wherever his unit served, Rodionov tried to be friendly with the locals in the area, so much so that he was able to establish self-defence units from the very people who inhabited the region.[45] In addition to these static, village militia units, Dallin states that about 600 locals volunteered for Rodionov's SS brigade.[46] Relations with the local German authorities, who saw Rodionov and his unit as an intrusion into their 'domain', were less than cordial, however.[47] The start of 1943 brought on an increased demand for more anti-partisan units as Soviet guerrilla strength in the Soviet Union had vastly

Table 3.2. Soviet partisan estimates, March 1943.

Baltic States	9,000[48]
Army Group North	4,203
Belarusia	57,700
Smolensk/Bryansk/Orel (central Russia)	44,000
Ukraine	7,039[49]
Crimea	500

grown. Bach-Zelewski's plans to counter the growing guerrilla threat apparently included dramatically increasing the size of his collaborationist forces. The Druzhina SS Brigade was to be enlarged to some 5,000 men by additional recruitment among the local population and further drafts of volunteers from the German prisoner of war camps.[50] This increase in size also called for the expansion of the area of responsibility where Rodionov and his unit would operate. In March 1943 the estimated numbers of Soviet guerrillas operating behind the German front lines were as shown in Table 3.2.

The Druzhina SS Brigade contained 164 machine-guns, forty mortars, ten 45mm anti-tank-guns and five 76mm field guns. In July 1943 Gil was approached by the commander of the local partisan unit, who convinced him to defect. Colonel Gil duly defected to the partisans a month later, on 16 August 1943. There were approximately 150 German and Belarusian auxiliary police attached to the brigade. Gil hanged the entire German cadre staff of ninety men and killed those Belarusians who opposed the defection by the bulk of the Russian brigade. Several Czarist-era officers were simply placed under arrest and sent through the lines to be tried in Moscow as traitors. The defection of the Druzhina SS Brigade men was a severe blow to the morale of German anti-partisan forces and their collaborationist allies. The Germans eventually caught up with Gil and his deserters, and Gil himself was killed on 14 May 1944 during another anti-partisan drive, *Unternehmen Frühlingsfest* (Operation Spring Festival). After Gil's defection, the Germans officially disbanded the Druzhina Brigade but some 300–500 men remained who had not defected for one reason or another. Some were away training or on other duties, some were sick or wounded. This rump force continued to be used by the Germans well into 1944 but always, of course, under close scrutiny and employed alongside reliable forces in case a second desertion should be attempted.

Available commands and local forces

Table 3.3 lists the rear area field commands in Belarus and the Bialystok District between 1942 and 1944. These commands controlled the army forces that served to garrison the rear areas and also took part in anti-partisan operations within their area of control.

Table 3.3. German Army Field Commands in Belarusia and the Bialystok District.

Command	City	Period Served
392nd Higher Field Command	Minsk	1942–1944
399th Higher Field Command	Bobruisk, Polotsk	Bobruisk (1942–1944), Polotsk (1943)
400th Higher Field Command	Baranovichi	1943–April 1944
579th Higher Field Command	Brest Litovsk[51]	1941
812th Field Command	Molodechno	1942–1943
813th Field Command[52]	Mogilev	1942–1943
812th Field Command	Minsk, Slutsk	Minsk (1941–1942), Slutsk (1943)
551st Field Command	Lida	1 March 1943–1944
749th Field Command	Polotsk, Lepel	Polotsk (1941–1942), Lepel (1943)
181st Field Command	Lepel, Velikiye-Luki	Lepel (1943), Velikiye-Luki (1944)
754th Field Command	Pinsk, Polotsk, Yanov	Pinsk, Polotsk (1943), Yanov (1944)
191st Field Command	Mogilev	1941–1942[53]
199th Field Command[54]	Kobryn[55]	1943–1944
820th Field Command	Beriza	1944
549th Field Command	Bielski[56]	1941
550th Field Command	Stari-Dorogi	1942–1943
581st Field Command	Bobruisk, Shlobin	Bobruisk (1941–April 1942), Shlobin (1943–1944)
244th Field Command[57]	Vitebsk, Borisov, Vitebsk	Vitebsk (1941), Borisov (1942–1943), Vitebsk (1944)
516th Field Command	Borisov	1944
815th Field Command	Vitebsk, Polotsk, Gorodok	Vitebsk (1941), Polotsk (July 1942–January 1943), Gorodok (1943/44)
619th Field Command	Lachva, Mosyr[58]	1943
197th Field Command	Neskin	April 1942, 1944
683rd Field Command	Orsha	1941–1943
194th Field Command	Pinsk, Polotsk	1944
660th Field Command	Vileika/Glebokie, Postavy	Vileika (8 Feb. 1942–1943), Glebokie (1943), Postavy 1944
528th Field Command	Rogachev	10 May 1941–1942
250th Field Command	Slonim	November 1943–1944
282nd Local Command	Vitebsk	1942
427th Local Command	Vielke	1941
593rd Local Command	Vetrino	1944
848th Local Command	Chasniki	1944
525th Local Command	Starobin	1943
508th Local Command	Svislotch	1943
309th Local Command	Slutsk	1942

Command	City	Period Served
343rd Local Command	Slutsk	1943–1944
360th Local Command	Slavkovitschi	1944
552nd Local Command	Shuravitschi	1944
737th Local Command	Shlobin	1943
846th Local Command	Senno	1942
858th Local Command	Sapolje	12 June 1942–1944
363rd Local Command	Rogachev	1943
930th Local Command	Polotsk	1944
335th Local Command	Polotsk	1943
431st Local Command[59]	Podvoloczyska	1941–1942
292nd Local Command	Schventschionys, Pinsk	Schventschionys (1941), Pinsk (1943)
760th Local Command	Pinsk[60]	1942–1944
311th Local Command	Pasherevizy	1944
737th Local Command	Paritschi	1942–1944
842nd Local Command	Orsha	1942–1943
844th Local Command	Niesviez	1943–1944
619th Local Command	Mosyr[61]	1944
843rd Local Command	Mogilev	1942–1943
292nd Local Command	Mogilev	1941
850th Local Command	Grodno[62]	1941
906th Local Command	Minsk, Orsha, Sherven	Minsk (autumn 1941), Orsha (1942–1943), Sherven (1943)
650th Local Command	Minsk	1943
352nd Local Command	Minsk	1942
411th Local Command	Minsk	1941
436th Local Command	Minsk	1941
864th Local Command	Metvedy	1941
340th Local Command	Marina-Gorka	1943
845th Local Command	Luniniec	1942–February 1944
355th Local Command	Lida	1942–1943
851st Local Command	Lepel, Logoisk	Lepel (1941–1943), Logoisk (1943)
278th Local Command	Krupka	1943
532nd Local Command	Krugloye	1941
685th Local Command	Kostyukovitschi	1943–1944
353rd Local Command	Korma, Chechersk	Korma (1941), Chechersk (1941–1943)
889th Local Command	Koydanov	1943
452nd Local Command	Kobrin	1942
935th Local Command	Iasionovo	1944
352nd Local Command	Hansevicze	1942
763rd Local Command	Gorodok	1942
827th Local Command	Gomel	1942–1943
339th Local Command	Glebokie	1942, 1944
256th Local Command	Postavy, Glebokie	Postavy (1941), Glebokie (1943–1944)

Command	City	Period Served
262nd Local Command	Rossono, Schumilino, Drisa, Beschenkovichi	Rossono (1941), Schumilino (1941), Drisa (1943), Beschenkovichi (1943)
532nd Local Command	Cholopenichi	1944
194th Local Command	Bychov	1941–1942
327th Local Command	Brest-Litovsk[63]	1941
899th Local Command	Brest-Litovsk	1942, 1944
335th Local Command	Braslav	1944
Local Command Borisov[64]	Borisov	1941, 1943
841st Local Command	Boguschevskoye	1941–1942
273rd Local Command	Bobruisk	1943
264th Local Command	Baranovichi	July 1941–Sept. 1944
826th Local Command[65]	Baranovichi	1941–1942
425th Local Command	Kobrin, Berezina-Kartuska	Kobrin (1942–1944), Berezina (1944)
344th Local Command	Berezina	1943–1944
79th Local Command	Beschenkovichi	13 Oct. 1941–31 March 1942
929th Local Command	Berezina, Zabinka	Berezina (1943), Zabinka (1944)

Table 3.4. Einzeldienst figures during the second killing sweep of the Jewish population, 1942.[66]

Region Service	Eastland *Schutzpolizei* and *Gendarmerie*	Ukraine *Schutzpolizei*	Ukraine *Gendarmerie*
German Police	4,428	3,849	5,614
Indigenous Police	31,804	14,163	54,794

The number of volunteers that the Germans could employ in the Gendarmerie and other police forces was important because many of these indigenous auxiliary policemen took part in assisting the Germans in the second killing wave that began in the spring of 1942. Their knowledge of the countryside, the people and the language was extremely valuable.

Operation Jacob: 8–12 January 1943

This operation was a drive launched east of Stolpce between Slutsk and Minsk. The principal units employed in this drive were Police Regiment 2; the 5th and 12th Lithuanian Self-Defence Battalions; and the 18th and 271st Latvian Self-Defence Police Battalions. In addition, local Gendarmerie units, including the 6th, 11th and 21st Gendarmerie Platoons (motorized), also took part in the operation. The operation netted 600 partisans killed and another 1,100 partisan suspects apprehended. It seems that those apprehended were

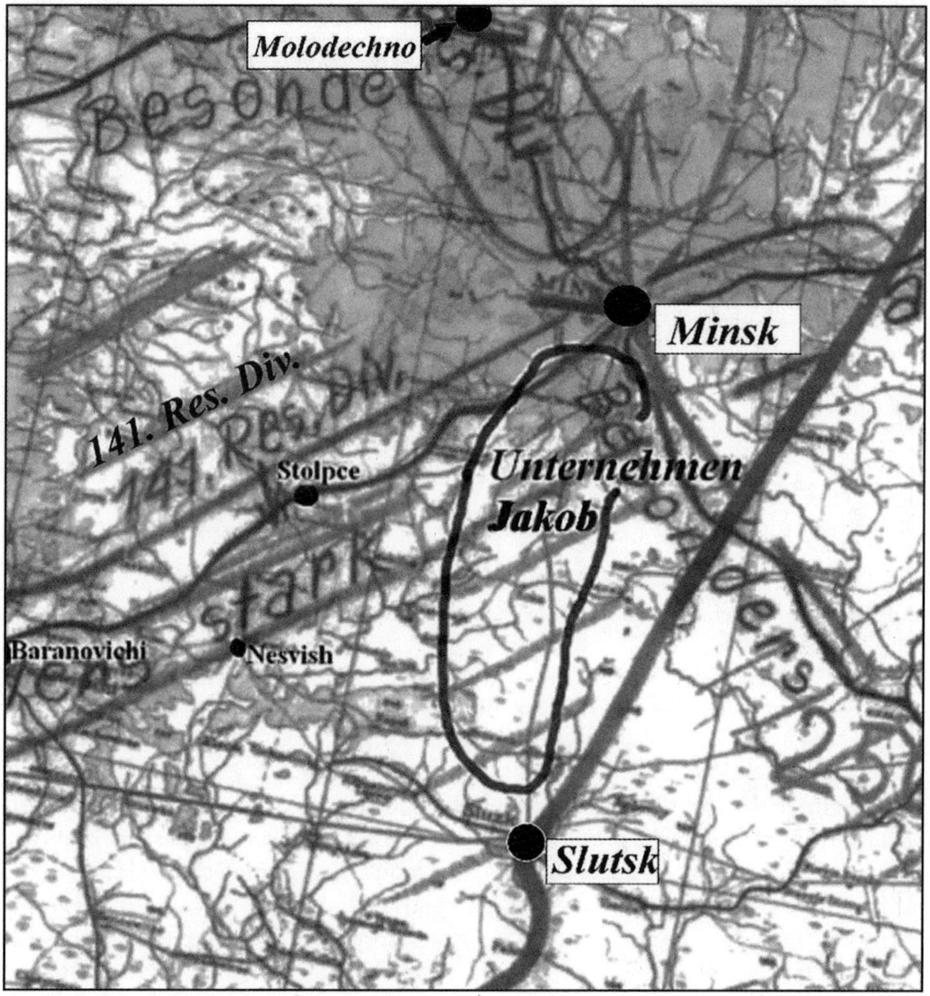

Map 23. Area of operations for Operation Jacob.

mostly killed since fewer than 500 were reported to have been drafted for work in Germany.[67]

Unternehmen Erntefest I (Operation Harvest Festival I): 18–27 January 1943

This anti-partisan drive centred on guerrilla units in the Cerven-Osipovichi area northwest of Bobruisk and was also meant to cover the Slutsk–Minsk highway.[68] The armoured company that had originally been attached to Police Mountain Infantry Regiment 18 was detached from the unit in early December 1942 when the regiment was transferred to Finland[69] and was

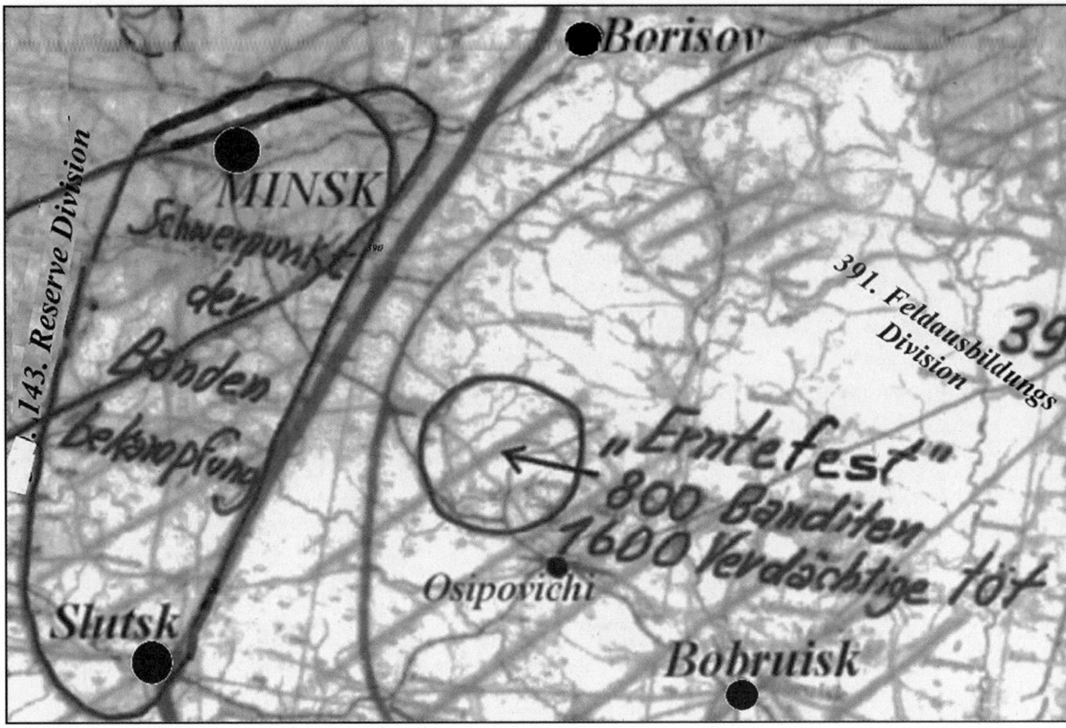

Map 24. Area of operations for *Unternehmen Erntefest I.*

instead sent to Police Regiment 2.[70] This armoured company, which included four platoons with six Steyr armoured cars and ten French Renault light tanks, was used by Police Regiment 2 during Operation Harvest Festival. One of the Renault tank platoons was employed with SS Sonderkommando Dirlewanger during this operation. Other police units involved included the I. Battalion of Police Regiment 23. Other units which took part in Harvest Festival I included the 633rd and 635th Eastern Battalions, the 271st Latvian Self-Defence Battalion, the 57th Belarusian Self-Defence Battalion,[71] and a platoon from III. Battalion of the 18th Panzer Regiment (formerly the 18th Panzer Battalion). According to the anti-partisan map shown, Operation Harvest Festival I ran for ten days and netted a total of 2,400 people killed – 800 during the fighting and another 1,600 shot after they were apprehended. These figures are close to estimates from one source, which listed 805 partisans killed in battle during the drive while another 1,165 'suspects' were shot after being captured.[72] Only 34 men, probably Red Army soldiers, were actually taken prisoner and sent to the rear.[73] I would tend to believe the figures scrawled on the anti-partisan warfare map, since they seem to indicate a primary reference source, but hasten to affirm author French MacLean's figures as being very close to those listed in the German *Bandenlagekarte* (anti-partisan map), affirming the numbers of people killed during the operation. Doubtless the local Russian civilian population added to the body count.

Operation Franz: 7–14 January 1943

This operation was conducted against the approximately 2,000–2,500 partisan troops located in the Berezino-Cerven region east of Minsk, bordering Piruvov-Most just, Verselov, Grodsyanka and Koleyna. One German-language source states that the operation began on 7 January 1943,[74] although a recent English-language study on the SS Sonderkommando Dirlewanger states that the operation began as early as 28 December 1942. Both sources agree, however, that two major SS and police battlegroups took part. SS Battlegroup Kutschera was to attack the partisan region from the north, while SS Battlegroup von Gottberg was to attack the area from the south.[75] Reports from the field stated that the guerrillas here were operating in mostly captured German Army uniforms, thus complicating the operation since it would be difficult to discern from a distance who was a guerrilla and who was a member of the Axis forces.[76]

SS Battlegroup Kutschera was composed of the following units:

- III. Battalion of Police Regiment 2
- 57th Belarusian Self-Defence Battalion[77]
- SS Sonderkommando Dirlewanger
- 633rd Eastern Battalion
- 634th Eastern Battalion
- 112th Police Signals Company
- Self-Defence Artillery Battalion for Special Employment[78]

In addition to these forces, elements of the 4th Police Panzer Company also took part in the operation as a part of SS Sonderkommando Dirlewanger. This newly created police tank company was on its way to its assigned unit, Police Regiment 13, when three of its armoured platoons were diverted to SS Battlegroup Kutschera and used in the drive. The 1st and 2nd Platoons each had three Steyr armoured cars, while the 3rd Platoon operated five captured French Hotchkiss light tanks.[79] Records show that two of the Hotchkiss tanks were attached to SS Sonderkommando Dirlewanger during this action.[80] SS Battlegroup von Gottberg was composed of Police Regiments 10 and 24, and the remainder of the 4th Police Panzer Company.

The results of Operation Franz were summed up in a report dated 16 January 1943, which stated that the operation had ended on 14 January 1943 with the following results: 1,143 partisans killed and 882 partisan suspects executed, for a total of 2,025 killed. The overwhelming majority of the partisan suspects were most likely Russian peasants who lived in the region. In addition, an additional 1,000 residents who were deemed fit for work were forcibly deported and sent to Germany. One 76mm gun, two 45mm anti-tank guns, 280 rifles and 12,000 rounds of rifle ammunition were captured, along with 100 grenades, 625lbs of dynamite and a wireless radio set. The

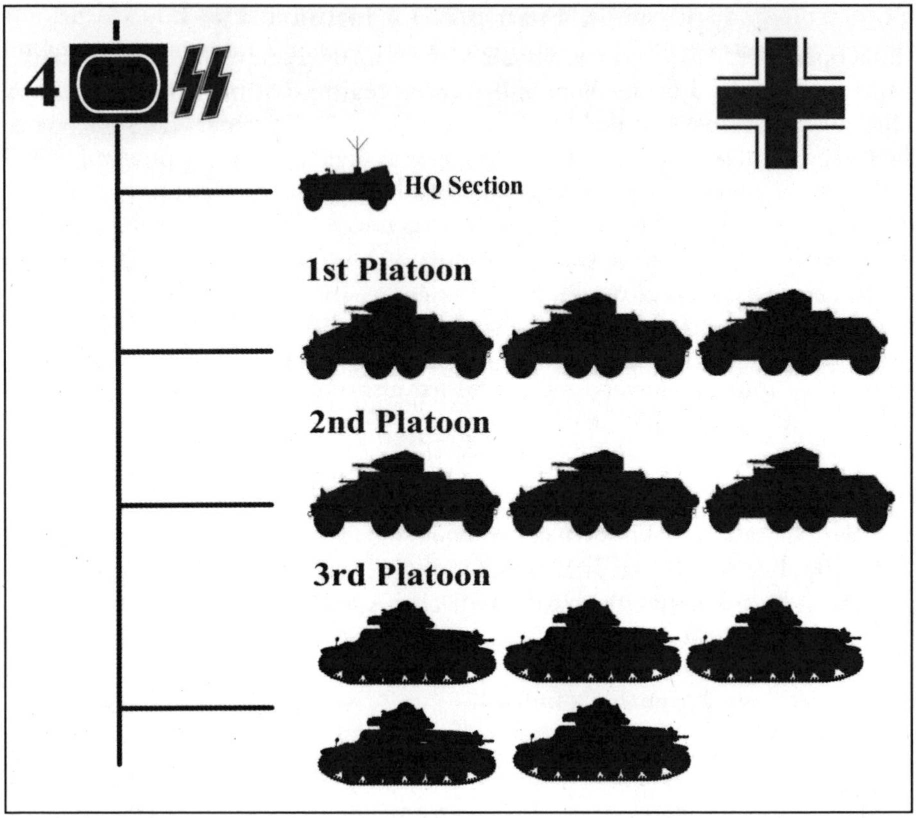

Figure 2. The 4th Police Tank Company in December 1942. This unit, like all other German police forces, received the honorary title 'SS' in February 1943.

operation also netted the Germans 2,000 head of cattle, 200 swine, 120 sheep, 143 horses, 100 sleighs and 60 tons of grain.

Operation Albert: 5–10 February 1943

This was a relatively small operation aimed at the 7th railway line from the western boundary of Bobruisk upstream of the Berezina river to Usda. Several partisan units were operating in this area and intelligence reports stated that these guerrillas could travel from Belarus into central Russia and back at will.[81] SS Lieutenant General Erich von dem Bach-Zelewski gathered together the following SS and police forces:[82]

- II. Battalion of Police Regiment 14 (commander: Police Lieutenant Colonel Otto Peter)
- Police Regiment 24 (commander: Police Lieutenant Colonel Gassler)
- 555th Security Battalion of the 286th Security Division.

The II. Battalion of Police Regiment 14 was the only unit from this regiment to take part in the operation. The I. and III. Battalions, plus the regiment's 13th, 14th and 15th Companies had been sent to Army Group South in December 1942 to bolster the 8th Italian Army. The bulk of Police Regiment 14 was attached to the 385th Infantry Division, which was fighting under the Italian 8th Army command.[83] According to one source, at this time the bulk of the I. Battalion of Police Regiment 14 was composed of Ukrainian auxiliary policemen.[84] It should be noted that the standard arrangement adopted when creating the police rifle regiments was one German police battalion (always the I. Battalion), and two battalions composed of Ukrainian volunteers (always the II. and III. Battalions). As far as the police regiments are concerned, they were supposed to be composed of pure Germans, or at the very least a mixture of pure Germans and ethnic Germans.

Unternehmen Kugelblitz (Operation Lightning Bolt): 22 February–8 March 1943

In late February 1943 the 3rd Panzer Army directed the 201st Security Division and elements of the II. Luftwaffe Field Corps to launch an attack against the partisan centre located in the Surazh Rayon northeast of Vitebsk.[85] Specifically, the towns and surrounding regions around Vitebsk, Gorodok, Gurki and Lake Senniza were to be targeted.[86] The commander of the 201st Security Division, Generalmajor Jacobi, was placed in charge of the drive. In this operation, the 201st Security Division would employ Cossack and Volga-Tartar auxiliary forces alongside units from the 3rd and 4th Luftwaffe Field Divisions.[87] The 720th Infantry Training Regiment from the 391st Field Training Division, created on 31 August 1942 and stationed in Vitebsk, was also used. The Volga-Tartar unit employed in this drive was the 825th Volga-Tartar Infantry Battalion, which had been raised in Poland in late November 1942 and sent to the 3rd Panzer Army in early 1943.[88] In addition, the 601st Security Regiment, the 631st Cossack Battalion and the 2nd Bicycle Regiment, plus one Jäger regiment, also took part in the action.[89] This last-mentioned unit was most likely a regiment from the 5th Jäger Division, which during this period was operating between Nevel and Surash. At this time the southernmost regiment of this division was the 56th Jäger Regiment, under Colonel Hachtel.[90] It was therefore very probable that it was the 56th Jäger Regiment that was temporarily assigned to this anti-partisan operation.

The area of operation was referred to as the so-called 'Vitebsk corridor', which had gained notoriety on both sides of the front lines as an area where the Red Army could slip in men and supplies to guerrilla forces behind the German lines relatively unimpeded. This was because the sector basically

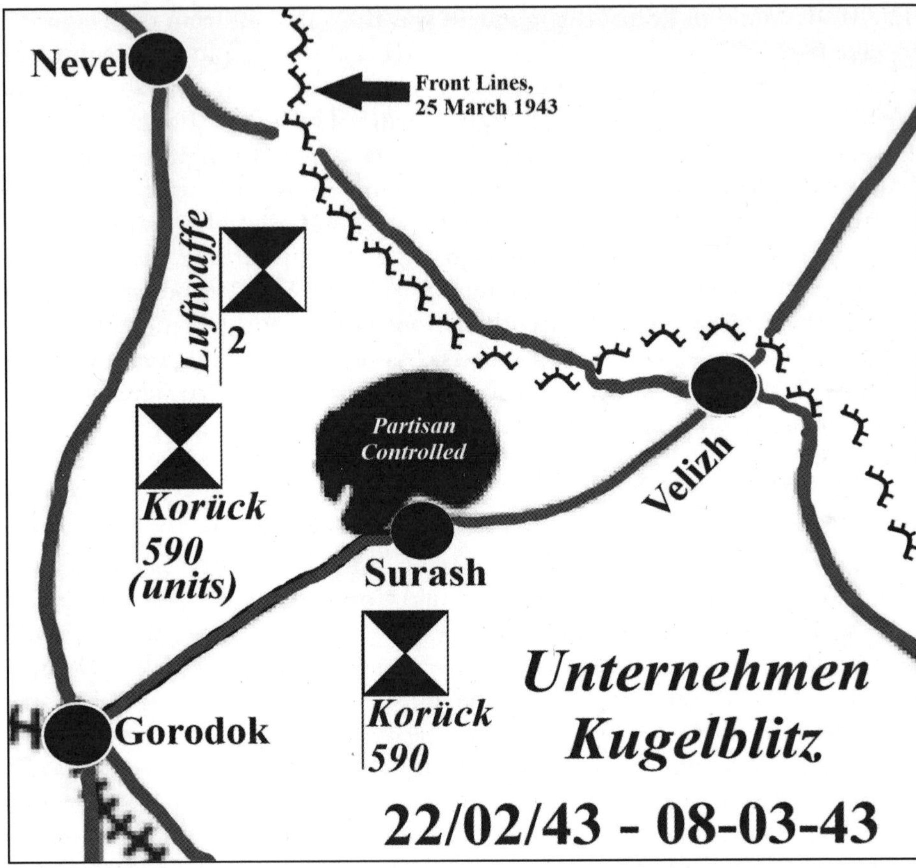

Map 25. Area of operations for *Unternehmen Kugelblitz* (Operation Lightning Bolt).

consisted of a thin line of strongpoints situated some 2–3 miles apart and manned by Luftwaffe infantry troops who, for lack of enough forces, had left the local partisan units alone to travel unimpeded through these wide gaps running through swamps and forests. Partisan forces here numbered some 5,000 men.[91] The operation was deemed a partial success, with about 3,700 guerrillas being killed in the operation.[92] In addition, because the Germans cleared the entire region of foodstuffs, a serious food shortage began to develop. Two more operations after *Kugelblitz* finally caused the Soviet partisan command to take notice and they attempted to fly in supplies so that their partisan units there could continue to operate. The head of the partisan movement, General Ponomarenko, made it a priority to supply the local partisan brigades with food stores flown in from Soviet-controlled territory.[93]

Chapter 4

Collaboration in 1942

The 1st Russian National SS Brigade

In the previous chapter we encountered Vladimir Vladimirovich Gil, *aka* Gil Rodionov. Gil was approached by the SS Security Service in 1941, a move that would lead to the formation of the Druzhina SS Brigade. In 1942 the SS Security Service had not yet absorbed the Abwehr – the German Armed Forces intelligence apparatus. The SD was therefore in direct competition with the Abwehr to become Nazi Germany's chief intelligence-gathering service. Copying the actions of the leader of the Abwehr, Admiral Wilhelm Canaris, the SS Security Service also moved to create its own experimental Russian volunteer unit for planned operations behind the Soviet lines. This decision was taken purely for competitive reasons, given that Walter Schellenberg, who headed Department 6 of the Reich Security Main Office, was attempting to outdo his army equivalent, the Abwehr. The formation was variously named, but most often referred to as *SS Druzhina Verbände* (SS Druzhina Formation). The unit had its early beginnings in February 1942 when a battalion-sized group was organized near Osintorf, near Smolensk, and later stationed in Nevel. At this time the Abwehr's competing Russian unit, the Graukopf (Grey Head) Brigade, had an initial strength of two battalions. A month later, in March, the SS Druzhina formation was transferred to Glebokie, where it remained until September 1942.[1] There, it was attached to the Rear Area Commander Army Group Centre.[2] From Glebokie it launched a number of successful anti-partisan operations. In March 1943 it comprised 150 officers, 1,050 men, 60 artillery pieces, 95 machine guns, 18 mortars and 200 sub-machine guns,[3] and by April that year it was up to a strength of four battalions. By July 1943 it totalled a force of 3,000 men and was the size of a small brigade. This formation would prove to be the most effective indigenous anti-partisan unit in the German arsenal in Belarusia until its defection to the partisans on 13 August 1943.[4]

In November 1942 the Druzhina unit had been transferred from the *Sicherheitsdienst* to SS and police control. This was done for operational reasons, given that the SS and police were directing the anti-partisan war. Like the Graukopf Brigade, the Druzhina SS Brigade would eventually suffer from morale problems brought about for three main reasons: first, the lack of a cohesive German policy towards the people in the East insofar as what the Germans could and would offer as a replacement to Stalin and communism; secondly, continuing German atrocities against the Soviet civilian population forced many in the brigade, especially its leadership corps, to decide whether they wished to serve a domestic or a foreign despot; and thirdly, the German defeat at Stalingrad and at Kursk clearly foreshadowed the downfall of Nazi Germany and signalled to the collaborator forces that they had backed the wrong horse. In the end, most of the Druzhina men figured that if they had to serve a tyrannical regime, they were better off with a domestic tyrant rather than a foreign one. Once again, German arrogance and ignorance had played a role in undermining what might have been the beginnings of a large anti-communist Russian army. What makes the German stupidity so amazingly profound is that this recipe for disaster repeated itself again and again. The Soviet partisan command could only sit back and gloat at the manner in which the Germans were waging the war in the USSR. Nazi policies in the East guaranteed that these attempts to raise the Soviet people against Stalin and communism would ultimately fail. Yet in spite of German ignorance, some eastern volunteers continued to fight alongside them, apparently choosing the Germans over Stalin.

Action and reaction: massacres and mutinies in the East

By the time the Western Allies invaded France in June 1944 many eastern battalions had already been transferred to the West from the East. This had started in 1943, when the German Army in the West had been ordered to send one German battalion from each division in France and the Low Countries to the Russian front in exchange for two eastern battalions. The decision to do this had come from the Armed Forces High Command with no consideration whatsoever about the political implications and demoralizing effect of placing eastern volunteers in a position where they would have to consider firing at American, Canadian, British or French troops. When the Allies landed in France in 1944 some of these eastern battalions fought them to the bitter end, while others simply surrendered or offered only token resistance. In some cases there were mutinies, and small wonder, given that these volunteers were facing an 'enemy' with whom they had no quarrel. Mutinies and defections were not a new phenomenon, however, for as early as 1942 they were already a common occurrence. One such mutiny took place in the early morning of 18 September 1942 and is significant because it happened close to the time of the German high water mark in Russia. Thus, this mutiny did not occur as a result of opportunists seeing German reversals, but as a direct result of the oppressive nature of the German occupation, the attitude of the majority of the Germans towards the Russians, and the ambivalent attitude of the German military, and particularly the Nazi government, regarding the status and future of Russia and her people once Stalin and Communism were defeated:

> The staff and the 2nd Company of Ost Bataillon Berezina were based in Ljuban, about 90 kilometers [56 miles] southeast of the town of Bobruisk. On September 18, 1942 a combined force of three German members of Secret Field Police Group 707, 70 men of the Order Service, plus 102 Russians of the 2nd Company under the command of Russian Sergeant Sorwin, left their camp at 2:00 am. They were to reconnoiter the area and bring in the harvest. After two and a half hours the men of the 2nd Company stopped the column and suddenly machine-gunned the three Secret Field Police men and two *Ordnungsdienst* men while seriously wounding three others. Sergeant Sorwin thereupon explained to the men of the 2nd Company they were to defect to the partisans and those members who didn't want to go would be killed on the spot. When the column once again continued the march the complete *Ordnungsdienst* group and 35 men of the 2nd Company managed to leave the traitors after a brief firefight, returning to base. Sixty-seven mutineers with three light machine guns and two mortars defected to the partisans. The ring-leaders were mostly former Soviet army officers. Three more soldiers of the 2nd Company defected from the base in Ljuban in the afternoon. The following investigation netted four more soldiers who had connections with the partisans. The Secret Field Police . . . shot these soldiers. The causes of the rebellion were: (1) no action and therefore a lot of time to fraternize with the local populace who harbored the partisans; (2) family ties with the partisans (one sergeant had a partisan brother); and (3) insufficient German cadre personnel (the remaining soldiers of the 2nd Company demanded German officers). The action taken to avoid future occurrences has been the transfer of the battalion and its restructuring.[5]

It is quite telling that no mention was made of possible grievances which these men might have had, or the conditions of the Russian civilians with whom they were accused of fraternizing. What is clear is that the Germans wanted as little contact as possible between their soldiers in the East and the local civilian population. This was meant not only to discourage any ties with possible guerrilla sympathizers, but also to keep these eastern soldiers from finding out as little as possible about civilian conditions under Nazi rule. Often the peasantry would be brutalized. The Soviet partisan command encouraged its forces to commit war crimes themselves, in order to provoke the Germans into responding, and German atrocities against civilians were common. Where cases such as these did not occur, the Soviet partisans were more than ready to provoke any apparently benevolent German commander by slaughtering any hapless German whom they could lay their hands on:

> One would spy out one or two German soldiers, bestially mutilate and kill them, then freeze the corpses, often in the posture of the Nazi salute, and stand them at road intersections. The enraged SS would seek revenge on the nearby villages: shoot innocent people, burn them alive in their huts, confiscate cattle and devastate the entire land. Usually for one German killed, the SS retaliated on 100 natives.[6]

Thus, even if a local region, area, town or hamlet was governed by a relatively lenient or 'enlightened' German administrator, the guerrillas did their best to undermine whatever trust the local inhabitants had in him. In most cases the German Army commander was completely incapable of preventing his SS counterpart from committing any acts against the local population that would prove detrimental to the German cause. In some instances the German Army even took part in such atrocities. Incidences of mutinies and desertions continued throughout the war and increased in frequency. On the night of 5/6 October 1943 the entire 1st Company of the 668th Eastern Battalion, then operating in the German 16th Army sector, defected to the partisans after murdering nearly all the members of their unit's German cadre personnel. The Russian battalion staff thereupon revolted as well. They and the other companies left in the unit were disarmed. The formation was officially dissolved on 17 December 1943. These and countless other cases make it painfully clear that the eastern volunteer movement was far from perfect. On the contrary, it had been, and continued to be, a hodge-podge of quick fixes, half-promises, mistrust and deception. The movement was not even governed by a set of basic established rules and codes until mid- to late 1943 and it wasn't until 1944 that Hitler reluctantly agreed to the establishment of a 'Russian Army of Liberation', but he never quite trusted the Russians. By then the Nazis had long since lost the opportunity to win over the people of the Soviet Union. The conclusion must be drawn that were it not for Stalin's tyranny, hardly any of the Soviet Union's diverse peoples would have rallied to the German side. As the partisan movement rose, the Nazi repression of the local population increased. This in turn caused further resentment and defections, and it became common policy and practice within the German command to disarm collaborator units that showed the slightest inkling of unreliability and transfer them to France, Italy, the Low Countries, Norway, Denmark and the Balkans. One estimate quotes a figure of about 176 Russian, Belarusian, Ukrainian, East Orient, Caucasian and Cossack battalions withdrawn from the Soviet Union and sent to the West in order to prevent them from defecting.

As stated earlier, these eastern battalions were traded on a 2:1 ratio for German battalions from the West which were sent to the Russian front. In September and November 1943 sixty eastern volunteer battalions were exchanged for thirty German infantry battalions. By the end of 1943 the German Armed Forces still possessed a reported 370 eastern battalions and an additional 130,000 eastern volunteers acting as *Hilfswilligern* (volunteers), referred to in short form simply as 'Hiwis' within German divisions.[7] (This number later changed in June 1944 when 200 *Ost* battalions were available to the Wehrmacht.) In September 1943 some 15,000 eastern troops were transferred from the Eastern Front to other theatres of war, and by October thirty-four eastern battalions had arrived in the West, with twenty-three more on their way. Between November and December 1943 a further 25,000 eastern

Map 26. Eastern troop units stationed in France, June 1944.

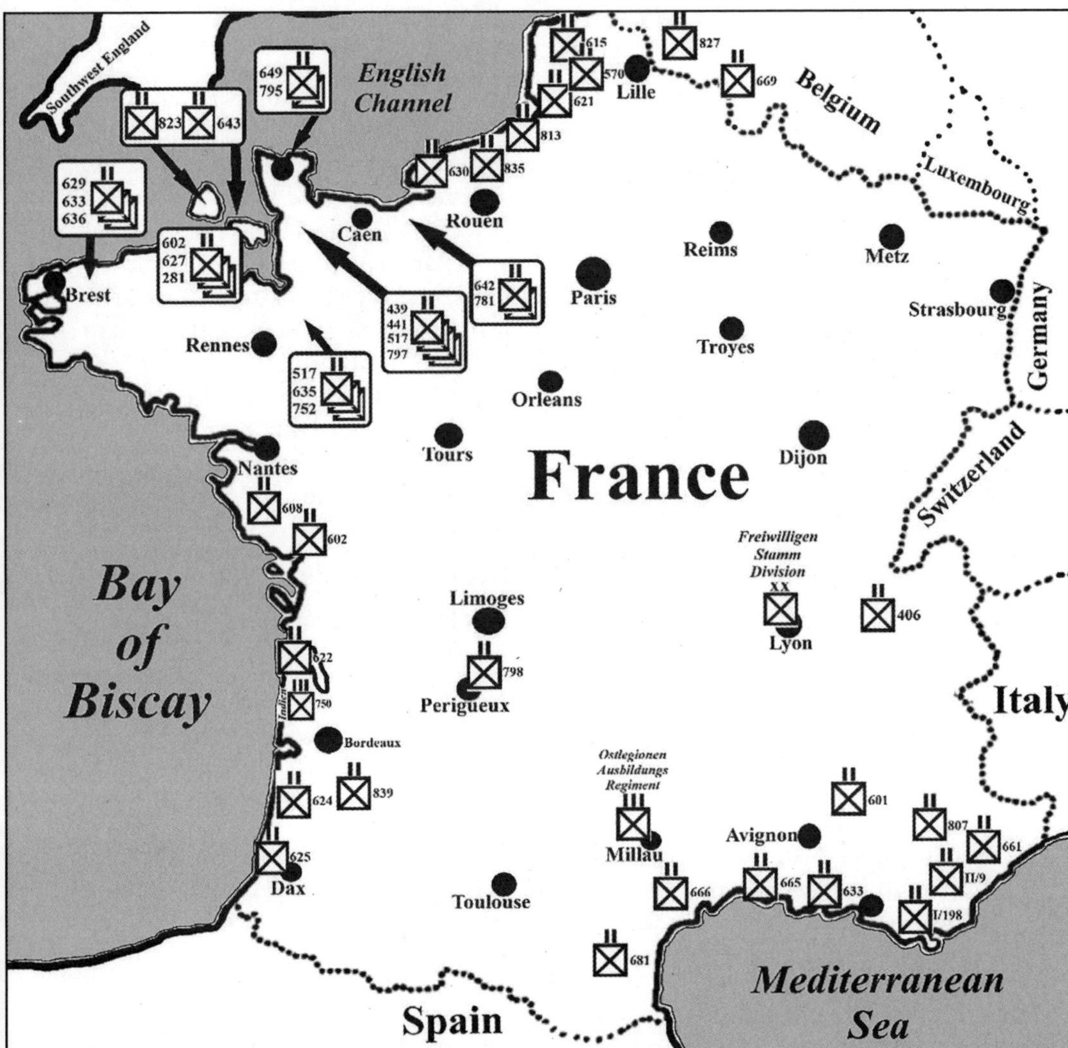

soldiers had been shipped out of the Soviet Union. These units were distributed roughly on the basis of one or two battalions per German division. By April 1944 most of the eastern battalions had been officially incorporated into German divisions stationed in the West, typically becoming the either the III. or IV. Battalion of a regiment within these divisions.

The transfer of these eastern volunteer units from the eastern battlefields consequently eliminated the very reason why the men in these units had supposedly volunteered in the first place: to aid in the destruction of communism in the USSR. Further demoralization and desertions were the end result. When these eastern troops were employed against the Western Allies from 1944, it was no surprise at all that some units simply surrendered or defected to the Allies. Some of them even killed their German cadre staff before defecting.

Creation and employment of volunteer units in Belarus, 1941–1944

It was clear from the beginning of the occupation of White Russia that independence was not going to be offered to the Belarusian people. The hope, however, was that after the war was over and the Soviet Union was defeated, the Germans might relent and allow for the creation of a separate Belarusian state that would be allied to a triumphant German Reich. Of course, this was merely wishful thinking on the part of the Belarusian collaborators, but the Nazis never openly stated how they intended to rule the eastern territories after the war was over, so the dream of an independent or semi-independent White Russian state, however unlikely, persisted. In order to prepare the way for just such an eventuality, the civilian political leaders of the White Russian collaborator government attempted to imbue the Belarusian forces being raised by the Germans with nationalism. The belief was that if units felt a national kinship, they could later be used as the basis for a White Russian national army. In order to achieve this, the following proposals were made:

- to spread nationalist ideology, whenever possible, directly among the Belarusian officers and NCOs of these various White Russian battalions;
- to instill a nationalist Belarusian spirit in the staffs of these auxiliary or volunteer units; and
- to subordinate the various collaborator units, whenever possible, to a Belarusian civilian or military governing body, with the least possible control by the Germans.

It was hoped that these steps would help prepare the way for an eventual Belarusian National Army. Originally, this programme was imposed only on White Russian volunteers in the collaborationist police force and by mid-1942 the number of Belarusian volunteers numbered 4,580 men, located in static units throughout the countryside.[8] These units were formed in the early period of the occupation of Belarusia and were principally referred to as 'home-defence' units, which the Germans called *Heimatschutz*. They were raised in the countryside from local villagers and farmers, who were then tasked with protecting their crops, villages and towns from Soviet and Polish guerrillas. On 29 June 1942 the General Commissioner of Belarusia, Wilhelm Kube, announced the creation of the *Korpus Belaruskay samaakhovy* (Corps of Belarusian Self-Defence, or KBS). A Belarusian civilian advisory panel was established, referred to as the *Belaruskaya narodnaya samapomach* (Belarusian Popular Self-Defence, or BNS). In order to give this new force an air of legitimacy, the BNS 'approved' the creation of the German-sponsored KBS. The commander of the Belarusian police at this time was Franz Kushel, a former Polish Army captain. In early July 1942 Kushel met with representatives of the SS and Police Leader White Russia in order to plan and create the KBS combat formations. The structure of the KBS was to be organized as follows:

Corps' HQ command in Minsk
1st Division in Minsk and Slutsk
2nd Division in Baranovichi
3rd Division in Vileika

These 'divisions' were little more than wishful thinking on the part of the civilian collaborator government. The KBS battalions that were raised were static, poorly clothed, armed and equipped, and under direct German Order Police control. The Germans had no intention of allowing larger formations to be created. Nevertheless, in spite of their limitations, these static defence forces proved useful in augmenting the German rear area defences in Belarusia. By the second half of 1942 some 15,000 Belarusian volunteers were serving in twenty static, self-defence KBS battalions. As static formations, these battalions could never be employed in operations against the partisans, but merely served as defence forces. The German command also assured itself that these units never came under one unified Belarusian command. Each static battalion was also subordinate to the local German Gendarmerie (rural police) or *Schutzpolizei* (protection police) post. The men in these units were armed with a variety of weapons of varying number, quality and nationality, while their clothing varied from civilian attire to Polish and Red Army uniforms. Their one identifying factor was the 'pursuit' cap badge and the white-red-white armband worn on the left sleeve. (The colours were the national Belarusian colours.) In many cases the armbands were handmade and rather crudely done. In 1942 the German order police instituted a recruitment drive in Belarusia, as they had done in Ukraine and the Baltic States, in order to create combat battalions to fight the guerrillas directly. However, the

Belarusian self-defence battalions were never as numerous as those raised in Ukraine and the Eastland (Baltic) region. Those in the *Ordnungsdienst* (Order Service), for example, amounted to 251 NCOs and 3,528 men by July 1942.[9] These men were considered *Hilfspolizei* (auxiliary policemen). In addition, the first three Belarusian self-defence battalions were created in July 1942 and named the 46th and 47th Self-Defence Guard Battalions and the 48th Self-Defence Front Battalion. Like all Belarusian numerical designations, they were prefaced with *Weissruthenische* (White Ruthenian) for easy recognition. These battalions were raised and initially stationed in Minsk.[10] While the 46th and 47th were designated as *Wach* (Guard) battalions, the 48th was deemed employable against the partisans as a *Front Bataillon* (front-line combat battalion). Towards the end of October 1942 the German railway command also established a Belarusian Railway Guard Battalion, which would eventually contain 1,000 men divided into five companies of roughly 200 men each. These companies were located and employed along the main railway lines in Belarusia as follows:

1st Company in Minsk
2nd Company in Stolpce
3rd Company in Baranovichi
4th Company in Lida
5th Company in Krulevschizna

Lastly, in December 1942 plans were enacted to create an SS Security Service battalion made up of Belarusian volunteers. This formation was created in early 1943. Initially it contained two companies of 200 men each but was later expanded to three companies, with an eventual strength of about 1,000 men. The officers were predominantly German SD personnel, although a few lower-ranking Belarusian officers also served in the unit, principally to translate German orders into the local language.

The Belarusian Police

The first Belarusian auxiliary police units were formed in the eastern part of Belarusian territory even before the 'General District White Ruthenia' was established by the Germans. The creation of these formations was at the initiative of the Germans, who were concerned about increasing the numbers of security troops in the rear of Army Group Centre. The result was that by 1942 dozens of Belarusian auxiliary police units, termed *Ordnungsdienst* (order service auxiliary policemen), were operating in eastern Belarus. The units were created principally by the Belarusian émigrés Dimitry Kosmovich and Mikhail Vitushk and were made up of infantry and cavalry formations, mostly led by former Red Army officers. These units were largely manned by recruiting men from German prisoner of war camps, so the troops were a mixture of volunteer civilians and recently released prisoners of war, organized into companies of between 100 and 150 men each. Various procedures were introduced in order to persuade the locals to join or assist these collaborationist formations. The mission of the auxiliary police units entailed food requisitioning, protecting the harvest, tax collecting and general police duties. It is important to note that in some cases these *Ordnungsdienst* groups cleared some regions of Belarusia without the presence of German troops. In August 1941, in the region of Polesie and Mozyr, Belarusian nationalist forces conducted sweeps that bagged numerous Red Army stragglers, some partisan forces and even a few NKVD groups. The White Russians were aided by the 10,000-strong Ukrainian nationalist guerrilla force led by M. Borovtsa. This force was part of the *Ukrayins'ka povstans'ka armiia* (UPA, the Ukrainian Insurgent Army). The Germans did not participate in this drive, but merely observed. In the regions that were no longer under the control of Soviet forces but not yet under full German control, White Russian nationalists established a civilian administration, even publishing newspapers, and ended collectivization by redistributing the land to the peasants. In Polesie armed Belarusian units were spontaneously organized and began operating as a local constabulary. These indigenous police forces operated irrespective of the Germans, who only began to organize control of the region around October 1941.

The degree of autonomy offered to Belarusian collaborators by the Germans varied from region to region and from town to town. In one area the Germans allowed schools to reopen, while in others they were closed. The same thing occurred with regard to farm collectives, where some were ordered to be maintained while in other regions more enlightened German administrators allowed them to be shared amongst the farmers, although this ran contrary to standing German orders to maintain the Soviet collectives. Chaos reigned, especially in the first year of the war, as the Germans struggled to decide exactly what they wanted to do with their newly conquered territories. Unfortunately for the pro-German collaborationist movement, there were more unenlightened German administrators than good ones who understood that the only way to defeat Stalin and Stalinism was to offer the Soviet people a better alternative to communism. The most common German civilian administrators were knuckle-dragging, low-brow types, who had little or no experience in dealing with any foreign people. If lucky, they were the recipients of 90-day crash courses in 'schools' which taught foreign administrative rule. In reality they learned nothing that would help them to understand the very people they were to administer.

These men were quickly nicknamed *Goldfasanen* (Golden Pheasants), after the golden epaulets worn on the shoulders of their brown Nazi Party uniforms. Most were middle-aged men who had gone through the defeat of the First World War and the humiliation of the Treaty of Versailles, and then the depression of the 1920s. To them, hatred and bitterness had become a way of life. They brought that hatred and a desire to 'even the odds' with them to the East. The recipients of their wrath turned out to be those people they meant to rule and administer. Most had little or no administrative experience whatsoever. After the creation of the Belarusian General District by the Germans, responsibility for maintaining order there was assigned to the SS and Police Leader White Russia, which at this time was led by SS Brigadier General and Major General of the Police Carl Zenner, who held this post from 14 August 1941 until 22 May 1942. In due course, all Belarusian police forces created from the population were reformed under his tutelage and given the title of auxiliary police officers; the Germans initially referred to them as *Hilfspolizei*, but later the term *Schutzmannschaft* (self-defence) was employed. The term literally meant 'protective guard', but was used to denote the indigenous auxiliary police volunteers. City and rural (*Gendarmerie*) police were also formed from Belarusian volunteers once the Germans had occupied all the Belarusian cities and the larger towns. This was also done in conjunction with the local civilian collaborationist government.

In July 1941 the émigré Dimitry Kosmovich became the Chief of all the Belarusian Auxiliary Police, with his headquarters in Minsk. The local police chief of each region supervised the auxiliary police volunteers, but regionally they were still subject to the local SS and Police Leader command. The two principal duties of the auxiliary police were maintenance of order in the occupied areas and surveillance of the local population, with emphasis on checking the papers of suspicious persons. As the partisan threat grew, the Germans attempted to enlarge the White Russian auxiliary police. They also attempted to make them more mobile and thus more flexible in order to better deal with the growing partisan menace. A meeting was held at the beginning of October 1941 at the headquarters of Army Group Centre regarding this growing partisan threat.[11] The meeting had two major results. First, the decision was made to employ, whenever possible, regular German Army units in the suppression of partisan activity. Secondly, the Nazi belief that *Jeder Jude ist ein guerrillakämpfer* (Every Jew is a guerrilla fighter) was brought to its hateful fruition when the decision was made that in the fight against the partisan threat, the German Army was to take part in targeting any Jews within their area of operation. The first demonstration of this new policy was the murder of 150 Jewish men, women and children in the central Belarusian town of Krucha on 10 October 1941 by members of the 3rd Company of the 691st Infantry Regiment (339th Static Infantry Division), which at the time was serving as part of the German rear area security forces of Army Group Centre. In connection to this effort to improve the effectiveness of the auxiliary police, the OKW (German Armed Forces High Command) eventually published instructions on how to deal with the partisan menace. The notes taken at the meeting held in early October 1941 at Army Group Centre headquarters were added to other directives on how to deal with the guerrilla threat and published in early December 1941. The new pamphlet was titled *Sonderanweisungen zum Kampf gegen Partisanenbanden* (Special Instructions for Fighting Partisan Bands). In particular, it stressed that

> the use of local auxiliary groups in the struggle against the guerrillas is justifiable and necessary. The knowledge of the local region, climate and language makes it possible for these indigenous troops to apply guerrilla tactics against the partisans and combat them more effectively.[12]

Thus, according to this new German directive, the employment of indigenous collaborationist forces alongside German troops was of great importance in successfully dealing with the partisan threat. The new directive also allowed for further recruitment of the local population, even at the static level, where villagers were recruited to serve as static self-defence forces called *Heimatschutz* by the Germans. The static defence units were easily armed with leftover Red Army rifles and pistols. The rapid withdrawal and destruction of Red Army forces in Belarus during the summer and autumn of 1941 had permitted the gathering of many weapons. The principal role of the *Heimatschutz* was the guarding of crops and livestock against theft by either Polish or Red Army partisans. Apparently, the rapid German advance in the summer months of 1941 had prevented the Red Army from fully mobilizing a large number of able-bodied men of military age before the Soviet Army withdrew from Belarusia. These men were now selected for service by both the Germans and the White Russian collaborator authorities. On 16 July 1942 control over the forming Belarusian collaborator units was handed over to the Germans and thus the Chief of Police for the General District Belarusia, SS Brigadier General and Major General of the Police Eberhard Herff, assumed control of these units. The BNS civilian advisory council had no choice but to agree with the wishes of SS General Herff. However, in order to create the appearance that the KBS was under Belarusian control, SS General Herff permitted the appointment of Belarusian officers to high posts within the KBS. The result was that by April 1943 the Supreme Command of the BNS was staffed as follows:

Chief of the KBS – Ivan Ermachenko
Chief of Staff of the BNS Headquarters – Lieutenant Colonel Joseph N. Gut'ko
Chief Inspector of KBS Military Units – Captain Franz Kushel[13]

The men joining the KBS had little or no military training, and there was a desperate shortage of trained NCOs and officers. Kushel tried to alleviate the situation by starting a three-month officers' training course in order to train capable officers. The first course began in August 1942 and the initial graduating class included 260 officer candidates. After the end of this first course, each of the new officers was assigned throughout the countryside. It was expected that these officers would in turn help to train the NCOs in the various battalions. In April 1943 the Germans dismissed the local self-governing representatives of the BNS in Minsk. The various BNS battalions were now allocated directly to the local German police commands. The self-defence battalions were allocated to railway protection or police duties, or were sent to Germany as forced labourers. Citing the reasons why the KBS was dissolved, Colonel Klemm, Chief of the Field Gendarmerie in the General District White Russia, stated in April 1943:

> First, despite numerous requests, not enough quantities of weapons have been supplied. Secondly, as soon as the KBS came into being, its Belarusian soldiers and their families became targets of terrorist activity by the bandits and gangsters [guerrillas]. Thirdly, with certain exceptions, these volunteers were unreliable, and yielded easily to enemy propaganda. There have been cases where large KBS patrols, armed with rifles and automatic weapons, have voluntarily gone over to the bandits.[14]

As stated earlier, the creation of Belarusian self-defence battalions began in earnest in 1942 and was carried out in three stages: June–August 1942, September–October 1943 and February–March 1944. The result was that by April 1944 eleven self-defence battalions had been raised. In addition, a self-defence artillery battalion and a self-defence cavalry battalion were also created, giving a total strength of over 3,000 men:

45th Self-Defence Security Battalion
46th Self-Defence Security Battalion
47th Self-Defence Security Battalion
48th Self-Defence Front Battalion
49th Self-Defence Security Battalion
49th Self-Defence Front Battalion
64th Self-Defence Front Battalion[15]
65th Self-Defence Front Battalion
66th Self-Defence Front Battalion
67th Self-Defence Security Battalion
69th Self-Defence Front Battalion
56th Self-Defence Artillery Battalion
68th Self-Defence Cavalry Battalion

Each battalion contained four companies and a headquarters staff. Ideally, each company was to comprise 124 officers, NCOs and men. In reality, the companies varied from being understrength to overstrength (depending on losses and recruitment). Each company was organized around three rifle platoons and one machine-gun platoon. Although Polish or Belarusian officers led the companies and platoons, the battalion headquarters staff consisted of one German officer and nine German NCOs. The Belarusian self-defence battalions were charged with various tasks that included: protection of the rear area of the German Army against espionage and sabotage; protection and defence of the railways, roads, crossroads, intersections and lines of communication; defence of all economic and military depots, warehouses, buildings, barracks and airfields; and employment of units against partisan forces during anti-partisan drives. Non-Belarusian units also operated in White Russia. These included Polish, Latvian, Lithuanian, Ukrainian, Turkestani and Cossack formations. In July 1942 the following non-Belarusian units were stationed in Belarusia: the 3rd, 12th and 255th Lithuanian Self-Defence Battalions, the 26th and 274th Latvian Self-Defence Battalions, the 51st, 52nd, 53rd and 54th Ukrainian Self-Defence Battalions, and the 201st Polish Self-Defence Battalion. In May and June 1943 the following non-Belarusian units were operating in White Russia: the 600th Cossack Battalion (in the region of Mogilev), the 622nd Cossack Battalion (Polotsk), the 623rd Cossack Battalion (Vitebsk), the 624th Cossack Battalion (Polotsk/Vitebsk), the 4th (Independent) Cossack Regiment (Osipovichi), the 5th (Independent) Cossack Regiment (Rechitsi) and the 786th Turkestani Infantry Battalion (Zhlobina).

On 22 June 1944 the Red Army launched its summer offensive, mocking the German invasion date of three years before. This summer offensive would end up destroying most of Army Group Centre and would liberate all of Belarusia. Those German divisions that were not immediately smashed by the massive Soviet assault reeled back in disarray and confusion. Attempts to establish a solid defence line proved impossible. One of the indigenous units not destroyed or mauled by the Soviet offensive was the 13th Belarusian SS Security Service Battalion, which had been stationed in Vileika at the start of the Red Army offensive. Given the increasingly difficult military situation, the morale of the battalion was not good. Tensions were running high between the German cadre staff and the Belarusian NCOs and men. All of the battalion's companies were led by German SS security service officers, except for the battalion's 'Alarm Company', which was led by Lieutenant Bandyk. This company had been raised in August 1944 after the battalion had withdrawn to Poland.

According to one source, what happened next was an attempt by the German battalion commander to appoint a German SS captain of the security service as the new Alarm Company commander. Bandyk absolutely refused to step down and instead took his 150 men and deserted to the Polish partisans, along with some other Belarusian officers who now deserted the battalion. After this event the Germans combed through the battalion, seeking out those

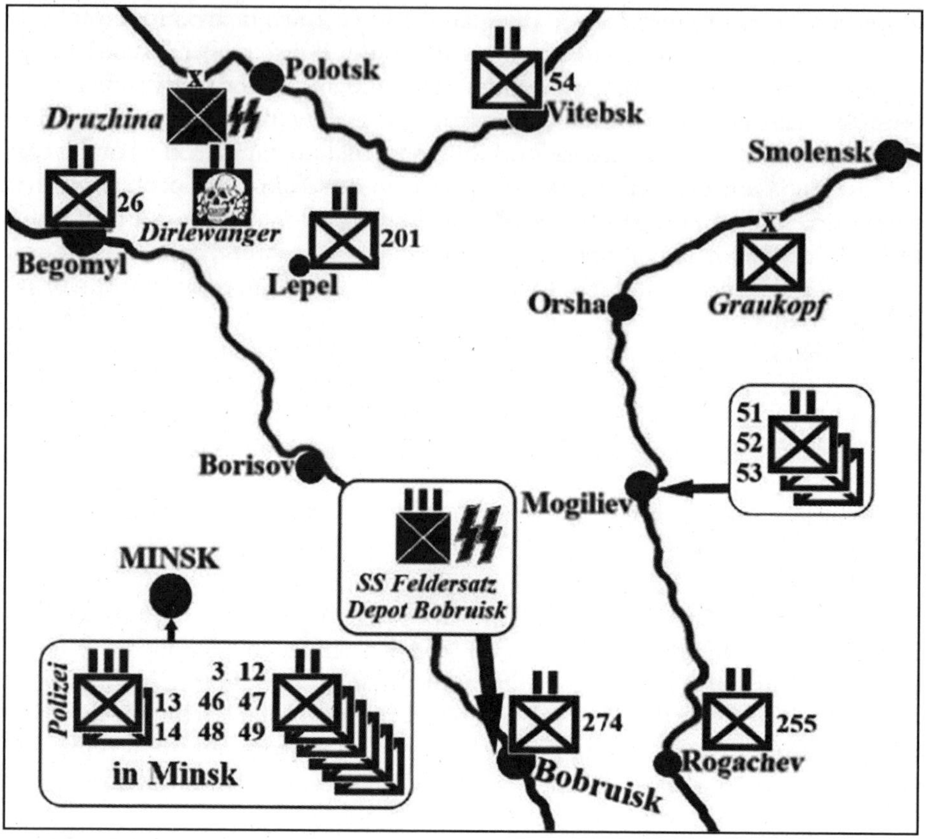

Map 27. Location of German and locally raised units in Belarusia, July 1942.

men they thought were unreliable. Those deemed untrustworthy were transferred over to General Vlasov's Russian Army of Liberation, which was then forming inside Germany. The remaining men of the battalion were then sent to Arensberg in East Prussia, where they remained in September and October 1944. Major Kushel visited the battalion in October and was surprised to discover that it still possessed about 600 officers, NCOs and men. The Germans then decided to split the battalion into company-sized units and scatter them throughout Germany. In this way, 85 men were sent to Lebrechsdorf, 260 were sent to Breslau, 112 were sent to Trieste, 89 were sent to Nikachev along the Polish-Belarusian border, while 21 men were actually transferred to SD headquarters in Berlin. The Germans reversed their action in December 1944 when they opted to transfer the remaining Belarusian personnel from the SD to the newly created 30th Grenadier Division of the SS White Ruthenia. These transfers continued into January 1945. Strangely, the twenty-one Belarusians who had been sent to Berlin never left the German capital and even took part in the defence of the Reich Main Security Office at Prinz-Albrecht-Straße 8 during the battle for Berlin. The battle for Berlin certainly had its moment of irony. For nearly six years the Third Reich had conquered most of the nations of Europe, but now it would be those same Europeans who would help to defend the German capital: Russians, Belarusians, Ukrainians, Estonians, Latvians, Swiss, Frenchmen, Spaniards, Dutch, Danish, Norwegians, Belgian Walloons, Flemish volunteers and even Arabs from the Middle East all fought alongside the Germans vainly attempting to defend the German capital against the Red Army. These men were the ones who had sided with the Nazis during the war. They were, as author David Littlejohn described them, the patriotic traitors.

The auxiliary support received by the Germans in Belarusia became quite significant from the second half of 1942 onwards. The following tables clearly illustrate this significance to the German command and elucidate the strength of the German police, security police and auxiliary police forces at the end of 1942. Table 4.1 lists the indigenous forces as they stood on 1 October 1942 in the region of Belarus and the Baltic States (the so-called Eastland region). Table 4.2 lists the numbers of Order Police and Security Police forces which were available to the Germans in Poland and the USSR as of December 1942.

German use of locally raised collaborationist forces was significant, not only to the history of the anti-partisan war, but to the Holocaust as well. The

Table 4.1. German and foreign *Ordnungspolizei* and SD personnel, 1 October 1942.[16]

Station Post	Germans	*Ordnungspolizei*	Self-Defence
Tallinn, Estonia	591	5,110 Estonian OD men	5,385 Estonian *Schuma*
Riga, Latvia			
Order Police	1,000	9,000 Latvian OD men	9,000 Latvian *Schuma*
SD	987	563 Latvian SD men	–
Kaunas, Lithuania	456	8,757 Lithuanian OD men	7,917 Lithuanians
Minsk, Belarus	1,394	8,374 Belarusian OD men	1,456 Belarusians
Total:	4,428	31,804 OD men	23,756 *Schuma*

Table 4.2. German Order and Security Police in Poland and the USSR, December 1942.[17]

Region	*Ordnungspolizei*	*Sicherheitspolizei*	Total for Region
General Government (Poland)	11,400	2,200	13,600
Northern Russia	4,093	800	4,893
Central Russia	7,000	750	7,750
Southern Russia and Ukraine	12,900	2,000	14,900
Total	35,393	5,750	41,143

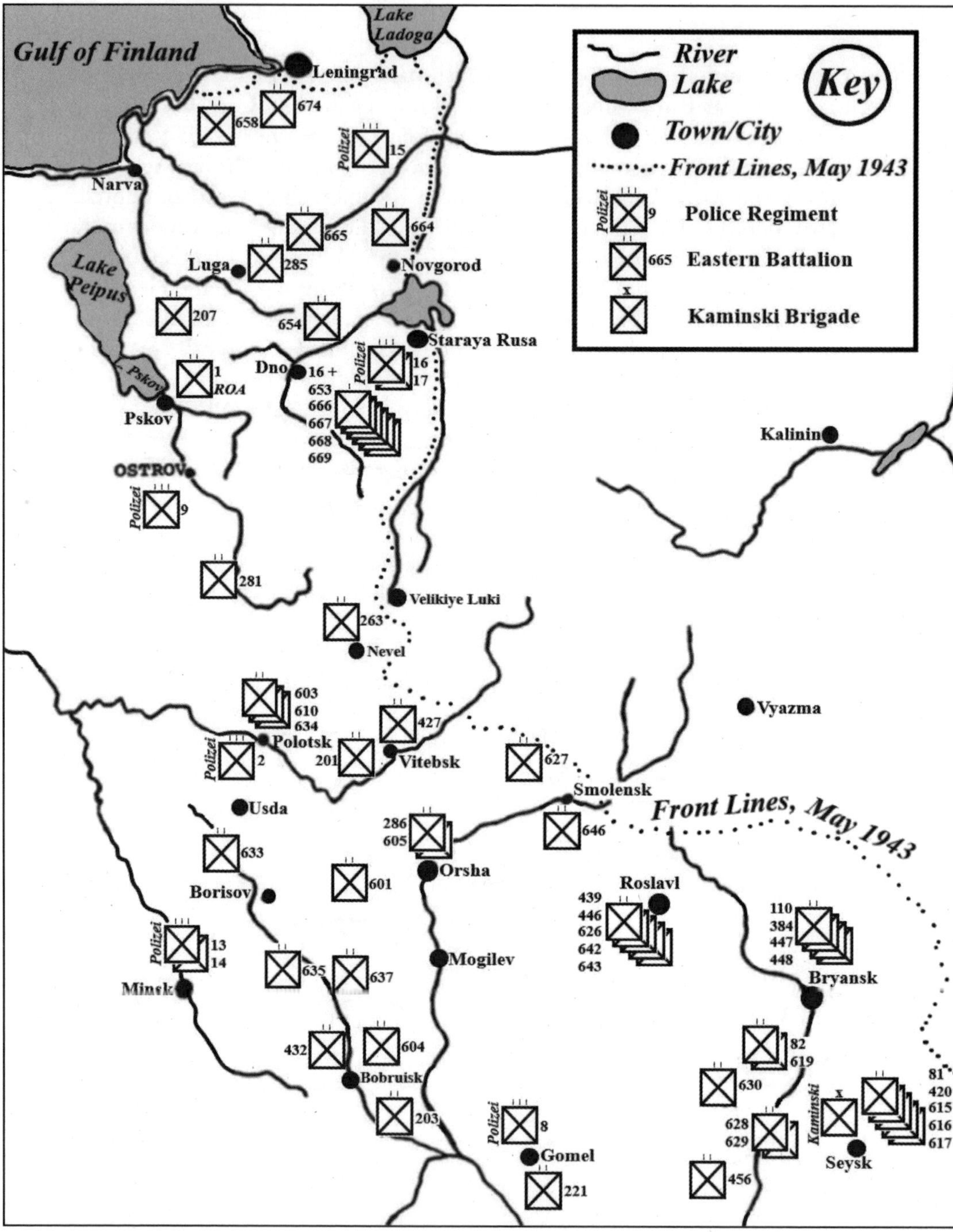

Map 28. German police and locally raised units in the region of Army Group North and Central Russia, autumn 1942–spring 1943.

SS/SD, police and army all employed these forces to various degrees. Their actions, criminal or not, must be attributable not only to these units, but to the German commands to which they were assigned. Therefore, if collaborationist units were employed by a German army garrison command and they committed a war crime, they would be directly responsible for that crime, but the army command would be indirectly responsible because the crime occurred while under their control.

Chapter 5

The war against the Jews and partisans in Ukraine and southern Russia, 1942

Resettlement and the Jewish Question in Ukraine

A report by *Wirtschaftsinspektion Süd* (Economic Inspectorate South) on the economic and military situation in the region of Ukraine for the month of April 1942 is quite illuminating. An ominous account on page nine of this lengthy report states that about 1,600 Jews had been 'resettled' in the town of Piryatin:[1] 'In Piryatin during the Easter holiday 1,600 Jews were resettled.'[2] What is significant about this Wehrmacht report on the economic state of Ukraine is that, according to historian Martin Gilbert, 1,530 Jews were murdered in Piryatin in April 1942.[3] This is the exact time period of the report by Economic Inspectorate South, which leads us to speculate that perhaps the army economic office was employing the genocide code-word *umgesiedelt* (resettled) to indicate that an *Aktion* had taken place at Piryatin in April 1942.[4] If true, then this would implicate the army because it had obvious knowledge of the massacre and was trying to cover up the killings by listing the Jews as 'resettled'. It could also be that perhaps the Wehrmacht economic office transported those Jews to the town, where they were killed later that month. But even if the latter is the case, then the German Army is still implicated since it helped in the process of elimination by concentrating the Jews in one place, thus facilitating the killings. Finally, if these unfortunate Jews are one and the same, we should raise the official level of Jewish dead at Piryatin, since the Germans themselves in this document are admitting to 'resettling' 1,600 and not the lesser figure of 1,530 listed by Gilbert.

A detailed, six-page-long situation report by the 774th Field Command of the 444th Security Division, dated 19 March 1942, dealt with the 'Jewish question'. At this time, the headquarters for this garrison command was at Genichesk, straddling the easternmost isthmus into the Crimea and on the coast of the northwestern part of the Sea of Azov. However, by May of that same year this garrison command was shifted west, to Skadovs'k, but still in the Kherson Oblast.[5] The report was split up into various sections, one of which was clearly labelled '*Judenfrage*' (Jewish question). It said, 'in the region of the garrison command, with few exceptions, all traces of the Jews have disappeared'.[6] What is telling about this report is that this garrison command was speaking of a large region of land under its control which before the war contained about 53,000 Ukrainian Jews.[7] Although we do not know how many Jews from the Kherson Oblast were able to escape eastwards before the Germans occupied the region in the autumn of 1941, we do know that in Genichesk alone, which had a pre-war Jewish population of 1,776, no Jews survived the killing squads of Sonderkommando 10a when it moved through the town in September 1941.[8] It appears that in the autumn of 1941 the 774th Field Command made a complaint to Sonderkommando 10a about the murder of Jews in their area – not the fact that the Jews were being killed, just the manner and location of their murder:

> From Beserovka arrived parts of the Sonderkommando after Genischesk where a short-term dispute with the garrison post there occurred because of 'Jew matters'. The garrison headquarters complained about the executions of the Sonderkommando – to be sure not because of the crime itself, but rather because it took place in the direct vicinity of the inhabitants and the quartered soldiers. The officer of the execution felt himself 'misunderstood', and was offended, emphasizing this in his letter of reply, as well as his men in the execution of the murder operation, about which nothing had been criticized. No one showed empathy to the murdered victims, and further collaboration between the Sonderkommando and the [Wehrmacht] garrison headquarters was not questioned.[9]

Indeed, the note made by the army officer writing the 19 March 1942 report which stated that all traces of the Jews had disappeared was affirming two things: first, the efficiency with which the Nazi murder commandos had swept through this region of Ukraine, and secondly, the continued support, or at the very least the tacit approval, of the army garrison command of the goal to eliminate all Jews from German-occupied areas. But this Wehrmacht campaign, like the efforts of their counterparts in the SS, was not merely against the Jewish race. The I/882nd Local Command, one of the subcommands of the 774th Field Command, noted in another report, dated 9 April 1942, that in the region of Melitopol its army troops had discovered forty Romany who had lived out the winter of 1941/1942 in the Beloserka Kolkhoz and, according to the army report, had incited the local Ukrainian population not to work. The report casually stated that all forty were shot.[10]

Anti-partisan operation by Vesseloye, near Ivanovka, 23 May 1942

Ivanovka is located in the Luchansk Oblast, near Krasny Luch. This operation was launched under the command of the I/746th Local Command, which was subordinate to the 774th Field Command, which in turn was responsible to the 444th Security Division. The operation was launched after it was discovered that there were Russian deserters or possibly partisans in a forest area about 4 miles northeast of Vesseloye. One Local Command officer, *Oberleutnant* (First Lieutenant) Dumröse, together with *Leutnant* Jendrich and ten German soldiers, plus five Russian auxiliary policemen and four officials from Agriculture Command Vesseloye, moved to the area and engaged the enemy from the north. Simultaneously, *Obersturmführer* Hardt and ten men from the SS and Police Command at Melitopol, together with eight men of the Ukrainian *Hundertschaft* of the 444th Security Division, advanced from the west.[11] During the operation it was reported that several of the enemy surrendered but were shot on the spot. The after-action report stated that the apparent leader of the band was Jewish.[12] The report specifically stated the manner in which the German command had come to this conclusion. Apparently, the Germans had taken the trouble to pull down the trousers of the dead Russians in order to see who was circumcised and who was not. This once again shows the German obsession with identifying Jews as members of the partisans.

Bread and Salt

When the Germans entered Ukraine in the summer of 1941, Stalin's government was in crisis and reeling from the blow of the invasion. Most of Ukraine's population greeted the invaders with bread and salt, the traditional Ukrainian welcome gift. On 20 August 1941 Adolf Hitler established the Reich Commissariat Ukraine. Twelve days later, on 1 September 1941, Hitler appointed Erich Koch as Reich Commissioner for Ukraine. With this title came the power not only to decide civil administrative duties, but also to administer and employ the *Ordnungspolizei* (Order Police) and the *Geheimstaatspolizei* (Secret State Police) in Ukraine as he wished. Koch's primary goal was the exploitation of the people and the resources of the land for the Third Reich. His very first official act was the signing of an order closing all Ukrainian schools. When he was asked if the decision was imprudent, he was quoted as saying: 'If I meet a Ukrainian worthy of being seated at my table, I must have him shot.'[13] With this kind of attitude towards the very people he was supposed to rule, it didn't take too long before Ukrainians began reconsidering whether they had acted too hastily in welcoming the Germans.

Whack-a-Mole in 1942: partisan attacks and German moves

On 30 April 1942 the 1st and 2nd Companies of the 692nd Military Field Police Battalion were moved to an area between Zaporozhye and Genitschesk, where they performed rail line security. By 26 May both companies had been ordered to cover a stretch of railway line between Visilyevka and Novo Alekseyevka[14] as the growing partisan threat called for rapid redeployment of forces. Given the vast expanse of territory that needed to be covered, even shifting troops quickly could not guarantee that the guerrilla threat would disappear in a region that had just been swept. To the officers in charge of anti-partisan operations, it must have felt like a constant game of Whack-a-Mole. On 8 May 1942 the 698th Military Field Police Battalion was located in Krasnoarmeyskoye. On 16 May the 311th Police Battalion was shifted to coastal defence duty around Novo Moskovsk. On 18 May this police battalion was located in Snamenka, but by 24 May it was sent to the area between Visilyevka and Novo Alekseyevka.[15] It moved there by way of Frusenki, Spaskoye, Vasilyevka and Pavlograd.[16] That same day the 17th Latvian Self-Defence Battalion was attached to the 444th Security Division, but relegated to the Higher SS and Police Leader Dnepropetrovsk headquarters for tactical control.

A report by the secret field police, written from detailed interrogations of captured parachutists, yielded the information that the local population was willing to support the Soviet partisan group operating in the forest area around Beloschitzkaya, in the region controlled by the 194th Field Command. On 6 June 1942 the 692nd Military Field Police Battalion was again ordered to move, this time to Lubny. Since the winter of 1941 and spring/summer of 1942 this area had been the base of a 150-man partisan 'battalion'. Although the report was dated 28 May 1942, the captured paratroopers were said to have been shot between December 1941 and February 1942, indicating that the Wehrmacht's rear area command, 194th Field Command, may have captured these Red Army paratroopers over a period of several months. The importance of this report is that it documents Soviet paratroopers being shot after interrogation. Clearly this was another war crime, since captured soldiers in uniform, even paratroopers, were entitled to be treated as prisoners of war.[17] Article 3 of the 1929 Geneva Convention stated the following:[18]

(a) it requires humane treatment for all persons in enemy hands, without discrimination;
(b) it specifically prohibits murder, mutilation, torture, the taking of hostages, unfair trial, and cruel, humiliating and degrading treatment;
(c) it requires that the wounded, sick and shipwrecked be collected and cared for;
(d) it grants the ICRC[19] the right to offer its services to the parties to the conflict;
(e) it calls on the parties to the conflict to bring all or parts of the Geneva Conventions into force through 'special agreements'; and

(f) it recognizes that the application of these rules does not affect the legal status of the parties to the conflict.

The fact that the Soviet Union had not subscribed to the Geneva Convention of 1929 gave some technical cover for the Germans to kill in the USSR with wanton disregard. Whether it was a lowly *landser* in a line regiment or rear area command,[20] or a military policeman, or a secret field police member, it did not matter. Everyone in the *Ostheer* apparently had a free pass to disregard the Geneva Convention while fighting in the East. The illegal orders that were passed down from the Armed Forces High Command and Army High Command all emanated from Berlin, where a legion of Nazi technocrats worked to establish a twisted legal framework that allowed mass murder in the East on a grand scale.

The same report dated 28 May 1942 stated that between 2 and 15 May a group of fifty Soviet paratroopers had landed and joined the local partisan band in the area of Spichevaki. Part of the 415th Regional Defence Battalion managed to track the group through Senkov, Lochviza, Lubny and Chorol, in the area under the jurisdiction of the 213th Security Division. The chase then proceeded south of Nikopol, in the operational region of the 444th Security Division, and it was there that many of the paratroopers were apprehended and quickly shot. It was during this period of time that the division received substantial reinforcements.[21] On 3 August 1942 a divisional order from the 444th Security Division complimented the three secret field police groups for their actions. According to this command, the commanding officer of the 444th Security Division personally approved of the manner in which these secret field police groups had so far operated:

> The Division would like to address Secret Field Police Director Grosseck [and] his staff of the 711th, 720th and 726th Secret Field Police Groups for their conduct within the Division during the eastern campaign. We are indebted to you for the smooth and rapid manner in which you have dealt with the bandits and supervised illegal elements within the divisional area.[22]

Commander of the 444th Security Division, Lieutenant General Wilhelm Rußworm, had been replaced by Lieutenant General Adalbert Miculicz on 4 March 1942.[23] This means that Rußworm, who had led the division from 1 April 1941 until 4 March 1942, and had an intimate knowledge of the actions of the army units under his command, did not issue the divisional order dated 3 August 1942. It is clear that *Generalleutnant* Miculicz did. But did he know of the atrocious behaviour of his divisional units? As the divisional commander, he had access to all reports, including those of his predecessor. It stands to reason that Miculicz knew exactly how the war behind the front lines was being waged, and apparently approved. When he commended these troops for their performance, he in effect gave his blessing to the brutal manner in which his men were comporting themselves. This is a good segue to detail some of those divisional units operating in Ukraine and Army Group South, and their actions.

Geheim Feldpolizei forces in the region of Ukraine and Army Group South

GFP-725 would initially see employment under the 6th German Army and operated in the region of Army Group South well into 1944, when it was attached to the 8th German Army. The initial officer in charge of GFP-725 was Field Police Commissioner Ignatz Roisel. He fell in battle on 18 April 1942, fighting Red Army parachutists who had landed behind German lines to help organize another partisan group. On 14 June 1942 Kurt Arlt was the Field Police Director, with the army equivalent rank of major, and head of all secret field police units in the region of Army Group South. Previously he had been in charge of the secret field police units assigned to the 213th Security Division.[24] From February to April 1942 Secret Field Police Superintendent Richard Sithof was in charge of GFP-708, GFP-721 and GFP-730. All of these units were currently performing security duties in the operational area of the 105th Hungarian Light Infantry Division (in the region of Army Group South). From 8 May 1942 Sithof's successor was Field Police Commissar Karl Eschweiler, who would end the war with the rank of senior field police director. The senior field police director in the 444th Security Division was named Schmidt.[25] From September 1941 until October 1942 Field Police Director Hans Stephainski was Senior Field Police Director for Army Group South. From 1943 to 1945 this position was taken by Field Police Director Joachim Kaintzik. The leader of GFP-730 in June 1943 was Field Police Commissar Moll, while the leader of GFP-708 in April 1943 was Field Police Commissar Forejtnik. Some secret field police officials were made responsible for several secret field police units within a higher division or army/rear area command. These posts often had a high turnover of commanders:

Senior field police director for the groups in the Hungarian 105th Infantry Division: GFP-708, GFP-721 and GFP-730
- 2 April 1942: Senior Field Police Director Sithoff
- May–July 1942: Field Police Commissar Dr Heinrichs
- 27 August 1942: Field Police Director Karl Eschweiler[26]

Senior field police director for groups GFP-706, GFP-719 and GFP-725
- February–July 1942: Field Police Director Kurt Arlt

Senior field police director for the 213th Security Division: GFP-706, GFP-719 and GFP-725
- 30 August 1942: Field Police Director Kurt Arlt

Senior field police director at Commander Army Area South 103
4 January 1943: Field Police Director Friedrich Walz

Senior Field Police Director for the 444th Security Division: GFP-711, GFP-720 and GFP-726
Field Police Director Schmidt

Senior Field Police Director for the 454th Security Division: GFP-708, GFP-721, GFP-726 and GFP-740
Field Police Director Sithoff, then Field Police Director Hochgräbe

In July 1942 the 403rd Security Division was transferred to the region of Army Group South. GFP-706, which was operating under this security division, was also transferred. The leader of GFP-706 from March to April 1942 was Field Police Commissar Jakobs; from May 1942 it was Field Police Commissar Beuys. GFP-708 was employed under the 454th Security Division of the Commander Rear Army Area South. Its secret field police commanders were as follows: 25 January 1942, Field Police Commissar (?); February–April 1942, Field Police Commissar Haimann; March–June 1942, Field Police Commissar Gerhahn; July–August 1942, Field Police Commissar Haimann; October–November 1942, Field Police Commissar Lamy; 25 December 1942, Field Police Commissar Haimann.

Following in the wake of the German Army, the security divisions operating in the region of Army Group South began moving eastwards, covering the rear of the advancing army group as it headed towards the Caucasus and Volga river bend region. On 19 August 1942 the 311th Police Battalion was sent from Botyevo Zaraderovka towards Taganrog. Three days later this police battalion became the II. Battalion of the newly created Police Regiment 6.[27] On 29 August 1942 GFP-711 was moved from Salsk to Voroshilovgrad and assigned, for tactical operations, directly to the commander of Army Group A. However, the 444th Security Division was still to be kept informed of all sabotage and espionage activity in which this police battalion was engaged.[28] On 9 September the local pro-German collaborationist militia at Mechetinskaya turned over a Red Army first lieutenant to GFP-711, who immediately shot him on the pretext that he was missing identifying documents.[29]

Adaptive counterinsurgency tactics

When the Germans reached the Caucasus mountains, the rear area forces paused and the commanders reflected on the topography that they now had to face. In order to adapt to the changing conditions of guerrilla warfare and to operate more effectively in the mountains and forests of the Caucasus region, the German security forces altered their tactics. By the end of August 1942 the 444th Security Division had established small hunter groups, operating in much the same fashion as the US Army's long-range reconnaissance patrols during the Vietnam War. These groups were called *Jagdkommandos* (Hunter Commandos) and they were given specific orders on how to operate:

> On August 31, 1942 an 'instruction for the Jagdkommandos' drawn up by [Adolf] Heusinger came into effect which required the use of the most inhuman and savage methods with regard to the population of occupied areas. Heusinger's demands were to act by surprise and without mercy, 'to remove burdensome witnesses noiselessly', 'to kill everyone who falls into the trap'. Among the troops Heusinger translated into reality the directive 'On the Struggle Against the Guerrilla Movement in the East'. This directive prescribed that 'all captured guerrillas are to be shot or hanged ... every commander is responsible for guerrillas (including women) captured in combat being shot or, even better, hanged'. Heusinger sanctioned the shooting of hostages and the razing of villages 'where guerrillas find any support'.[30]

The idea for these new formations and their more drastic tactics appears to have been drawn up by the Operations Chief of the Wehrmacht High Command, Lieutenant General Adolf Heusinger. Here again we see the criminal orders being expanded upon by army officers, on the pretext of fighting the guerrilla movement.[31] This also shows how the very brutal manner in which the war in the East, especially the anti-partisan struggle, was being waged, was embraced by many German Army soldiers and officers, sometimes with great zeal. On 1 September 1942 GFP-610 was in action in the area of Ssalsk. A day later the II. Battalion of Police Regiment 6 reported capturing one partisan and what they referred to as 'five communist functionaries'. These six people were reportedly shot while trying to flee.[32] Whether they did actually attempt to flee, or the police simply used that excuse to kill them, we will never know.

A *Kriegsgliederungkarte* (war situation map) dated 23 September 1942 listed the II. Battalion of Police Regiment 6 (ex-311th Police Battalion) as garrisoning Rostov under the control of the 200th Field Command.[33] In fact, the battalion had entered Rostov in August, following in the wake of the German capture of that city in late July.[34] Another report, dated 3 September 1942, stated that since 25 August 1942 the 444th Security Division had shot 525 Red Army soldiers and suspicious persons its men had captured, including 2 officers, 12 'communists' and 48 Jews. On that same day the diary also noted that in the region of Orlovskaya the 14th Company of the 360th Infantry Regiment had apprehended three bandits and shot them 'while trying to escape'.[35] If we are to believe this report, it appears that the 444th Security Division had a large number of its captured prisoners attempting to run away. This type of report should be questioned, since claiming that prisoners were shot while trying to get away was an easy way to cover up illegal shootings,

The sign reads: 'Attention: Bandit Region. Only travel with an escort.' By the spring of 1943 entire regions of the German rear areas along the Eastern Front were completely controlled by the partisans. (*Bundesarchiv*)

The guerrillas felt safe enough in these partisan-controlled areas that they were able to create airfields, establish base hospitals and even parade their forces, as seen here. (*Bundesarchiv*)

German Armoured Train No. 21, somewhere in Russia in 1942. The growing partisan menace required stronger rear area security forces. Armoured trains provided additional striking power and protection for German security forces. *(Bundesarchiv)*

German security troops force a Russian from his home, some time in 1942. Of the estimated 16–24 million people that the Soviet Union lost during the Second World War, approximately 8–13 million were civilians. *(Bundesarchiv)*

A German armoured police company using a captured French Panhard 178 armoured car during an anti-partisan operation in the winter. German police forces employed a vast array of captured weaponry. *(Bundesarchiv)*

An execution of Russians by SS troops. It is not possible to ascertain whether the victims were Jews or not. A large anti-tank ditch has been dug, at the edge of which the victims were made to kneel. They would be shot from behind (usually in the back of the head). *(Author's collection)*

The Russian prisoners about to be murdered. (*Author's collection*)

Another view of the execution. In spite of the graininess of the photographs, it is clear that the men about to execute these Russians are SS. The camouflaged helmet covers suggest they are from a Waffen SS unit. The Waffen SS were the combat troops of the SS. Such killings were usually performed by men of the security police or SS security service, but these photographs attest to the participation of the Waffen SS. (*Author's collection*)

The Waffen SS squad just prior to or immediately after the executions. There is a Wehrmacht soldier on the far right, in the background, wearing a white coat. Two German Army officers are standing in the background. (*Author's collection*)

Two German Order Police officials stand alongside two auxiliary volunteer policemen by a sign that reads 'Sarig Rayon Post'. Rayons are administrative units of the USSR. Below, in both German and Ukrainian, are the words 'Ukrainian Self-Defence'. (*Bundesarchiv*)

Men of various ages lined up under army guard. Notice that the German soldier has attached his *Gewehrbajonett* (rifle bayonet) as a precaution. *(Bundesarchiv)*

German troops manoeuvre through snow and brush during an anti-partisan drive, somewhere in the Soviet Union. *(Bundesarchiv)*

A poor quality, but very rare image of members of the German Gendarmerie posing in front of a group of people they have just murdered in a village. *(Bundesarchiv)*

Russians being interrogated in the field during an anti-partisan drive, sometime in the spring of 1943. *(Bundesarchiv)*

By the beginning of 1943 the Germans faced a well equipped, well disciplined and large partisan force that controlled vast swathes of territory behind the front lines of the *Ostheer*. More and more anti-partisan units would be required in order to prevent a total loss of control by the German rear area forces. (*US Library of Congress*)

A photograph taken in the USSR of a soldier from a Luftwaffe field division, standing alongside a person dressed in a white polar bear suit and two policemen. To judge from the structure in the background, it is likely that this picture was taken somewhere behind the lines of Army Group North. It appears to be posed, and the men seem jovial and relaxed. The year was most likely 1942 or 1943. (*Author's collection*)

and is very difficult to disprove. On 13 October 1942 the 7th Company of Police Regiment 6 and the 4th Company of the 286th Security Battalion moved towards Yalta. The 5th, 6th and 7th Companies of Police Regiment 6 were located northeast of Voroshilovsk on 14 October 1942.[36] On 19 October the staff company of Police Regiment 6 was transferred from Yaschalta to Dshalga Malaya.

On 25 October 1942 the 5th and 6th Companies of Police Regiment 6 were stationed in Nemezko Chaginka.[37] On 12 November 1942 GFP-711 was in the region in and around Petrovaskoye, where it arrested seven 'suspicious people'. These suspects were shot for various reasons: one was in possession of a weapon, while another had enemy propaganda on his person. Two others were shot because they allegedly belonged to a [partisan] band, while the last one killed had been labelled a 'partisan supporter'.[38] Today it is incomprehensible that suspects would be executed on such flimsy evidence, even though the possession of a firearm and partisan propaganda hinted at these individuals being guilty of siding with the enemy. However, because both the Germans and Russians were ignoring the Geneva Convention rules, and were fighting the war in the East as a war of annihilation, such evidence was enough to cost lives.

Operation Rabbit Hunt: 6–15 February 1943

This drive, not to be confused with *Unternehmen Schneehase*, employed about 1,200 Army and police troops and was intended to eliminate the Kovpak Partisan Brigade in the Mamayevka Forest region and the area of Krasnoye-Gora, and the towns of Svetilovichi, Vyetka, Dobrush and Slynka. The Kovpak Partisan Brigade had been an especially active guerrilla unit operating on the border between Army Group Centre and Army Group South. In retrospect, 1,200 men was too small a force to root out, encircle and destroy the partisans, but the undertaking was conducted nonetheless. It would not be until early June that a sufficiently large force was gathered that would eventually evict the Kovpak and Saburov Partisan Brigades from this region. The area of operations for the brigade under Sidor Kovpak was in the Chernigov region in 1941–1942.[39]

Part of the 221st Security Division, whose headquarters was stationed at Gomel and whose area of responsibility covered Gomel, Krichev, Potschep and Staodub, was asked to supply units for the operation. SS Battlegroup Schimana attacked the partisan region from the northwest, while the 221st Security Division, employing the I/169th Local Command headquarters, attacked from the northeast.[40] At this time, SS Battlegroup Schimana comprised one battalion from Police Regiment 2, the 12th Police Tank Company, SS Sonderkommando Dirlewanger and III. Battalion of Police Regiment 13. From the south, one regiment from the 143rd Reserve Division was to move

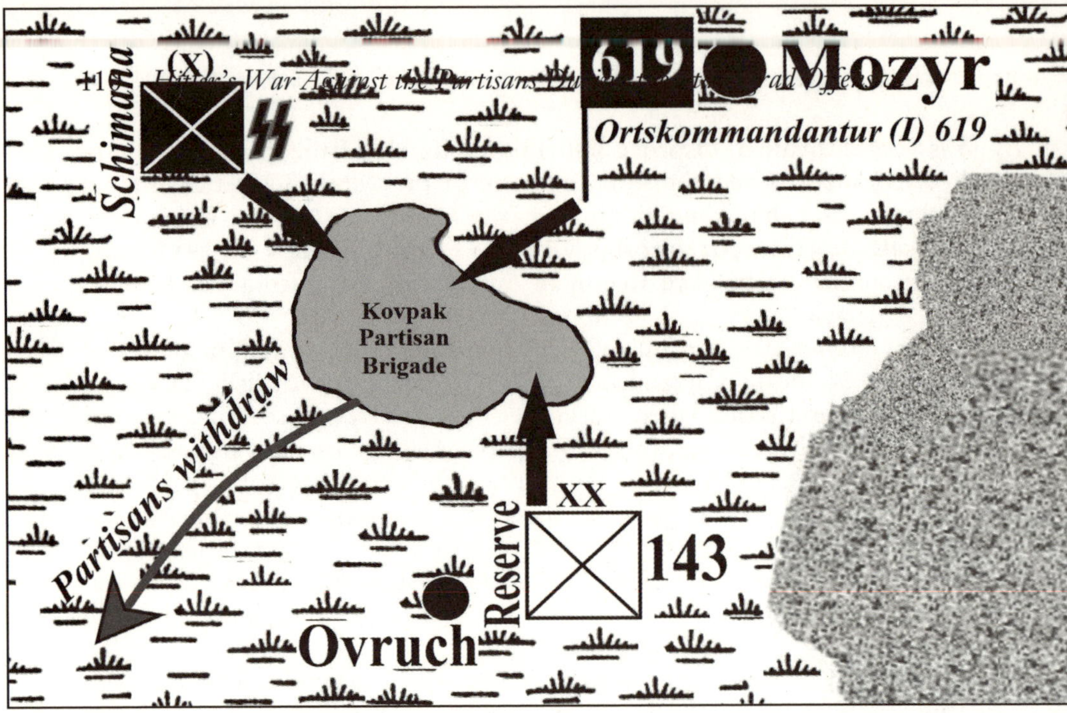

Map 29. Operation Rabbit Hunt was intended to snare the Kovpak Partisan Brigade.

north to block the guerrillas. The Kovpak Partisan Brigade had been able to re-establish itself throughout the northern part of the Chernigov Oblast during the winter of 1942/1943.[41] The German units employed in this operation included the I. Battalion of Police Regiment 8, plus the 45th Security Regiment. The drive netted few results as Kovpak's forces evaded the relatively small German force and withdrew in a southwesterly direction.

Operation Horning: 8–26 February 1943

At the beginning of the second week of February 1943 the Germans launched Operation Horning[42] in the region of the Pripyat Marshes. The drive begun on 8 February and lasted until 26 February 1943. The units involved in this operation included the following SS and police forces. Again, as in Operation Harvest Festival II, they were split up depending on their staging area:

Battlegroup East – HQ of Police Regiment 2

I., II. and III. Battalions of Police Regiment 2
Artillery Battery Borisov of the 1st SS Infantry Brigade (motorized)
Police Artillery Battalion of the 18th Police Mountain Infantry Regiment[43]
Battalion Rodionov (from the Druzhina SS Brigade)

Battlegroup North – HQ of Police Regiment 23

I. Battalion of Police Regiment 23
SS Penal Battalion Dirlewanger

57th Belarusian Self-Defence Battalion
112th Police Signals Company (motorized)
Polizei Panzer Kompanie 12

Battlegroup West – HQ of Police Regiment 13
III. Battalion of Police Regiment 13
18th Latvian Self-Defence Battalion
1. Battery of the 56th Belarusian Self-Defence Artillery Battalion
II. Mine Detection and Bridge Construction Battalion of the Technical Emergency Service[44]

Battlegroup South – HQ of Police Regiment 10
I. Battalion of Police Regiment 10
I. Battalion of Police Regiment 11 (reinforced)
103rd Ukrainian Self-Defence Battalion[45]
One (unspecified) Baltic Schutzmannschaft battalion
Heavy Weapons Company Kolstedt

Battlegroup Southeast – HQ of the 103rd Slovak Infantry Regiment
Two battalions of the 103rd Slovak Infantry Regiment

For Special Employment
Planes from Brobruisk Air Force Bomb School (Stuka Ju-87s).
11th Police Signals Company (motorized)
One battalion of SD (SS security service) troops

Map 30. This German wartime map indicates the location of *Unternehmen Hornung*.

Enemy losses included 2,219 killed in the field, with another 7,378 given over to the secret field police and SD for 'special handling' (i.e., shot after interrogation). Sixty-five prisoners were captured and not executed. Also apprehended during the operation were 3,300 Jews, who were eventually murdered. German losses included two killed and twelve wounded, with an additional twenty-seven Russian volunteers also wounded. The Germans captured 4,000 marks in Ukrainian currency, 2 trucks, 185 *panje*-wagons, 205 sledges, 172 rifles, 14 pistols, 6 light machine guns, 2 heavy machine guns, 5 submachine guns, a Russian-made 47mm anti-tank gun, about 150 grenades and 7 heavy explosive mines, complete with large quantities of explosives. In addition, 21,173 rounds of rifle ammunition, 559 horses and foals, 844 pigs, 9,578 cattle, 5,700 sheep, 222.8 tons of grain and 32.8 tons of linen were taken. It is obvious from the disparity between the number of weapons captured and the number of people killed that the Germans had targeted the local civilian population, perhaps in order to improve their statistics regarding the number of partisans killed. A letter written and sent from SS Lieutenant General Kurt von Gottberg to SS Lieutenant General Maximilian von Herff on 8 March 1943, after the conclusion of Operation Horning, listed the numbers of captured and killed partisans, as well as German losses during the operation:

> Operation Hornung has had the following results: Enemy dead: bandits: 2,219; suspected bandits: 7,378; prisoners: 65; Jews shot: 3,300; own losses – Germans: 2 dead, 12 wounded; local auxiliaries: 27 dead, 26 wounded.[46]

This letter clearly indicates that the Russian civilian population, both Jews and non-Jews, suffered terribly during these anti-partisan drives in which entire regions were 'cleansed' of people in order to make them inhabitable, and thus impossible for the guerrillas to gain support and supplies from the local population. It was irrelevant to the Germans whether the local peasants supported the guerrillas or not. If the support was eliminated, then the guerrillas would run into shortages of foodstuffs, vital local intelligence and other resources. The tactic was harsh and brutal. That the Germans had to resort to this also showed the increasing frustration and desperation on the part of the Germans.

Operation Gizo: 3–19 March 1943

This drive was basically a continuation of *Unternehmen Hasenjagd* (Operation Rabbit Hunt), which took place between 6 and 15 February 1943, and was devised specifically to deal with the Kovpak Partisan Brigade. At this time Kovpak's force was located in the southern region of the Pripet Marshes north of Slovechno. The partisans of this brigade even had a small airfield located within their area of control, enabling men and supplies to be flown

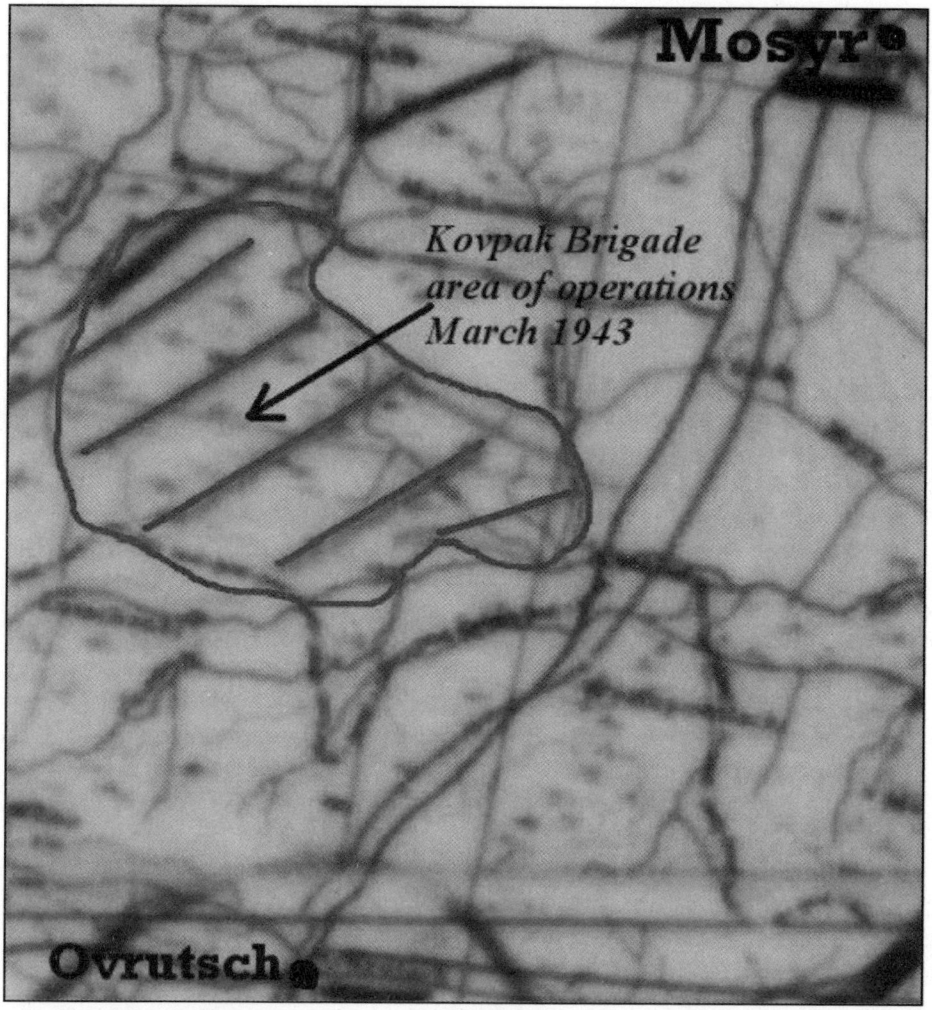

Map 31. German anti-partisan warfare maps had located the region where the Kovpak Brigade was operating in March 1943.

in from unoccupied Russia. Units involved in this drive included both Army and police forces (specifically, SS Battlegroup Schimana, elements of the 143rd Reserve Division and units from the 619th Field Command located in Mosyr, which included Police Regiment 2 and Police Tank Company 1).[47]

The Kovpak Partisan Brigade was led by Sydir Kovpak, a Red Army officer of humble beginnings. He was born in Ukraine in 1887 to peasant parents. Apparently, he served well during the First World War, winning several medals for bravery in the Czarist Army. After the war he joined the Communist Party and fought in the Russian Civil War (1917–1923). When the

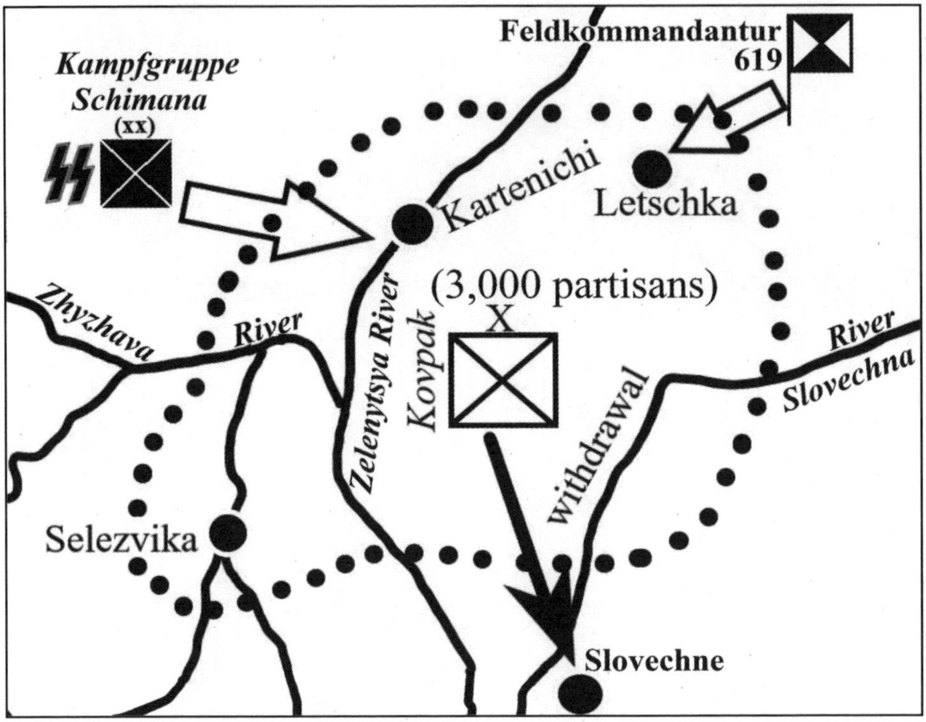

Map 32. The Kovpak Partisan Brigade was able to escape the trap by moving south-southeast to the Jewish settlement of Slovechne (sometimes spelled Slovechno), from where it continued moving in a southwesterly direction.

German invasion was launched, he eventually formed a guerrilla force that initially operated in the regions of Sumy and Bryansk. German anti-partisan drives eventually forced Kovpak to move his brigade south, through the Pinsk Marshes, also known as the Pripyat Marshes and through the regions of Kiev, Zhitomir, Rivne, Homyel and Volyn. Numerous German anti-partisan drives tried to destroy the brigade, but Kovpak's men always managed to escape complete destruction. These partisans also fought against the Ukrainian Insurgent Army (OUN) which was seeking independence for Ukraine from both Stalin and Hitler. During its movement from central Russia to Ukraine the Kovpak Brigade cooperated with two important partisan formations: the Fedorov and the Saburov Partisan Brigades.

The Federov Partisan Brigade was led by Colonel (later Major General) Oleksiy Fedorovych Fedorov. The Saburov Partisan Brigade was led by Colonel (later Major General) Alexander Nikolayevich Saburov. The Federov unit came from the Chernigov region and the Saburov unit came from the Bryansk region.

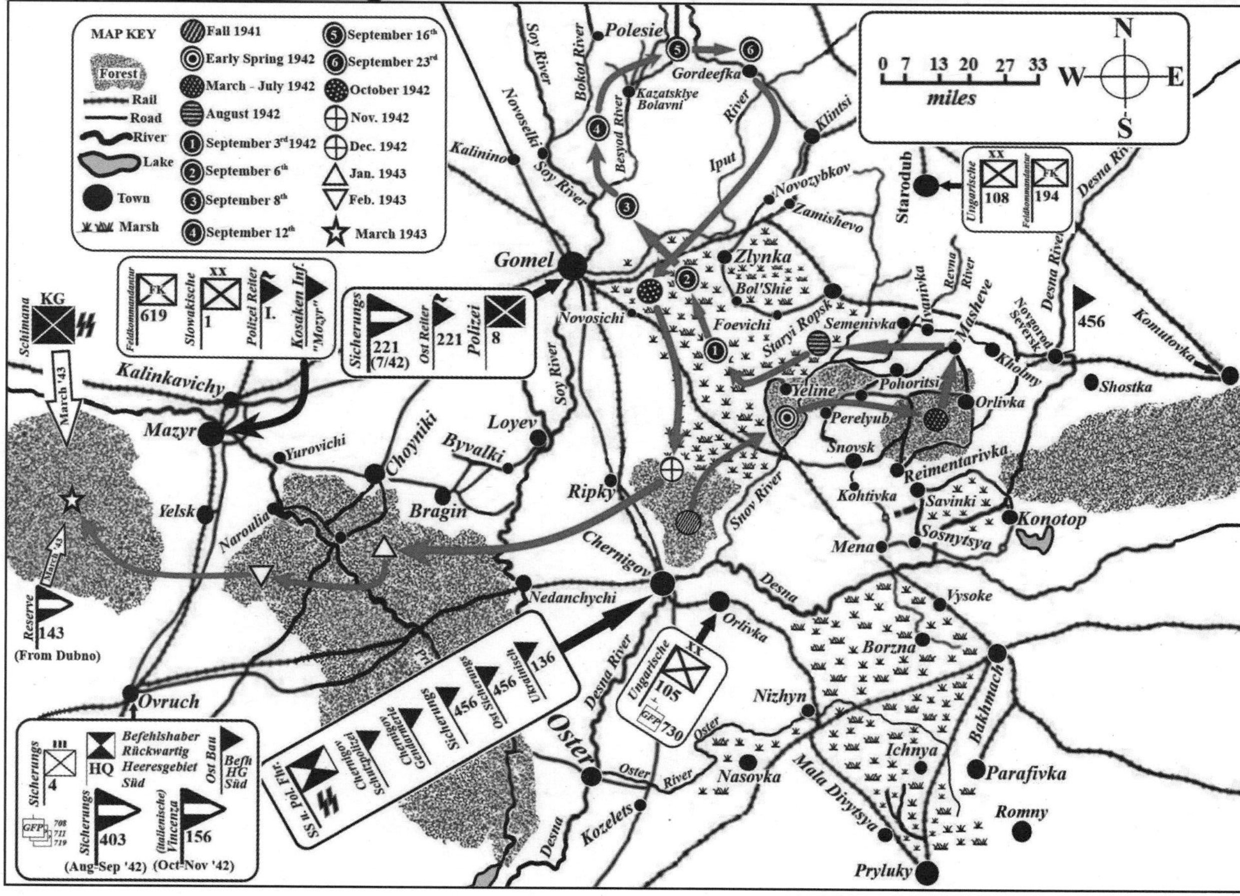

Map 33. Movement of the Federov and Kovpak Partisan Brigades between the autumn of 1941 and the spring of 1943. After having failed to destroy the partisans during Operation Rabbit Hunt, the Germans tried again a month later to destroy both the Federov and Kovpak Partisan Brigades in the region southwest of Mozyr.

Chapter 6

Stalingrad and its consequences

The situation just before the Red Army offensive

The German rear area divisions moved into southern Russia in late July 1942, following the German advance of Army Group South. Although still operating behind the lines, in September 1942 part of the 444th Security Division had to be brought up to the front lines just north of Elista. The German 16th Motorized Infantry Division (nicknamed the Greyhound Division) was stationed in Elista and was performing screening duty for the 4th Panzer Army. The German forces on the front lines of the Don river bend at Stalingrad and in the Caucasus Mountains were all hard-pressed for additional forces. As had occurred during the winter of 1941/1942, the German command called upon the rear area forces behind the lines to support operations on the front lines. This situation was exacerbated by Hitler's demand that both Stalingrad and the Caucasus oil fields of Grozny and Maikop be taken simultaneously. This was a strategic mistake as the Germans simply did not have sufficient forces to accomplish both tasks. Their forces were seriously overstretched and their flanks had to be covered by weak Axis armies. The Red Army saw the weakness in the German positions and in the third week of November 1942 they acted on that weakness.

By 13 November 1942 the 2nd Battalion of Police Regiment 6 (ex-311th Police Battalion) was located as follows: battalion staff at Malaya Dsalga, the 5th Company at Kiyevka, the 6th Company at Tachta and the 7th Company at Yaschalta.[1] Just six days later, on 19 November 1942, the Red Army launched their winter counteroffensive in the Stalingrad sector and the entire 444th Security Division was placed on standby readiness. On 23 November 1942, just as the 444th was preparing for action at the front for the very first time, an order regulating how much food was to be distributed to the local population was released by the Commander Rear Army Area South 103. This headquarters was in charge of the rear areas immediately behind the front lines of Army Group South, while two other rear area commands were responsible for similar security and economic duties behind the areas of Army Group North (Commander Rear Army Area North 101) and Army Group Centre (Commander Rear Army Area Centre 102).[2] The Commander Rear

Map 34. While the 16th Motorized Infantry Division and part of the 444th Security Division performed screening missions on the Kalmyk Steppe, further down, in the Caucasus Mountains, elements of the 1st Panzer Army were trying desperately to reach the important oil-producing centre at Grozny.

Army Area South 103 published the following food restrictions which were to be implemented behind the lines:

> For the population that performs long-term heavy physical labour, the following food portions are assigned: meat and meat products – 200 gr., fat – 150 gr., bread – 2,500 gr., potatoes – 3,500 gr. For children under 14 years of age and Jews: rations as listed under section 'a': for the population that performs no work worth mentioning: no meat and meat products; fat – 70 gr., breads – 1,500 gr., and potatoes – 2,000 gr.[3]

The order for this specific caloric food distribution was, in effect, a death sentence for the remaining Jewish population (including the children) under the control of Rear Area Army Commander South, since the number of calories allotted was not sufficient to sustain a child, let alone an adult. Historian Kiril Feferman has recently argued that food distribution practices by the German occupation forces were a possible catalyst for Holocaust-related deaths.[4] In effect, he states that by creating a food shortage in the region of the Crimea, the Germans justified the killing of the Jewish population there as a way to eliminate excess mouths to feed. It should be noted that adult Jews were not exempt from forced heavy labour, so the rations which they were to receive were wholly inadequate for the vigorous labour imposed on those assigned to work in lieu of being killed outright. This system worked in the death camps in Poland, and seems to have been employed behind the front lines of the German armies operating in the USSR.

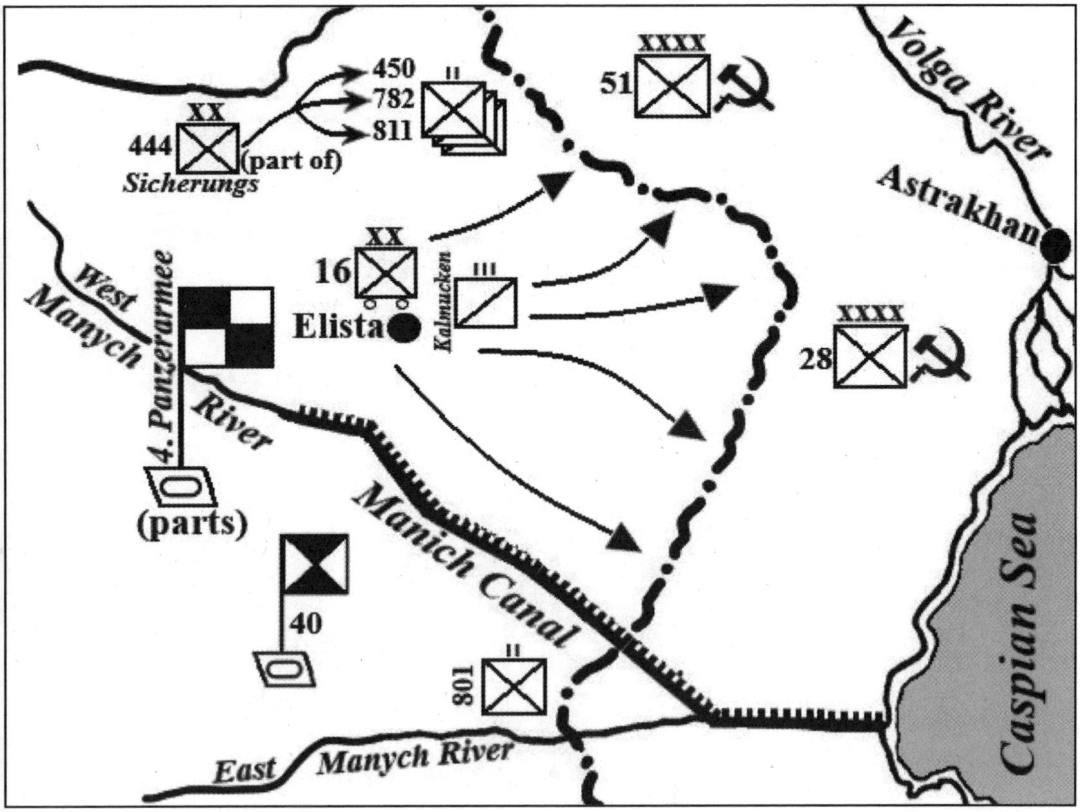

Map 35. As early as September 1942, some elements of the German rear area security forces were sent to the front lines in order to bolster German screening forces protecting the link between Stalingrad and the Caucasus Mountains.

Also on 23 November 1942 the II. Battalion of Police Regiment 6 (minus the 5th Company) was directed to move towards Derbetovka. The transfer order stated that the battalion was to be attached to the 16th Motorized Infantry Division, which was already operating on the Kalmyk Steppe, south of Stalingrad. However, by 2 December this order had been countermanded and the former 311th Police Battalion was instead ordered to join the newly created 15th Luftwaffe Field Division, which was in the process of being established in the area of Saalsk.[5] On 21 December 1942 the police battalion was located at Velichayevskoye. All of these moves were part of the German reaction to the Soviet winter counteroffensive, which was now about a month old. The 213th Security Division now put down roots in and around Kremenchug, in order to perform security and garrison duties there.[6] Part of the 444th Security Division was still performing similar tasks just northwest of Voroshilovsk (present-day Stravropol), while the 454th Security Division was doing the same between Rostov and Armavir. In Armavir itself the Germans had brought up the 381st Field Training Division (commander: Major General Hellmuth Eisenstuck), which prepared new German recruits for service in the line regiments.

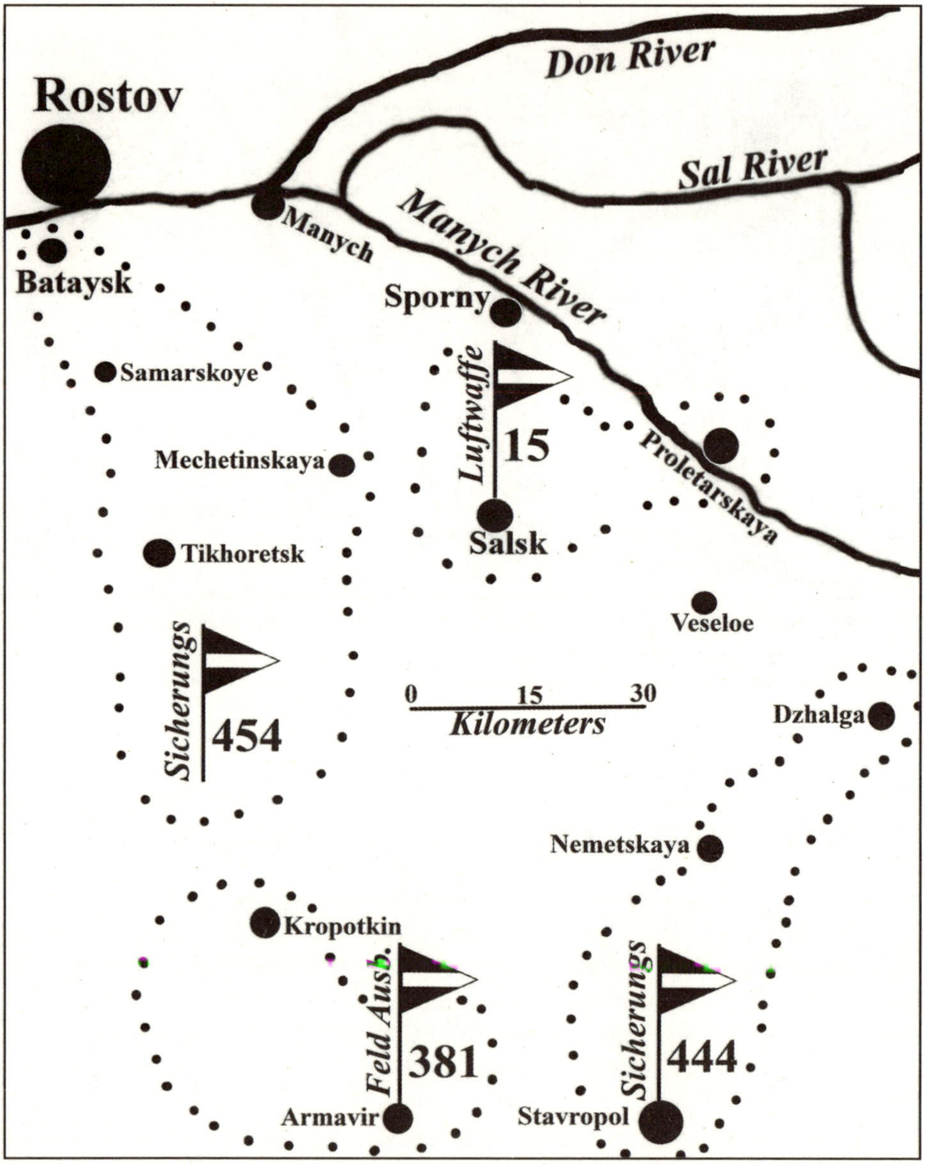

Map 36. Location of German rear area forces south of Rostov, December 1942–January 1943.

The idea was to employ these training units to augment the security divisions. Almost certainly these recruits received some sort of political indoctrination in addition to their military training, although we cannot say how much of an influence that indoctrination had on the manner in which these recruits treated the local Soviet civilian population, or the way they prosecuted the war. In October 1942 this division arrived in the rear area of Army Group A in the Caucasus region.[7] A detachment from the 444th Security Division was diverted to front-line fighting towards the end of December and was shifted to the Vladimirovka region. On 28 December 1942 the II. Battalion of Police Regiment 6 was in the region of Urochainoye-Vladimirovka-Levokumskoye, under the *Generalkommando z.b.V. F.* (Corps Command for Special Employment F). This police battalion had been diverted from its assigned task of joining the 15th Luftwaffe Field Division and was instead employed as part of a detachment from the 444th Security Division, which needed to beef up its hard-pressed divisional components.[8] Its sister battalion, the I. Battalion of Police Regiment 6, was on its way to Divnoye at the time. Other units of the 444th Security Division which made up the battlegroup attached to Corps Command for Special Employment F were the II. Battalion of the 360th Infantry Regiment, together with the 4th and 6th Artillery Batteries from the 221st Artillery Regiment, plus the I. Battalion of the 360th Infantry Regiment, supported by the 5th Artillery Battery of the 221st Artillery Regiment.[9]

On 1 January 1943 Corps Command for Special Employment F ordered a general retreat.[10] A document from the division listed the organization of the 444th Security Division at this time.[11] As of 1 January 1943 the division consisted of various units that had survived the Stalingrad campaign.[12] On 17 January 1943 the 444th Security Division was still attached to Corps Command for Special Employment F. The I. and II. Battalions of Police Regiment 6 were still part of the division, with the I. Battalion located in Kiyevka and the II. Battalion at Malaya Dshalga.[13] On or before 23 January 1943 the II. Battalion of Police Regiment 6 was withdrawn from the front lines and placed in reserve in the town of Uspenskaya for one of the two tactical areas delineated by the division for operational purposes – *Abschnitt Süd* (South Sector). Yet during all of this time the division listed no record of killings on the pretext of combating the partisans. The military situation simply did not allow for the employment of parts of the division to prosecute the ideological war. While this was unfolding, the commanders of both Army Group South (Manstein) and Army Group A (Kleist) began to clamour for moderation in the fight against the guerrillas, especially with regard to relations with the local populace.[14] For the most part, however, these sentiments seemed to be the exception rather than the rule.

The Soviet winter offensive, which had begun on 19 November 1942, would eventually force the commitment of German police forces to the front lines. This decision, made out of necessity, given the need for front-line forces, would have negative consequences for the police forces operating behind the front lines in the USSR. In particular, the fierce fighting that would take place between the Donetz and Don rivers would eventually cause grievous losses. Between January and February 1943 four German police regiments – 6, 8, 14 and 15 – were wiped out in front-line action.

Map 37. The military situation around Krasnodar, December 1942–January 1943. Partisan forces were instrumental in forcing the Germans to withdraw to the defensive positions of the 125th Infantry Division in January 1943. The men of the 97th and 100th Jäger Divisions were obliged to travel in large groups behind their own front lines on account of the partisan threat.

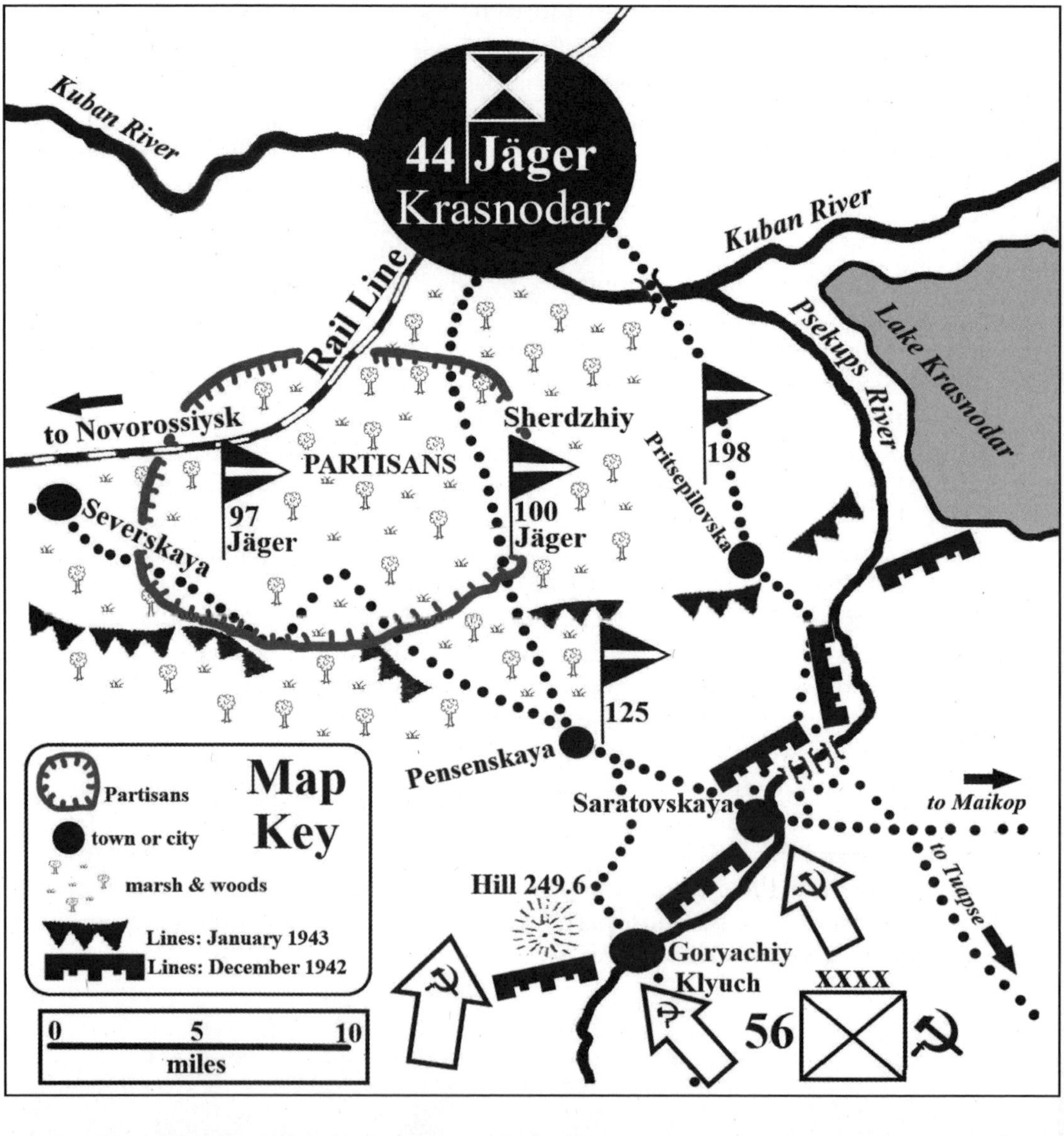

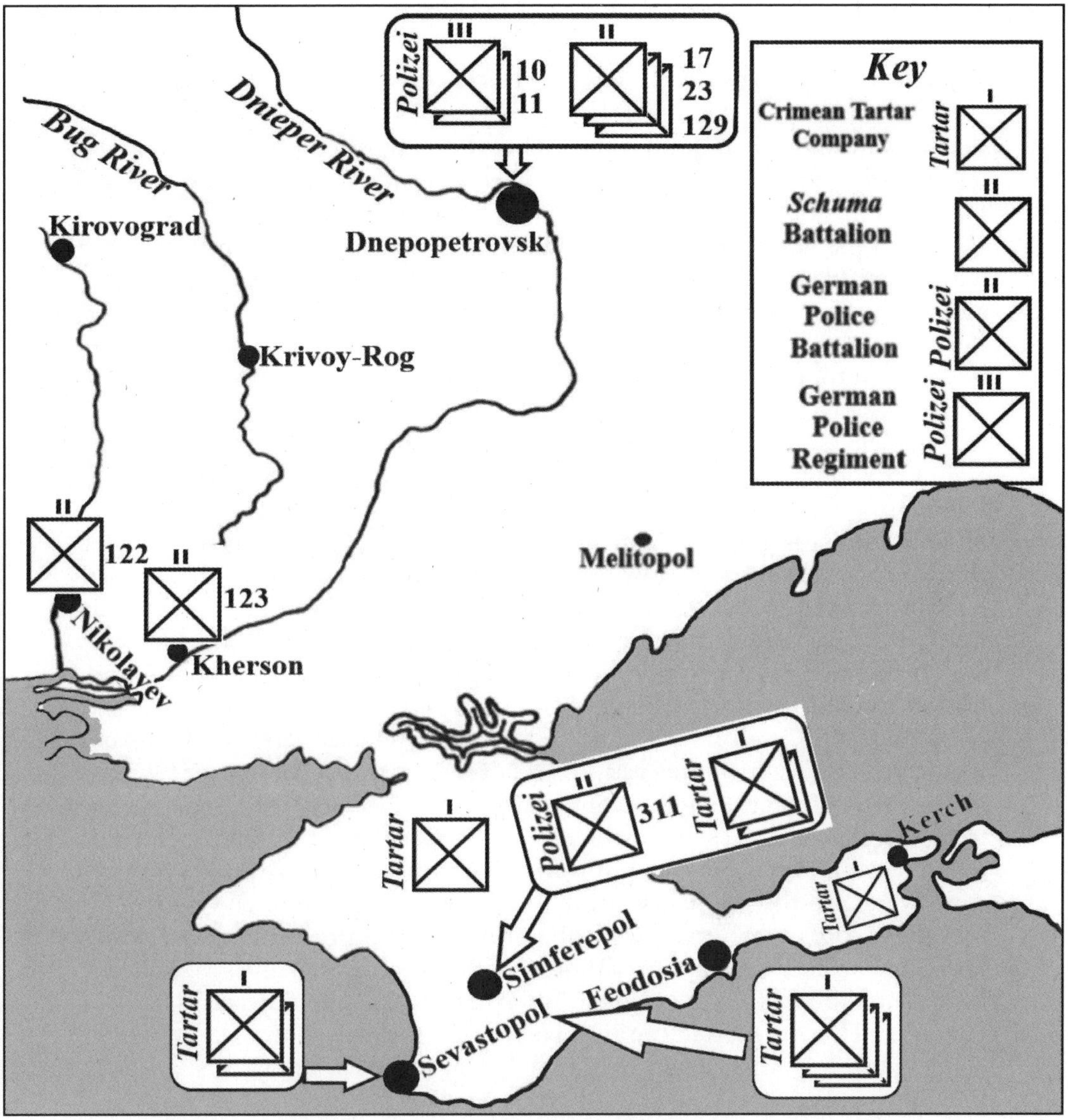

Map 38. German police and locally raised units in southeastern Ukraine and Crimea, July 1942.

Police Regiment 14, in particular, had performed miserably against Russian front-line forces. In January 1943 the unit was temporarily attached to the 385th Infantry Division. After first allowing themselves to be surrounded, the men of Police Regiment 14 withdrew in panic in order to escape the Red Army trap, leaving behind all of its heavy equipment. Shortly thereafter, what remained of Police Regiment 14 was destroyed by two small infantry companies of Russian troops. The German embarrassment was made all the worse given the proximity to troops from the Italian 8th Army, who complained to the German high command that the rapid collapse of Police Regiment 14 had endangered their front lines.[15]

It was around this time that the 782nd Turkestani Infantry Battalion was temporarily attached to the division. This battalion was one of dozens of pro-German units organized from the various peoples of the Caucasus and other regions of the USSR.[16] At the time, the pro-German 450th, 782nd and 811th Turkestani Infantry Battalions were recorded by the 444th Security Division as moving through the towns of Ilinskaya, Tichorezk, Novoroshdestvenskaya, Beresanskaya and Novokursunskaya towards Timoshevskaya, under orders to be attached to XL Panzer Corps, near Fastovezkaya, about 10 miles north of Tichorezk (Tikhoretsk).[17]

Kalmuck Cavalry Battalion Dr Doll, a cavalry formation created from Kalmuck volunteers and led by a German liaison staff, was transferred to the 3rd Panzer Division on 22 January 1943 and was located west-northwest of Bela Glina as the lynchpin between the 3rd Panzer Division and the 444th Security Division.[18] Tikhoretsk was on the road to Rostov. The Turkic formations from the Caucasus had been created from Muslim volunteers who were partly inspired by their hatred of Bolshevism, a term which the Germans employed fully to recruit these peoples and which merged their anti-communist and anti-Semitic beliefs.[19]

Author Paul Carell[20] states that at the end of January 1943 the Germans, whose principal units in the area of Tikhoretsk were the 3rd Panzer Division and the 111th Infantry Division of the German XL Panzer Corps, were racing from there to try to reach Rostov before the Russians captured the city and trapped all the German forces still in the Caucasus.[21] With those two divisions were also the remnants of the 444th Security Division and units from the Army Corps for Special Employment F, as well as pro-German Caucasian formations which now had to withdraw with their German allies. Meanwhile the I. Battalion of Police Regiment 6 was attached to the northern sector by Pavlovka. This only lasted until 27 January 1943, when both battalions were relegated to the 3rd Panzer Division and sent to Yekaterinovskaya.[22] At this time the 3rd Panzer Division was part of XL Panzer Corps, which was operating on the right flank of the Army Corps for Special Employment F.[23] This transfer, however, only lasted a few days and by 1 February 1943 both police battalions were back with the 444th Security Division.[24]

Throughout the crisis winter in southern Russia both the 444th Security Division and the 454th Security Division continued to serve in the front lines on an emergency basis. As can be ascertained by their history, this prevented their sustained employment in anti-partisan operations during this period. That the number of shootings and summary executions of partisans and partisan suspects, as well as anti-partisan operations, dropped to almost zero is an indicator of that involvement in front-line combat. What does this show? It shows that while these security divisions operated behind the lines, they consistently behaved in a manner that caused the deaths of countless Jewish and non-Jewish civilians, as well as captured Red Army soldiers. The various accounts described so far attest to this murder spree. The criminal orders and subsequent commands assured that this behaviour continued and was actually encouraged and commended. Therefore, it is obvious that these Wehrmacht units implemented the ideological war to the best of their abilities.

After the Stalingrad campaign, the security divisions were able to withdraw from the Caucasus and were soon regrouped. While the 454th Security Division was quickly reconstituted and employed both as a front-line unit and in the rear, the 444th Security Division would linger as a cadre staff until it was finally disbanded almost a year later. It had taken losses while part of the division had been committed to front-line fighting. The withdrawal from the Caucasus region continued into February 1943, when the remnants of the 444th Security Division withdrew alongside the LVII Panzer Corps. During this time the 444th Security Division operated in various groups, one of which was named Combat Group Krause, which contained the I. and II. Battalions of Police Regiment 6. The III. Battalion of Police Regiment 6 had been destroyed in January 1943 while serving with the 8th Italian Army. On 3 February 1943 both police battalions, alongside an assault gun battery, were operating around the town of Koissug.[25] On 16 February 1943 the II. Battalion of Sonderverband 287, one of the famous Brandenburg commando regiments, was attached to Combat Group Krause in the region of Troizkoye. This occurred because on 17 February the I. Battalion of Police Regiment 6 was withdrawn from the division due to heavy losses, although it was still being listed as operational as late as 30 January 1943. On 16 February 1943 the remnant of the I. Battalion of Police Regiment 6 was transferred to the 454th Security Division.[26]

A later document states that the unit was disbanded on 31 March 1943 when the 1st, 2nd and 3rd Companies of Police Regiment 6 (i.e., units from the I. Battalion) were lost. However, this police battalion was still listed as part of the order of battle for the division as late as 23 March 1943. This order of battle was: around Mius and the coastal region, behind the 111th Infantry Division and the 454th Security Division (which at this time were serving in the front lines) were the following forces under the command of Major Menke. (The 454th Security Division would be reduced to a cadre by May 1943 and would remain in that condition until about November or December 1943 when it was finally disbanded):

I. Battalion of Police Regiment 6 (led by Police Major Haase)
2nd Company of the 551st Military Field Police Battalion
I. Cavalry Battalion of the 444th Eastern Cavalry Battalion[27]
II. Cavalry Battalion of the 444th Eastern Cavalry Battalion
2nd Company of the 444th Eastern Cavalry Battalion (detached)

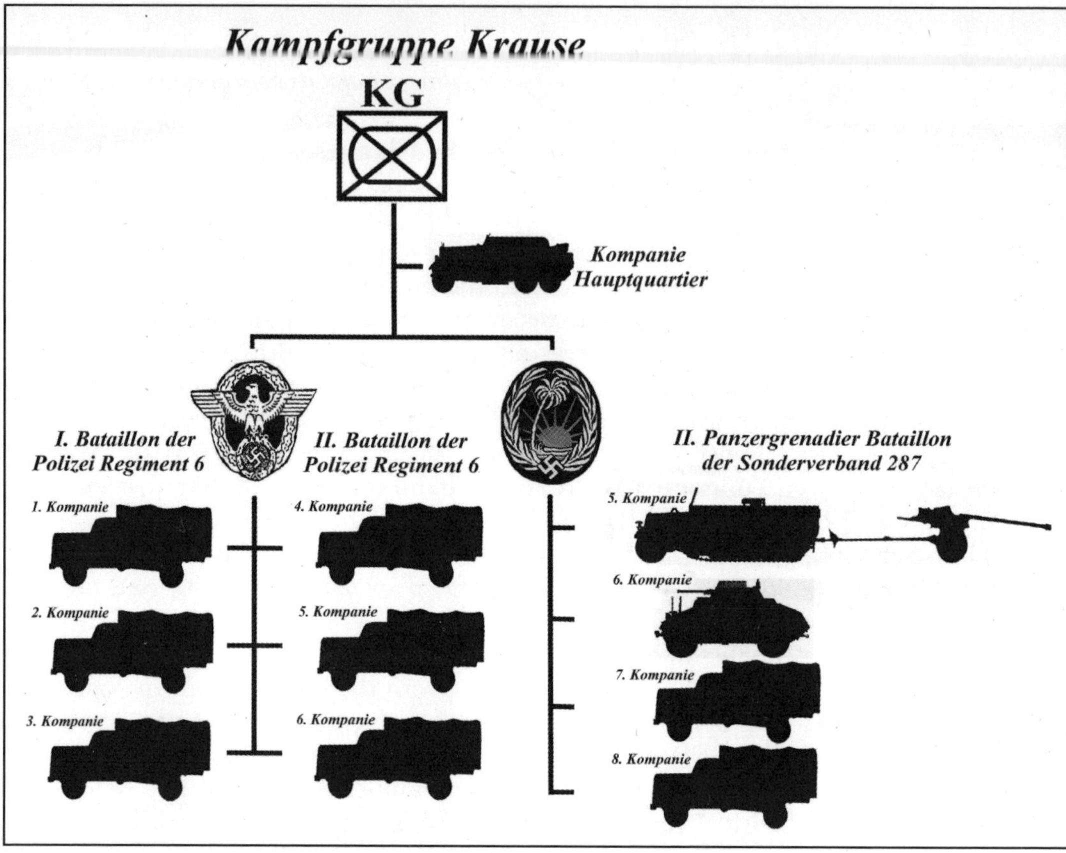

Figure 3. Combat Group Krause, January 1943.

In the coastal region by Budenovka were forces under the command of Colonel Hahn:

- 326th Bicycle Guard Battalion (led by Lieutenant Colonel Beermann)
- 503rd Electrical Backup Battalion (an electric cable maintenance security battalion, commanded by Captain Raisch)
- 1st–3rd Companies of Battalion Dreihaus (led by Captain Dreihaus). This was formerly a Reich Labour Service construction battalion that had been converted into a guard battalion (the 126th Guard Battalion) on 8 May 1941
- Eastern Training Battalion Kranz (a training battalion for Russian volunteers, commanded by Major Kranz)
- Cossack Cavalry Regiment 1 von Jungschultz (commanded by Cavalry Captain Hacke)
- Kalmuck Cavalry Formation Dr Doll (comprising three cavalry battalions of Kalmuck volunteers around a German cadre staff)
- I/457th Local Command
- One platoon from the 1st Company of the 571st Military Field Police Battalion

Throughout this time the II. Battalion of Police Regiment 6 remained with the 444th Security Division. A war situation map clearly lists the II. Battalion as being stationed northeast of the coastal town of Budenovka, west of Taganrog.[28] A table of organization document for the 444th Security Division dated 12 March 1943 lists the II. Battalion of Police Regiment 6 as still being part of this security division's organization. On 3 April 1943 the 1st Company of the 571st Military Field Police Battalion was mentioned in the division's operational history, recording that it was being attached to the 200th Field Command. On 25 April 1943 the 444th Security Division was reorganized and new units were assigned to its organization:

Infantry units
602nd Security Regiment
46th Security Regiment
Eastern Training Battalion
Battalion Dreihaus

Bicycle and Cavalry units
326th Bicycle Guard Battalion
Cossack Cavalry Regiment 1 von Jungschultz

Signals unit
828th Signals Battalion

Support unit
3rd Company of Driving Column 360

By 5 May 1943 the 444th Security Division was reforming just south of Kirovograd.[29] By May 1943 it had been reduced to a mere battle group and its surviving component parts were split up among the 111th Infantry Division and Korück 558 behind the lines of the German 8th Army. The 454th Security Division would continue to operate in the region of Army Group South until the summer of 1943.

After Stalingrad

The Stalingrad debacle provoked the Nazis into renewing their efforts to instill the proper political motivation and will to prosecute the war in the East. The defeat at Stalingrad had sapped the morale of many men serving in the *Ostheer*. Field Police Director Kurt Arlt, senior official within GFP-725,[30] then operating with the 213th Security Division, demonstrated this when he established lectures within his unit in order to lift the morale of his men. The significance of these lectures was obvious: they were meant to renew the resolve of the men in these units to prosecute the war with continued vigour:

> Political indoctrination in GFP units, as in virtually all Wehrmacht formations, intensified following the reverses suffered by the German Army

> before Moscow in the winter of 1941–42. Senior GFP officials performed indoctrination duties during visits to the field, lecturing their subordinates on subjects ranging from general political issues and current events to questions of race. For example, Feldpolizeidirektor Kurt Arlt, senior GFP official of the 213th Security Division, deployed in the southern sector of the front, lectured members of GFP Group 725 on 'The General Political and Military Situation'. Subsequent sessions included 'The 30th of January 1933 and Current Events', 'The History of Germandom in Poland', and 'The Evolution of the Greater German Idea'.[31]

Thus, it appears that even after their defeat at Stalingrad, the Germans intended to prosecute the war in the East in the same brutal manner in which they had conducted it so far. In fact, the criminal orders were once again reinforced and expanded upon in December 1942, while the battle for Stalingrad was still being decided. On 24 December 1942, a week after the Red Army had surrounded the German 6th Army at Stalingrad, Supplemental Order No. 1615/42 was released by Wilhelm Keitel. Written in an urgent tone that may be an indication of the pressures of the military situation in which the Germans now found themselves, its effect was to once again affirm the 'mandate for murder' of the previous 'criminal orders'. If any previous edict had been vague, the meaning of this order was crystal clear:

> The Führer is informed that some military men of the Wehrmacht combating partisans were brought to court martial for their behaviour. The Führer has ordered on this account: In the struggle with partisans the enemy uses fanatics, fighters with communist ideology, who cannot be scared by any repressions. Here, as never before, raises the question to be or not to be. This struggle has nothing to do with soldier chivalry or with obligations of the Geneva Convention. If the most severe measures in this struggle against the partisans in the East and in the Balkans as well are not applied, we fail with our forces to get rid of this plague in the near future. Therefore, the troops are obliged and have the right to apply in this struggle any method without restriction, stopping at nothing, even as regards women and children when this guarantees a success. Condescension of any kind is a crime against the German people and the soldiers at the front, who have to stand the consequences of partisan blows and cannot have any feeling of pity to the partisans or their accomplices ... Not a single German fighting partisans or their accomplices is to be brought to military court or to be subjected to disciplinary punishment for his actions in this struggle.[32]

If any German officer fighting with the *Ostheer* had any doubts as to the manner in which the war in the East was being waged, and especially the fight against the partisans (remembering here that being Jewish was made synonymous to being a partisan), then his doubts should have disappeared after reading Keitel's order of 24 December 1942. The point was very clear: everything was excusable within the context of fighting the guerrillas. The mandate which all of these orders sanctioned had been slowly expanded over the one-and-a-half-year period from June 1941 to December 1942. Anything could be justified by simply claiming that it was done in order to fight the guerrillas.

Order of Battle, Armed Forces Commander Ukraine

Command Staff

Commander: General of the Air Force Karl Kitzinger[33]
O3: Captain Dschenfzig
Chief of the General Staff: Colonel i.G. von Krause
O4: Lieutenant Karpf
Liaison Officer: Captain Dr Schafferdt
Ia: Lieutenant Colonel Gais
Quartermaster: Lieutenant Colonel i.G. Sichting
IIa: Major Scipio
Kdt. H. Qu.: Major Graf Chamaré
Law: Dr Mellinghoff
H.W. Nafü.: Oberst Meltzer
Ast.: Lieutenant Colonel Neumerkel
Commander of Patrol Services: Major Gebhardt
Armed Forces Inspector and Commander of the Battlegroup: Major General Feichtmeier
Transportation Officer: Major Kurek

Principal Headquarters and Combat Units[34]

393rd Senior Field Command – Zhitomir (later Kiev)
579th Senior Field Command – Luck (19 October 1941), then Rovno

- 899th Local Command – Brest-Litovsk
- 909th Local Command – Kovel
- 935th Local Command – Rovno

183rd Field Command Kamenec – Podolsk (19 October 1941)

- 357th Local Command – Schepetovka

454th Security Division – General District Zhitomir and Kiev

675th Field Command:

- 261st Local Command – Berdichev
- 275th Local Command – Gaissin
- 269th Local Command – Uman
- 285th Local Command – Pervomaisk

Table 6.1. Units under the Armed Forces Commander Ukraine.

Year	Date	Units
1941	September	393rd and 579th Senior Field Command
	November	393rd and 579th Senior Field Command, 108th Hungarian Light Division (from 27 November)
	December	393rd and 579th Senior Field Command, 108th Hungarian Light Division (until 3 December 1941)
1942	February	393rd and 579th Senior Field Command, 454th Security Division, Slovak Security Division, 10th Romanian Infantry Division
1943	June–October	393rd and 579th Senior Field Command, LVII Army Corps, with 143rd and 147th Reserve Divisions
	November	393rd and 579th Senior Field Command, Cadre staff of the 444th Security Division, VII Hungarian Army Corps, LVII Army Corps, with 143rd and 147th Reserve Divisions

- 298th Local Command – Bielaya-Zerkov
- 251st Local Command – Schopola

811th Field Command:
- 327th Local Command – Ovrutsch
- 325th Local Command – Korosten

Kiev City Command

195th Field Command:
- 328th Local Command – Kiev
- 368th Local Command – Kiev
- 123rd Hungarian Infantry Brigade – Proskurov
- 124th Hungarian Infantry Brigade – Staro-Konstantinov (later Schepetovka)[35]
- 102nd Regional Defence Regiment – Korzec
- 231st Regional Defence Battalion – Zwiahel
- 988th Regional Defence Battalion – Rovno
- 552nd Regional Defence Battalion – Luck
- 856th Regional Defence Battalion – Brest-Litovsk

Order of Battle: Commander of Rear Army Group South 103[36]

Principal Operational Employment in 1941:[37]

- 22 June–5 July 1941: following up the breakthrough by the San river
- 6–26 July 1941: following up the breakthrough by Kiev
- 5–31 August 1941: anti-partisan operations in the Pripet Marshes region
- 31 October–8 November 1941: anti-partisan operations in the Cherkassy region

Table 6.2. Forces under the Commander of the Rear Area Army Group South 103 Command.

Year	Date	Units
1941	1 July	444th and 454th Security Divisions, LVII Army Corps: 100th and 101st Jäger Divisions, Slovak Fast Brigade, 4th Security Regiment, 692nd Military Field Police Battalion
	7 Aug.	213th, 444th and 454th Security Divisions, 1st SS Infantry Brigade (motorized), 4th Security Regiment, 692nd Military Field Police Battalion
	3 Sept.	213th, 444th and 454th Security Divisions, 1st SS Infantry Brigade (motorized), Slovak Fast Brigade, 4th Security Regiment, 692nd Military Field Police Battalion
	2 Oct.	213th and 444th Security Divisions, part of 1st SS Infantry Brigade (motorized), Slovak Fast Brigade, 102nd and 108th Hungarian Light Divisions, 4th Security Regiment, 692nd Military Field Police Battalion
	4 Nov.	213th, 444th and 454th Security Divisions, Slovak Security Division, 62nd Infantry Division, 102nd Hungarian Light Brigade/Division, 108th Hungarian Light Brigade/Division (until 27 November 1941), 4th Security Regiment, 692nd Military Field Police Battalion
	4 Dec.	102nd Hungarian Light Division, 105th and 108th Hungarian Light Brigades, 4th Security Regiment, 692nd Military Field Police Battalion
1942	2 Jan.	102nd Hungarian Light Brigade/Division (until 30 January), 105th and 108th Hungarian Light Brigades/Divisions, 4th Security Regiment, Feldgendarmerie Abteilung 692
	Feb.–Mar.	Part of 454th Security Division, main body of 444th Security Division, 105th Hungarian Light Brigade/Division, 4th Security Regiment, 692nd Military Field Police Battalion
	Apr.–June	Part of the 444th Security Division, 4th Security Regiment,[38] 692nd Military Field Police Battalion
	4 July	213th Security Division (one regiment only), 444th Security Division, the staff of 403rd Security Division, 105th Hungarian Light Brigade, 692nd Military Field Police Battalion
	Aug.–Sept.	213th and 403rd Security Divisions, 105th Hungarian Light Brigade, 692nd Military Field Police Battalion
	Oct.–Nov.	213th and 403rd Security Divisions, 105th Hungarian Light Brigade, Italian Infantry Division Vicenza, 692nd Military Field Police Battalion
	1 Dec.	213th Security Division, 105th Hungarian Light Brigade, Italian 'Vicenza' Division, 692nd Military Field Police Battalion
1943	Jan.–Feb.	213. Sicherungs Division (partly), 105th Hungarian Light Brigade, 692nd Military Field Police Battalion
Commander Army Area South		
1943	4 Mar.	213th Security Division (parts), 403rd Security Division, 692nd Military Field Police Battalion
	Apr.–May	213th Security Division (parts), 692nd Military Field Police Battalion
	June–Sept.	213th and 454th Security Divisions, cadre staff of 444th Security Division, 692nd Military Field Police Battalion
	4 Oct.	Cadre staff of 444th Security Division, 692nd Military Field Police Battalion

Table 6.3. The 213th Security Division.

Year	Date	Corps/Army	Army Group	Place	Region
1941	Mar.–May	8th Military District[39]	–	Home	Silesia
	June	XVII Army Corps of 6th Army	South	East	Ukraine
	July	For special employment	South	East	Ukraine
	Aug.– Dec.	Rear Army Area South	South	East	Ukraine
1942	Jan.–July	Rear Army Area South	South	East	Ukraine
	Aug.–Dec.	Rear Army Area South	B	East	Ukraine
1943	Jan.–Feb.	Rear Army Area South	B	East	Ukraine
	Mar.–Sept.	Rear Army Area South	South	East	Ukraine
	Oct.	VII Army Corps of 4th Panzer Army	South	East	Kiev, Ukraine
	Nov.	XXVII Army Corps of 4th Panzer Army	South	East	Zhitomir
	Dec.	XIII Army Corps of 4th Panzer Army	South	East	Zhitomir
1944	Jan.–Feb.	XIII Army Corps of 4th Panzer Army	South	East	Vinnitsa
	Mar.–July	At the disposal of 4th Panzer Army	North Ukraine	East	Kovel
	Aug.	XLVII Panzer Corps of 4th Panzer Army	North Ukraine	East	Baranov

Table 6.4. The 444th Security Division.

Year	Date	Corps / Army	Army Group	Place	Region
1941	Apr.–May	8th Military District	–	Home	Silesia
	June	XLIX Mountain Army Corps of 17th Army	South	East	Ukraine
	July–Dec.	Rear Army Area South	South	East	Ukraine
1942	Jan.–July	Rear Army Area South	South	East	Ukraine
	Aug.–Dec.	Rear Army Area A	A	East	South Russia
1943	Jan.	Rear Army Area A	A	East	South Russia
	Feb.	At the disposal of 4th Panzer Army	Don	East	South Russia
	Mar.	At the disposal of Army Detachment Hollidt	South	East	South Russia
	Apr.[40]	XXIV Panzer Corps of 6th Army	South	East	South Russia
	May–Oct.	For special employment	South	East	Ukraine
	Nov.–Dec.	Armed Forces Commander Ukraine	South	East	Ukraine

Table 6.5. The 454th Security Division.

Year	Month	Corps/Army	Army Group	Place	Region
1941	Apr.–May	8th Military District	–	Home	Silesia
	June	XLIX Mountain Army Corps of 17th Army	South	East	Prezemysl, Ukraine
	July	For special employment under 17th Army	South	East	Vinnitsa, Ukraine
	Aug.–Sept.	Rear Area Army Group South	South	East	Ukraine
	Oct.	Rear Area Army Group Centre	Centre	East	Ukraine
	Nov.	Rear Area Army Group South	South	East	Ukraine
	Dec.	Armed Forces Commander Ukraine	South	East	Ukraine
1942	Jan.	Armed Forces Commander Ukraine	South	East	Ukraine
	Feb.–May	For special employment under 6th Army	South	East	Kharkov[41]
	June	XI Army Corps of 1st Panzer Army	South	East	Izium, S. Russia
	July	For special employment under 1st Panzer Army	South	East	Rostov, S. Russia
	Aug.–Dec.	Rear Area Army Group A	A	East	Caucasus
1943	Jan.	Rear Area Army Group A	A	East	Caucasus
	Feb.	For special employment under 4th Panzer Army	Don	East	Rostov, S. Russia
	Mar.	For special employment with Army Detachment Hollidt	South	East	Mius, S. Russia
	Apr.[42]	XXIV Panzer Corps of 6th Army	South	East	Mius, S. Russia
	May–Sept.	Rear Area Army Group South	South	East	Ukraine
	Oct.–Nov.	XLVII Panzer Corps of 4th Panzer Army	South	East	Kiev, Ukraine
	Dec.	For special employment under 4th Panzer Army	South	East	Zhitomir, Ukraine
1944	Jan.	LIX Army Corps of 4th Panzer Army	South	East	Vinnitsa, Ukraine
	Feb.–Mar.	XIII Army Corps of 4th Panzer Army	South	East	Rovno, Kovel
	Apr.–May	XIII Army Corps of 4th Panzer Army	N. Ukraine	East	Kovel, Ukraine
	June	For special employment under 4th Panzer Army	N. Ukraine	East	Kovel, Ukraine
	July	XIII Army Corps of 1st Panzer Army	N. Ukraine	East	Brody, Ukraine
	Oct.–Nov.	XLVII Panzer Corps of 4th Panzer Army	South	East	Kiev, Ukraine
	Dec.	For special employment under 4th Panzer Army	South	East	Zhitomir, Ukraine

Year	Month	Corps/Army	Army Group	Place	Region
1944	Jan.	LIX Army Corps, of 4th Panzer Army	South	East	Vinnitsa, Ukraine
	Feb.–Mar.	XIII Army Corps of 4th Panzer Army	South	East	Rovno, Kovel
	Apr.–May	XIII Army Corps of 4th Panzer Army	N. Ukraine	East	Kovel, Ukraine
	June	For special employment under 4th Panzer Army	N. Ukraine	East	Kovel, Ukraine
	July	XIII Army Corps of 1st Panzer Army	N. Ukraine	East	Brody, Ukraine

Conclusions

The beginning of the turning point

As 1942 gave way to 1943 the feeling in all major centres of power in the Third Reich must have been a kind of resigned acceptance that the war had turned against Nazi Germany. A nation of 80 million people was now fighting the world. No one in Germany spoke of it openly, but most were probably thinking it. The catastrophe at Stalingrad had reinvigorated not only the Red Army, but also the hopes of tens of thousands of partisans fighting behind the German lines. For the collaborators, the Stalingrad debacle showed that Stalin and communism were not just going to disappear. Many of the 85 million Soviet citizens under Nazi rule began to think about retribution if and when the Red Army returned. The second half of 1941 and first half of 1942 were filled with assassinations of village elders and town mayors, as well as police volunteers, especially those with the rank of sergeant or above. Stalin had directed that those collaborators be targeted as a way to stifle further assistance to the Germans by the Soviet populace. In the second half of 1942 the equation changed. The guerrillas no longer had to target every collaborator, given that many who had previously helped the Germans were now either avoiding being seen to assist the Nazis, or were actually approaching the partisan bands to volunteer as guerrilla fighters.

The partisan tactic of playing on the Nazi predisposition to anger, revenge and violence, especially whenever a German soldier was killed, was employed fully from the start of the partisan war. This was especially true if the murder was heinous. A partisan group would capture a German or group of Germans, murder and mutilate them quite bestially, then leave their bodies in some mocking pose where they would be discovered by German patrols. Of course, this guerrilla method was bound to provoke a Nazi reprisal that would kill innocent civilians. Thus, the population of the USSR was between a rock and a hard place. On the one hand, if a person collaborated with the Germans, they would be targeted by the partisans as a traitor; if they assisted the partisans, they would be targeted by the Germans. Even for those who tried to remain neutral, there was no winning. Inaction or lack of partisan support was enough for them to be labelled Quislings to the communist cause and subject to assassination. Not aiding the Germans, on the other hand, was tantamount to being a 'partisan helper' or 'partisan supporter' – also punishable by death. It was an impossible situation to be living in. In the end, the only choice for civilians, which gave them a slim chance of surviving the war with their skin intact, was to run to the woods and join the guerrillas.

To remain in a village or town was like being already dead, but still waiting for the moment of death. No one knew where the next partisan atrocity or attack would occur, and which local community would be targeted for retribution by the German command. Those who could escape headed for the woods, which explains the steady rise in the number of partisans throughout 1942. The first German military reversals on the front lines gave pause to those who hated the communist system so much that they were still willing to aid the German invader. Had they bet on the wrong horse? Then there were those volunteers who had witnessed the abysmal Nazi treatment of the Soviet population but were still willing to support the invader because of their hatred for Stalin and communism. However, by the second half of 1942 these individuals were less numerous than they had been during the first year and a half of the German invasion. The Nazis, with their racist and exterminationist policies, had done a lot to destroy what good will there may have been within the local population. The Nazis treated even those people who seemed friendly to them quite abysmally. It was thus that in the first year of the war the Germans threw away the one key to defeating the Soviet Union: the good will and support of the general population. But given Nazi ideology, fair treatment of a captive population was not possible. It was simply not in the psyche of the Third Reich.

Who won the war behind the lines in 1942?

Militarily speaking, and from the German point of view, the war behind the lines in 1942 proved to be a draw at best. The Germans could argue that in spite of the rise in partisans, especially in Belarus, the German rear areas were sufficiently well defended that supplies of men and war materiel heading to the front lines were not significantly disrupted by the guerrilla bands. That is the most optimistic appreciation of the German effort to nullify the partisan threat in 1942. One could argue justifiably that the year proved to be a tactical success for the guerrillas, because of the tried and tested belief that a guerrilla movement is successful if it can remain undefeated. I am reminded of former Secretary of State Henry Kissinger, who during the Vietnam War said: 'The conventional army loses if it does not win. The guerrilla wins if he does not lose.'[1] In the case of the Soviet partisans, not only were they not destroyed, but they grew significantly, especially in the second half of 1942. Thus, the argument that the Germans achieved a tactical draw is undermined by the fact that the partisan movement grew, and grew steadily. By the spring of 1943 entire regions to the rear of the German armies were infested and controlled by the partisans. This is why 1943 saw the greatest number of German anti-partisan operations. These will be discussed in a forthcoming work that will follow this study on the guerrilla and anti-partisan war in the USSR from the spring of 1943 to the spring of 1944.

The partisan concentrations in 1942

In the region of Army Group North the guerrilla threat continued to worry the German command. There were significant partisan attacks against railway lines, ammunition dumps, warehouses and bridges. These were especially troublesome in the regions west and east of Pskov, between Gdov and Narva, east of Luga, northwest of Novgorod, south and southwest of Tosno, west of Dno, surrounding Polotsk, west of Velikiye Luki, and southwest of Staraya Rusa. In the region of Army Group Centre the principal area of guerrilla activity was the forested areas around the city of Bryansk. The forests around Mogilev also presented a challenge to the German command. In the Bialystok District the partisans were concentrated in the Bialystok forest, northeast of Grodno. In Lithuania they were concentrated in the Nacha forest, while Belarus had large numbers of guerrilla bands in the Naliboki forest, just south of Lida, as well as all around Novogrudok and the forested region south of Baranovichi. Partisan forces were also operating in the Lipiczany forest just south of Slutsk, while guerrilla forces were also concentrated in the Naroch and Kozany forests north and northwest of Minsk. Partisans were also located north and west of Mozyr. In western Ukraine the partisans were concentrated around the towns of Sarny and Rovno. A small force was operating south of Dnepropetrovsk and a guerrilla force was located in the Crimean mountains, south of Simferopol.

The Soviet and German military situation at the start of 1943

As 1942 turned into 1943 the *Ostheer* was in a serious predicament. Although the 1st Panzer Army and what remained of the 4th Panzer Army had managed to squeeze their way out of a trap by reaching Rostov before the Soviet armoured forces, the withdrawal of German forces westwards continued unabated. The German 17th Army had managed to reach the Kuban peninsula in fairly good order, but now had the unenviable task of crossing the Kerch Strait into Crimea under fire and constant pressure from the Red Army. The Soviet 69th Army had recaptured Kharkov, while the 3rd Tank Army was trying to break through to Poltava in the German rear. Meanwhile the Popov Armoured Group had broken through the German lines at Izium and was driving south, deep into German-held territory. Its goal was to link up with Red Army forces driving west between Rostov and Voroshilograd. The goal was the capture of Stalino.

With Army Group South in chaos, the Red Army meant to take advantage by striking in specific areas under Army Groups North and Centre. This was planned in order to put further pressure on the Germans there, which in turn would hopefully prevent the transfer of vital divisions to Army Group South from the other army groups. In the north the Soviets chose to attack by Novgorod, as well as the region between Gorodok and Lake Ladoga, east of Leningrad. The plan worked, since Army Group North was unable to send any reinforcements to assist Army Group South. In the region of Army Group Centre nine Soviet armies – the 5th, 10th Guards, 20th, 29th, 30th, 31st, 33rd, 39th and 49th Armies – were pressing against German forces defending Rzhev. The situation there became untenable so that at the beginning of March 1943 the German 9th and 4th Armies, which were holding the Rzhev salient, were ordered to withdraw in order to shorten the front line. This operational withdrawal was codenamed *Unternehmen Büffel* (Operation Buffalo). Once the front line of Army Group Centre was shortened by the evacuation of the Rzhev salient, the Germans created a reserve of some twenty-two divisions.[2] This in turn allowed for forces to be diverted from Army Group Centre and sent to assist Army Group South.

For the Germans, the military situation in the spring of 1943 was particularly critical in the region of Army Group South. Luckily for the German command, guerrilla activity in eastern Ukraine was at a minimum. Nevertheless, the lack of sufficient forces kept the Germans reacting to Soviet moves instead of proactively trying to take command of the military situation. This began to change when Erich von Manstein launched a counterattack that would become known as the Third Battle of Kharkov (19 February–15 March 1943). In this classic battle of flanking manoeuvre, the Germans seized significant ground, recaptured the city of Kharkov and destroyed three Soviet armies, while forcing three more armies to withdraw. It was a spectacular victory and showed that the *Ostheer* was still capable of creating tactical successes on the battlefield. Adolf Hitler was impressed by von Manstein's success – so much so that it is believed that this tactical victory convinced the Führer that Germany was still capable of defeating the Red Army. This set the stage for the fateful Battle of Kursk four months later.

Appendix I

Russian volunteer formations, March 1942–April 1943

The following volunteer formations were raised between March 1942 and April 1943.[1]

March 1942

- Assault Group Tietjen. Continued to serve under Korück 582 of 9th Army, Army Group Centre. An artillery battery, 582nd Eastern Artillery Battery, with four Soviet-made 76mm guns, was added on 1 March 1942.

April 1942

- 207th Cavalry Battalion. Formed on 11 April 1942, with two cavalry squadrons. It was attached to the German 207th Security Division behind the lines of Army Group North.
- 246th Construction Battalion. This unit was formed from Russian prisoners of war for work for the German Army. Its German cadre staff came from the 246th National Labour Service Battalion, which had been virtually destroyed while fighting during the cold Russian winter of 1941/1942. The construction battalion was formed in the region of 4th Panzer Army, Army Group B, in southern Russia.
- Eastern Combat Battalion Dnieper. Formed on 29 April 1942, from Special Staff Hohlfeld.
- 617th Eastern Battalion. Formed on 28 April 1942, under Korück 532 of 2nd Panzer Army, Army Group Centre.
- 1st Prisoner of War Labour Battalion. Formed on 8 April 1942 in Arnsberg from Russian prisoners of war housed in the 20th Prisoner of War Camp near Thorn (Torun), Poland. The unit was organized by the 6th Reserve Construction Battalion. This battalion also contained a good proportion of Polish prisoners of war.
- Special Staff Hohlfeld. This headquarters unit was raised on 29 April 1942 in the region of Army Group Centre from a German cadre staff to control Russian volunteers. It helped to organize Eastern Combat Battalion Dnieper (a former unit of the Graukopf Brigade), and other

eastern battalions for employment in Belarus and the region of central Russia where Army Group Centre was operating.
- Special Staff Knoth. Same as Special Staff Hohlfeld, but stationed in Minsk, Belarus.

June 1942

- 188th Russian Security Battalion (Russische Sicherungs Abteilung 188). Formed from the 31st–34th Centuries (a series of company-sized Russian volunteer formations organized from the autumn of 1941 in the area of Army Group North under 18th Army).
- 189th Russian Security Battalion. Raised by grouping together the 35th–38th Centuries operating in the region of 18th Army.
- Eastern Combat Battalion Berezina. Formed on 15 June 1942, in Bobruisk, Belarus.
- 1st Prisoner of War Labour Battalion. Sent to northern Norway on 13 June 1942. It became an army troop of 20th Mountain Army.
- 410th Russian Security Battalion. Formed under X Army Corps, 16th Army, Army Group North.
- 510th Russian Security Battalion. Formed under X Army Corps, 16th Army, Army Group North.
- Partisan Hunter Battalion of the 16th Army. Formed from six Russian volunteer companies acting in an anti-partisan role. Also contained one artillery battery using captured Russian guns. Employed against the guerrillas behind 16th Army lines.
- 187th Finnish Security Battalion. Formed from Finnish volunteers using the 27th Century as the core of the unit. Employed in the area of 18th Army, Army Group North. This unit would eventually be transformed into a purely Russian battalion.

July 1942

- Eastern Combat Battalion Duna. Formed in Bobruisk on 14 July 1942 for use in the region of Belarus and *Heeresgruppe Mitte*. It was a former battalion of the Graukopf Brigade.
- Eastern Combat Battalion Pripyat. Formed in Bobruisk on 14 July 1942 for use in Belarus and the area of *Heeresgruppe Mitte*. It was a former battalion of the Graukopf Brigade.
- Eastern Combat Battalion Volga. Formed in Bobruisk from Sonderstab Knoth. It was a former battalion of the Graukopf Brigade.
- 46th White Ruthenian Self-Defence Guard Battalion.[2] Formed in Minsk, Belarus, where it operated for most of its history.
- 47th White Ruthenian Self-Defence Guard Battalion. Raised and stationed in Minsk, and employed in Belarus.

- 48th White Ruthenian Self-Defence Front Battalion. Raised and stationed in Minsk, and employed in Belarus.
- Eastern Artillery Battalion Schrader. Formed from three volunteer Russian artillery batteries, using captured Russian artillery pieces. It was led by Captain Ernst Schrader.

September 1942

- 207th Cavalry Battalion. Initially it comprised two squadrons of volunteer Russian cavalry. A third squadron was added on 7 September 1942.
- I. Volunteer Battalion of Korück 582. Formed from Assault Group Tietjen, which had been expanded from its original six companies into three Russian volunteer battalions. Employed in the region of 9th Army, Army Group Centre.
- II. Volunteer Battalion of Korück 582. Formed from Assault Group Tietjen, which had been expanded from its original six companies into three Russian volunteer battalions. Employed in the region of 9th Army, Army Group Centre.
- III. Volunteer Battalion of Korück 582. Formed from Assault Group Tietjen, which had been expanded from its original six companies into three Russian volunteer battalions. Employed in the region of 9th Army, Army Group Centre.
- 582nd Reserve Eastern Company. Raised to supply recruits for the above three battalions under Korück 582.
- 582nd Eastern Battery. An artillery battery (with Russian guns) formed to provide support for the three Russian volunteer infantry battalions listed above.
- 582nd Armoured Train. This was a Russian armoured train that had fallen into German hands. It was at the disposal of Korück 582.
- 601st Eastern Combat Battalion Berezina. Attached to 203rd Security Division. It was a former battalion of the Graukopf Brigade. Headquarters Staff and 2nd Company were based in the town of Ljuban, about 55 miles southeast of Bobruisk. A mutiny arose in the ranks of the 2nd Company on 18 September 1942. After it was all over, three German members of the 707th Secret Field Police Group were dead, along with two Russian Order Service members; three other men were wounded. In all, sixty-seven Russian mutineers with three light machine guns and two mortars defected to the partisans. The rebellion occurred for three reasons. First, the Russian volunteers witnessed the abysmal treatment that the Germans meted out to the Russian civilian population. Second, the Germans refused to establish Russian formations larger than battalion-sized units. Third, the realization that

Nazi Germany had no interest in establishing a post-war Russian government and simply wished to annex Russian lands.

- 603rd Eastern Combat Battalion Duna. Ordered to be formed 30 September 1942. Simply a redesignation of Eastern Combat Battalion Duna, a former battalion of the Graukopf Brigade.
- 604th Eastern Combat Battalion Pripyat. Ordered to be formed 30 September 1942. Simply a redesignation of Eastern Combat Battalion Propjet, a former battalion of the Graukopf Brigade.
- 605th Eastern Combat Battalion Volga. Ordered to be formed 30 September 1942. Simply a redesignation of Eastern Combat Battalion Volga, a former battalion of the Graukopf Brigade.
- 49th White Ruthenian Self-Defence Guard Battalion. Raised and stationed in Minsk, Belarus.
- 180th Prisoner of War Construction and Labour Battalion. Formed on 15 September in 1st Military District in East Prussia from Russian prisoners of war who volunteered for work. The battalion was sent to Oslo, Norway.
- 183rd Prisoner of War Construction and Labour Battalion. Formed in 1st Military District in East Prussia from Russian prisoners of war who volunteered for service. This battalion was also sent to Norway and stationed in Drontheim.

January 1943

Forming Cadre Battalion Russia. Established in the General Government (Poland) on 18 January 1943 from Russian prisoners of war.

- 412th Eastern Battalion. Formed by redesignating the Self-Defence Battalion of the XII Army Corps. It comprised four Russian volunteer rifle companies.
- 446th Eastern Battalion. Disbanded on 1 January 1943 and its two companies transferred to 82nd Eastern Battalion of 2nd Panzer Division.
- 82nd Eastern Battalion. Formed on 1 January 1943 from Anti-Partisan Hunter Company Zimmeck, and the 1st and 2nd Companies of 446th Eastern Battalion.
- 339th Eastern Battalion. Formed by the 339th Static Infantry Division, then fighting under the XLVII Panzer Corps, 2nd Panzer Army, Army Group Centre. Like the 446th Eastern Battalion, it initially comprised only two volunteer Russian rifle companies. The 339th began operations south of Kirov (east of Roslav, north of Bryansk).
- 555th Eastern Guard Battalion. Formed on 15 January 1943 in the region of 17th Military District in northern Austria. The battalion was

established using former Russian prisoners of war and served in the capacity of factory guard.

- 447th Eastern Battalion. Expanded from one battalion to two, redesignated as follows: I. Battalion and II. Battalion/447th Eastern Battalion. Both battalions continued to operate under XLVII Panzer Corps, 2nd Panzer Army, Army Group Centre.
- 556th Eastern Battalion. Formed on 15 January 1943 in 8th Military District (Silesia). It had three rifle companies but no headquarters staff.
- 701st Commander of Eastern Troops for Special Employment. Formed on 19 January 1943 from the German liaison command attached to Eastern Replacement Regiment Centre located in Bobruisk, Belarus.
- 709th Commander of Eastern Troops for Special Employment. Formed on 28 January 1943 from the 582nd Staff Officer for Eastern Troops. Controlled the following units: 628th, 629th and 630th Eastern Battalions, 582nd Eastern Replacement Company, 582nd Eastern Artillery Battery and 582nd Armoured Train.
- 134th Eastern Battalion. Formed using four rifle companies of Russian volunteers. Began forming in January but was deemed ready in March 1943. Served under the 134th Infantry Division of 2nd Panzer Army, Army Group Centre. Two additional platoons of Russian volunteers were in this German division's engineer battalion. This division had about 2,300 volunteers by April 1943, and an additional 5,600 Russian prisoners of war as acting as labourers. Russian volunteers thus amounted to almost 8,000 men in the 134th Infantry Division.
- 427th Eastern Battalion. Ordered to be formed in January 1943 under the German XXVII Army Corps, Army Group Centre. It was in action by May 1943.
- 667th Eastern Battalion. Formed on 14 January 1943 by simply redesignating I. Battalion of 16th Free Hunter Regiment. It was still operating under 16th Army, Army Group North.
- 668th Eastern Battalion. Formed in 14 January 1943 by simply redesignating II. Battalion of 16th Free Hunter Regiment. It was still operating under 16th Army, Army Group North.
- 669th Eastern Battalion. Formed on 14 January 1943 in the 16th Army area of North Russia, with a staff company and six companies. The battalion originated as the Partisan Hunter Battalion of the 16th Army and was known by this name from March to October 1942. From October 1942 to January 1943 it was known as III. Battalion of 16th Free Hunter Regiment (16th Army). It was redesignated a third time as 669th Eastern Battalion from 14 January 1943 to 6 July 1944, when it was finally renamed as 669th Russian Battalion.

- Ost Bataillon 633. Formed in the region of *Heeresgruppe Mitte* around mid-January 1943.
- Ost Bataillon 634. Formed in the region of *Heeresgruppe Mitte* around mid-January 1943.
- Ost Bataillon 635. Formed in the region of *Heeresgruppe Mitte* around mid-January 1943.
- Ost Bataillon 636. Formed in the region of *Heeresgruppe Mitte* around mid-January 1943.
- Ost Bataillon 637. Formed in the region of *Heeresgruppe Mitte* around mid-January 1943. It was attached to 3rd Panzer Army.
- Ost Bataillon 642. Formed on 15 January under 4. Armee, *Heeresgruppe Mitte*. It was formed from Russian volunteers, the 5. (Ost) Kompanie der Wachbataillon 582 and Ost Stab Kompanie 642 of Bataillon Hopfgartern.

February 1943[3]

- 448th Eastern Battalion. Disbanded and its two companies handed over *en masse* to the 339th Eastern Battalion. It was still employed under 339th Static Infantry Division.
- 339th Eastern Battalion. Increased in size from two companies to four by the addition of the two companies of the disbanded 448th Eastern Battalion, which had been serving under the headquarters of XLVIII Panzer Corps.
- 703rd Commander of Eastern Troops. Formed on 1 February 1943 under 3rd Panzer Army, Army Group Centre. This headquarters staff was used to control eastern battalions.
- 704th Commander of Eastern Troops. Formed under the 4th Army, Army Group Centre. This headquarters staff was used to control eastern battalions.
- 720th Commander of Eastern Troops. Formed in the region of Army Group South. This headquarters staff was used to control eastern battalions.
- 721st Commander of Eastern Troops. Formed in the region of Army Group South. This headquarters staff was used to control eastern battalions.
- 555th Eastern Guard Battalion. Sent to southern Russia for use as an army troop unit.
- 556th Eastern Battalion. Sent to southern Russia for use as an army troop unit.

March 1943

- 207th Eastern Cavalry Battalion. A 4th (reinforced) squadron was added to this cavalry battalion on 15 March 1943.

- 559th Eastern Construction Battalion. Formed on 15 March 1943. It was intended to be an infantry battalion but was redesignated a *bau* (construction) unit on 26 March. On that day it was renamed as Eastern Construction Battalion of the Commander of Army Group South. It was partially formed from parts of the German 246th Construction Battalion and contained four companies.
- 134th Eastern Battalion. Deemed fully formed and attached to 134. Infanterie Division.
- 643rd Eastern Construction Battalion. Formed on 23 March under Korück 559 of 4th Army, Army Group Centre.
- 46th Belarusian Self-Defence Guard Battalion. Still located in Minsk under the Commander of the Protection Police Minsk.
- 604th Eastern Battalion. Stationed in Gomel and attached to 221st Security Division.
- 221st Eastern Cavalry Squadron. Also stationed in Gomel. It had been raised in December 1942 as 221st Cavalry Century (squadron).

April 1943

- 1st Eastern People's Convalescing Battalion. Formed on 30 April 1943 in the General Government (Poland). This was simply a redesignation of Convalescent Battalion Russia.
- 711th Commander of Eastern Troops for Special Employment. Formed under 18th Army, Army Group North. Like all the other eastern troop command staffs, this headquarters staff was used to control eastern battalions.
- Regiment Staff Findeisen for Special Employment. Formed on 9 April 1943 by simply redesignating the 710th Commander of Eastern Troops in the area of 16th Army, Army Group North.
- 702nd Commander of Eastern Troops for Special Employment. Formed on 19 April under 2nd Panzer Army, Army Group Centre. It had been raised with the help of 532nd Eastern Staff for Special Employment, under Korück 532 of 2nd Panzer Army. This was simply a redesignation of Eastern Regimental Staff for Special Employment. Like all the other headquarters staffs, this command staff was used to control eastern battalions.
- Eastern Battalion Hansen. Formed on 25 April under 3rd Panzer Army, Army Group Centre.
- 46th Belarusian Self-Defence Guard Battalion. Located in Novogrudok, Belarus, under the Commander of the Order Police White Russia.
- 47th Belarusian Self-Defence Guard Battalion. Located in Minsk, Belarus, under the immediate control of the Commander of the Protection Police Minsk.

- 49th Belarusian Self-Defence Guard Battalion. Located in Minsk, Belarus, under the immediate control of the Commander of the Protection Police Minsk.
- 56th Belarusian Self-Defence Artillery Battalion. Located in Minsk, Belarus, under the immediate control of the Commander of the Protection Police Minsk. Initially contained two batteries of captured Russian artillery, but later a third battery was added. This battalion, along with other Belarusian battalions, was used to help create SS Brigade Siegling (named after Hans Siegling, its commander) in the summer of 1944. SS Brigade Siegling in turn served as the core of 30th Armed Grenadier Division of the SS (Russian No. 2).
- 454th Eastern Engineer Battalion. This battalion was raised by expanding on the 454th Eastern Engineer Company of the 454th Security Division, which was operating in the rear areas of Army Group South.

Appendix II

Lithuanian volunteer formations, 1941–1945

At the beginning of the German occupation, the Provisional Government of Lithuania urged members of the Lithuanian police to return to their former positions. An initial batch of about three thousand police officers of the former Independent State of Lithuania returned to work. This amounted to about 40 per cent of the pre-Russian and pre-German occupation numbers. The public police of Lithuania were divided into:

- city police precincts;
- regional and district police precincts; and
- self-defence battalions (with accompanying auxiliary police stations).

Police officers had the right to wear their former Lithuanian Police uniforms, but were obliged by the Germans to wear armbands on their left sleeve with the words 'In the service of the German Police' or 'In the service of the German Security Police'. On 22 August 1941 there were 1,849 full-time police positions assigned in 22 regions throughout Lithuania. On 1 August 1941 the regional police had 750 horses, 1,000 bicycles, 40 motorcycles, 10 passenger cars and 10 trucks for signals and communications duties. In August 1943 there were 4,043 Lithuanian policemen employed in the system of the public police of Lithuania. The activity of the Lithuanian police brought positive results for the German occupation since they helped to maintain order.

Germany therefore was able to use the Lithuanian police to achieve its goals, including fighting the partisans and assisting the Nazis in the Jewish Holocaust. On 25 July 1941 General Commissioner for Lithuania, Theodor Adrian von Renteln, assumed control of the country. What reward was given to the Lithuanians for helping to expel the Russians? Instead of allowing a Lithuanian government to assume control, the Germans banned it and jailed its leaders. In its place, they installed a seven-member Lithuanian *Generalrat* (Directorate or General Council), headed by General Petras Kubiliûnas.[1] They did, however, employ a small number of the Lithuanian partisan volunteers, organizing them into self-defence units of 500–600 men and placing them under German SS and police control. This occurred within a week of the German occupation of Kaunas. The Germans had succeeded in forming the

Table A1. Initial Lithuanian police battalions created in 1941.

Battalion No.	Station Post in 1941	Officers	Men	Battalion No.	Station Post in 1941	Officers	Men
1	Vilnius	10	334	4	Vilnius	8	253
2	Vilnius[2]	18	450	5	Vilnius[3]	22	288
3	Minsk, Belarus	24	607				

core of the so-called *Litauische Bataillone der nationalen Arbeit* (*Tautinio darbo apsaugos batalionas* or TDA), also known by the German term '*Hilfspolizei*'.[4] The majority of the TDA men were later organized into the *Schutzmannschaft* (self-defence) auxiliary police battalions. This was the beginning of the Lithuanian self-defence battalions. In short order, five Lithuanian battalions were created in the summer and autumn of 1941 (see Table A1 above).

Beginning in early 1942, the General Commissioner for Lithuania, Dr Theodor Adrian von Renteln, attempted to mobilize the Lithuanian male population with the explicit assistance of the Lithuanian General Council. This would have made it appear that the Lithuanian people themselves were mobilizing to aid the German war effort.

The issue of forced labour is yet another example of how poorly the Lithuanians were treated by the Germans. In 1943, while only 10,000 Latvians and 3,000 Estonians had been drafted for work in German factories, an estimated 40,000 Lithuanians had been forced to do so, many beginning in May 1942 when thousands had been sent to District Hesse to work in armaments factories there. By mid-1942 there were 19 Lithuanian self-defence battalions employed in the USSR and Lithuania.[5]

According to the Lithuanian General Council, in mid-1942 there were 16,000 Lithuanians in the self-defence battalions: 6,000 in the auxiliary police and 10,000 in the various other self-defence battalions.[6] In 1944 all Lithuanian self-defence units were redesignated as police battalions. A good number of the Lithuanian battalion members were drawn into the apparatus of destruction as prison guards, initially performing escort duty for those driven to mass execution sites and, finally, as shooters themselves. On the more extreme wing of these volunteers were the so-called Voldemarists, followers of Augustinas Voldemaras, the former charismatic prime minister and opponent of Smetona. They were thoroughly racist and neo-Nazi in their thinking, so they had no trouble fitting in to the newly formed Lithuanian Nationalist Party (LNP, *Lietuvių nacionalistų partija*). Its emblem was the swastika. The Lithuanian police battalions most implicated in the *Shoah* (Holocaust) were the 2nd Lithuanian Self-Defence Battalion and later the 12th Lithuanian Self-Defence Battalion, which was commanded by Antanas Impulevičius.

Table A1. Lithuanian Police Battalions in German Service.

No.	Date	Comments
1[7]	July 1941	Created on 31 July 1941 as the 1st Vilnius Self-Defence Battalion. Renamed 1st Lithuanian Police Front Battalion in July 1942. Disbanded in October 1944, the remnants going to the 21st Luftwaffe Field Division.
2	July 1941	Created on 31 July 1941 as the 2nd Vilnius Self-Defence Battalion. Renamed 2nd Lithuanian Police Guard Battalion in March 1942. Sent to Lublin, Poland, in July 1942 and used to guard prisoners of war and SS death camps. Broken up officially in April 1943.
2	Mar. 1943	A new 2nd Battalion was raised in March 1943 in Kaunas. On 31 July 1944 it became part of the 1st Lithuanian Police Regiment, which the Germans referred to as Lithuanian Regiment Siauliai. Employed under 5th Panzer Division 28 August–7 September 1944.[8] Removed from combat and reformed as a police unit in Danzig in October 1944. Took part in the defence of Danzig 15–30 March 1945.
3	July 1941	Initially created as a construction battalion on 31 July 1941 but renamed (Litauisch) Polizei Front Bataillon 3 in March 1942. Sent to Minsk, Belarus, in July 1942 where it remained for most of 1942 and 1943, principally fighting partisans in the surrounding countryside. Disbanded in Danzig in September 1944, with the remnants going to 2nd Lithuanian Volunteer Regiment, also known as 2nd Lithuanian Volunteer Police Regiment.
4	Aug. 1941	Formed as a self-defence battalion in Vilnius on 15 August 1941. Renamed 4th Lithuanian Police Front Battalion in March 1942. Sent to Ukraine in July 1942 and served there into 1943. Initially used to guard Durchgangslager 4 (Prisoner of War Transit Camp No. 4) in Stalino. In March 1943 it was rebuilt in Kaunas (Kovno), Lithuania. Two references state it was disbanded in November 1943;[9] another insists it was split up in November 1944.[10]
5	Sept. 1941	Formed in Kaunas as 5th Kaunas Self-Defence Battalion in September 1941. Renamed 5th Lithuanian Police Front Battalion in November 1941. In July 1942 transferred to Korück 584 behind the lines of 16. Armee. From 1 January to 22 March 1943 guarded the principal prisoner of war transit camp behind the lines of Army Group North. Later returned to anti-partisan warfare under Korück 584, and still listed under Korück 584 on 29 July 1943.[11] On 21 September 1944 disbanded because of heavy losses and poor morale but retained two companies, redesignated 5th Lithuanian Construction Battalion of Sonderstab Köhl, to be used as construction units building fortifications under Sonderstab Oberst Köhl (this staff controlled a number of construction units of *Heeresgruppe Kurland*). The 5th Lithuanian Construction Battalion remained part of Special Divisional Staff No. 300 from 6 to 22 November 1944 and under the control of Special Staff Colonel Köhl until 31 December 1944. Between 3 January and 14 March 1945 employed guarding Russian prisoners of war in Courland, Latvia, where it surrendered to Russian forces on 9 May 1945.

6	July 1942	Formed in Vilnius as 6th Lithuanian Police Guard Battalion in July 1942 and used to guard stationary posts. In September 1942 transferred to the Commander of the Order Police in Lithuania, located in Kaunas. Disbanded in November 1944 and part of the battalion was used to help form 256th Lithuanian Police Front Battalion.
7	Sept. 1941	Originally the 4th Lithuanian Self-Defence Battalion in Kaunas (Kovno), Lithuania, redesignated 7th Lithuanian Police Front Battalion in March 1942 and sent to Ukraine. In July 1942 it was located in Vinnitsa (south-southwest of Zhitomir), on the Bug river, guarding Russian POWs. The battalion was back in Kaunas by March 1943, when it was sent to guard Russian prisoners of war behind the lines of Army Group North. In June 1943 it returned to Kaunas.
8	Oct. 1941	Originally the 6th Lithuanian Self-Defence Battalion in Kaunas (Kovno), Lithuania, renamed 8th Lithuanian Police Front Battalion in March 1942. Sent to Vilnius that same month before transferring to Ukraine. In July 1942 guarded Russian prisoners of war behind the lines of Army Group South in the area around the town of Uman. Disbanded in November 1943.
9	Sept. 1941	Formed in September 1941 as the Kaunas Self-Defence Headquarters Staff. Expanded through recruitment and renamed in July 1942 as 9th Lithuanian Police Guard Battalion. Employed to guard stationary (fixed) installations. One source states it was used to form 1st Lithuanian Volunteer Police Regiment in Danzig in October 1944, while another source states it was used to form the 3rd Lithuanian Volunteer Police Regiment.
10	July 1942	Created in Panevezys in July 1942. Employed guarding stationary (fixed) installations in and around Panevezys. In September 1942 sent to Kaunas (Kovno). Part of the battalion was disbanded in February 1943, the remaining companies being employed under the 1st Luftwaffe Field Division, 6 April–30 July 1943.
10	June 1943	While the remnants of the old 10th Battalion were fighting alongside the 1st Luftwaffe Field Division, a new 10th Battalion was created in Kaunas and pronounced combat ready in June 1943. The remnants of the old battalion were withdrawn from the front lines and absorbed into the new battalion in July 1943. From that month the new 10th Lithuanian Self-Defence Battalion was deployed behind the lines of 16th Army, initially employed guarding Russian prisoners.
11	Sept. 1941	Formed as the 3rd Self-Defence Battalion in Kaunas on 13 August 1941 and while stationed in Vilnius in March 1942 renamed 11th Lithuanian Police Guard Battalion. Sent to Ukraine in July 1942, stationed in Korosten, where it apparently remained as a guard for about five months. In December 1942 moved to the area north of Polotsk and was attached to SS Battlegroup von Gottberg from 26 to 31 December 1943. Withdrawn from front-line action on 1 January 1944 due to heavy losses, and performed guard duty from 1 to 9 January 1944. In the meantime, it was also reformed. On 10–11 January 1944 it was temporarily committed once again, attached to the German 32nd Infantry Division of 16th Army. Returned to Korosten (northwest of Kiev) in late January 1944. Remained there on guard duties until the front lines reached it in late October 1943. While serving as part of the

		454th Security Division, it suffered heavy losses once again during the defence of Korosten in late November 1943.[12] Subsequently disbanded.
12	Aug. 1941	Formed as the 2nd Self-Defence Battalion in Kaunas on 7 August 1941. Reformed as 12th Lithuanian Police Front Battalion in Kaunas in July 1942 and sent to Minsk, Belarus. Remained there until June 1944 when it took part in the general withdrawal from Belarusia.
13	Aug. 1941	Formed as the 1st Self-Defence Battalion in Kaunas on 7 August 1941. Reformed in July 1942 as 13th Lithuanian Police Front Battalion and was sent to Korück 584 of 16th Army. From 1 January to 22 February 1943 it performed guard duty, then returned to fighting the partisans under Korück 584. It was still operating under the command of Korück 584 on 29 July 1943. In January and February 1944 it followed the general withdrawal of Army Group North back into the Baltic States, with the Red Army following close behind. In June 1944 the Soviet summer offensive brought the Red Army once again to the Lithuanian border, which they crossed on 5 July 1944. On 13 July the Red Army entered Vilnius. One account says that only the 13th Lithuanian Police Front Battalion remained in Vilnius, acting as the rear guard of the withdrawing German Army. Instead of withdrawing into East Prussia, the battalion was pushed northwards into Courland, Latvia. The defence of Vilnius and the withdrawal took a heavy toll on the battalion and in September 1944 it was reformed as a construction battalion and renamed 13th Lithuanian Construction Battalion. On 22 October 1944 attached to 12th Luftwaffe Field Division of 16th Army in the Courland pocket. From 6 to 24 November 1944 served under the command of 126th Infantry Division. From 29 November to 31 December 1944 attached to 32nd Infantry Division, being temporarily assigned to Group Lieutenant General Thomaschki from 14 to 31 December 1944. On 8 January 1945 came under the direct control of X Army Corps. From 13 to 28 January 1945 attached to the 132nd Infantry Division. From 19 to 24 March 1945 part of the rear area security by Pavilosta under Special Staff Colonel Köhl. From 28 to 30 March 1945 attached to Group von Gise, a battlegroup under the command of X Army Corps.
14	July 1942	Formed in Siauliai in July 1942 as 14th Lithuanian Police Guard Battalion. Performed guard duties in fixed emplacements and localities. In September 1942 transferred to the headquarters of Commander of the Order Police in Lithuania, in Kaunas. Served until the end of the war.
15	Nov. 1941	Formed in November 1941 as the Vilnius Railway Security Battalion and renamed 15th Lithuanian Police Front Battalion in July 1942; transferred to Baranovichi, in Belarus, to carry out guard duties and anti-partisan operations. From 12 September to 31 December 1942 transferred to the rear of Army Group North and placed under Korück 584 of 16th Army. Between 1 January and 22 February 1943 performed prisoner of war guard duty behind the lines of Army Group North. In July 1943 returned to Belarus to fight partisans there. In September 1944 became part of 2nd Lithuanian Volunteer Police Regiment.
251	Jul. 1942	Formed in Kaunas. Garrisoned Kaunas, Lithuania.
252	Jul. 1942	Formed in Kaunas. Garrisoned Kaunas, Lithuania.

253	Jun. 1943	Formed in Prienai, Lithuania. In April 1944 was located in Kaunas, Lithuania. On 13 July 1944 became part of 1st Lithuanian Volunteer Police Regiment.
254	Sept. 1942	Formed in Vilnius, Lithuania. In April 1943 stationed in Szarkovszcyna under the KdO of Belarus. Still stationed there in January 1944. In September 1944 became part of 2nd Lithuanian Volunteer Police Regiment.
255	Sept. 1942	Formed in Kaunas, Lithuania. In March 1944 it had 277 men and was attached to SS Battlegroup von dem Bach. In April 1944 it was stationed in Slutsk, Belarus.
256	Nov. 1944	Formed in Kaunas, Lithuania.
257	Apr. 1944	Located in Vilnius, Lithuania. On 13 July 1944 it became part of 1st Lithuanian Volunteer Police Regiment.
263	May 1944	Formed in May 1944 but disbanded in August 1944.
264	May 1944	Formed in May 1944 but disbanded in August 1944.
265	May 1944	Formed in May 1944 but disbanded in August 1944.
301	Mar. 1944	Created in March 1944 in Mariampole as part of Special Regiment Kaunas.
302	Mar. 1944	Created in March 1944 in Vilnius as part of Special Regiment Vilnius. Transferred into the Luftwaffe in May 1944 as airfield guards.
303	Mar. 1944	Created in March 1944 in Trakai as part of Special Regiment Mariampole. Transferred into the Luftwaffe in May 1944 as airfield guards.
304	Mar. 1944	Created in March 1944 in Vilnius as part of Special Regiment Vilnius. Transferred into the Luftwaffe in May 1944 as airfield guards.
305	Mar. 1944	Created in March 1944 in Kalvarija as part of Special Regiment Kalvarija. Transferred into the Luftwaffe in May 1944 as airfield guards.
306	Mar. 1944	Created in March 1944 in Vilnius as part of Special Regiment Vilnius. Transferred into the Luftwaffe in May 1944 as airfield guards.
307	Mar. 1944	Created in March 1944 in Mariampole as part of Special Regiment Mariampole. Transferred into the Luftwaffe in May 1944 as airfield guards.
308	Mar. 1944	Created in March 1944 in Ukmerge as part of Special Regiment Kaunas. Transferred into the Luftwaffe in May 1944 as airfield guards.
309	Mar. 1944	Created in March 1944 in Kalvarija as part of Special Regiment Kalvarija. Transferred into the Luftwaffe in May 1944 as airfield guards.
310	Mar. 1944	Created in March 1944 in Seredzius as part of Special Regiment Kaunas. Transferred into the Luftwaffe in May 1944 as airfield guards.
311	Mar. 1944	Created in March 1944 in Mariampole as part of Special Regiment Mariampole. Transferred into the Luftwaffe in May 1944 as airfield guards.
312	Mar. 1944	Created in March 1944 in Kalvarija as part of Special Regiment Kalvarija. Transferred into the Luftwaffe in May 1944 as airfield guards.

Appendix III

Latvian volunteer formations, 1941–1945

The Latvian contribution to the German war effort in the Second World War amounted to 104,000 soldiers. Latvians served in the Luftwaffe, the Kriegsmarine and the German Army. Most of the men who served fought in army battalions. In the case of Latvia, the Germans were able to raise two Latvian SS divisions: the 15th Armed Grenadier Division of the SS (Latvian No. 1) and the 19th Armed Grenadier Division of the SS (Latvian No. 2). Latvians also served, albeit in lesser numbers, in the German Order Police, as well as with the SS Security Service. What follows is a list of the principal Latvian self-defence battalions, with a brief history of each unit.

16th Latvian Self-Defence Battalion

This battalion was formed in Riga on 4 September 1941 and was led by Colonel Gustavs Mangulis until 11 December 1941. From 12 December 1941 until 30 January 1943 it was led by Lieutenant Colonel Rudolfs Kocins. It was incorporated into the Latvian SS Legion as the I. Battalion, Armed Grenadier Regiment of the SS 32 (Latvian No. 3). Between October and December 1941 the battalion fought at Dno, then Staraya Russa, performing railway security duties and anti-guerrilla operations. Between December 1941 and January 1943 it was assigned to rear area security behind 16th Army lines, but was sent into front-line action when it was brought into Cholm on 16 January 1942. There it was surrounded with other German forces and survived the siege in the spring of 1942. The battalion eventually returned to Latvia, where it was disbanded at Ilukste on 30 January 1943.

16E Latvian Self-Defence Battalion

This battalion was formed in Riga and Bolderaja on 21 March 1942 and was led by Lieutenant Colonel Osvalds Meija until 14 August 1942. On 18 May 1942 it was redesignated as 266E Latvian Self-Defence Battalion. It was stationed at Balderaja between March 1942 and November 1944. From 14 August 1942 until 9 February 1943 the commander of the battalion was Major Alfons Skrauja, who was succeeded by Major Nikolajs Tiltins, who led the unit between 9 February 1943 and November 1944. In November 1944 the battalion was transferred to Germany, where it was eventually absorbed into the 15th Armed Grenadier Division of the SS (Latvian No. 1).

17th Latvian Self-Defence Battalion

This battalion was formed in Riga on 21 December 1941 and was led by Major Alfons Skrauja until 21 July 1942. Between 21 July 1942 and May 1943 it was led by Captain J. Nikans. It was in the area of Lepel, Belarus, performing rear area security guard duty from December 1941 until May 1942, although one source states that the unit transferred to Ukraine in late March 1942 and was stationed in Dnepropetrovsk from May 1942 to May 1943, performing the same duties as in Belarus. While in Dnepropetrovsk, the unit was also responsible for providing guards for Prisoner of War Transit Camp No. IV, located in the area. The battalion's 4th Company apparently remained in Riga while the rest of the battalion was in Ukraine. The unit was finally disbanded in the autumn of 1943.

17E Latvian Self-Defence Battalion

This battalion was formed on 18 March 1942 in Kraslava[1] and was initially led by Lieutenant Colonel Raimonds Bebris. On 18 May it was redesignated the 267th Latvian Self-Defence Battalion. Between March and November of 1942 it was said to have been stationed in Kraslava, Latvia. In November 1942 it was sent to the Velikiye Luki region to perform anti-partisan operations, remaining there until July 1944 when it was pushed back, along with the rest of the German Army, into the Courland pocket in Latvia. It remained in Courland until the end of the war. One unconfirmed report says that the battalion commanders were Major Alfons Skrauja (21 December 1941–21 July 1942) and Captain J. Nikans (22 July 1942–May 1943). The same report claims that in May 1943 the battalion was disbanded and absorbed into the 25th Latvian Self-Defence Battalion. The company commanders were: 1st Company, Captain Jānis Purmalis; 2nd Company, Captain Augusts Sūna; 3rd Company, 1st Lieutenant Arnolds Vilks. The last commander of the battalion was Captain N. Plavenieks.

18th Latvian Self-Defence Battalion

This battalion was formed on 4 September 1941 in Riga, Latvia, and assigned Field Post No. 39350. The first battalion commander was Captain Karlis Bems, who led the unit until 16 December 1941. Colonel Karlis Lobe took command from 16 to 30 December 1941 and thereafter Colonel Arvids Kurse assumed control. Kurse was a former Latvian Army general who had accepted the rank of colonel under the Germans. He led the battalion until 21 February 1942, when Major Fridrichs Rubenis assumed command. Between September 1941 and May 1942 the unit was stationed in Riga. It moved to the Minsk region in May 1942, where it performed rear area security duties until May 1943, when it returned to Riga. In July 1942 the unit was stationed briefly in Stolpce under the Commander of the Protection Police Minsk. From Stolpce the unit planned, launched and took part in several anti-guerrilla operations. In June 1943 it was officially dissolved and its men were transferred into the Waffen SS. Major Fridrichs Rubenis led the battalion until 1 June 1943, when the formation was incorporated into the Latvian SS Legion as the III. Battalion of Armed Grenadier Regiment of the SS 33 (Latvian No. 4).

18E Latvian Self-Defence Battalion

This battalion was formed on 18 March 1942 in Liepaja (Libau) in Latvia and redesignated the 268th Latvian Self-Defence Battalion on 18 May 1942. Colonel Janis Rucelis led it until 1943, when Major Aleksandrs Tomass assumed command, remaining in the post until 3 February 1944 when the unit was officially disbanded. Between March and July 1942 the unit was stationed in Liepaja, but in July 1942 it was transferred to the Dnepropetrovsk region in Ukraine, where it performed guard duties and also took part in anti-partisan operations.

19th Latvian Self-Defence Battalion

This battalion was raised on 16 December 1941 in Riga. The first commander was Captain K. Porietis, who led the unit until 14 January 1942. Major Gustavs Praudins then led the unit until 7 August 1942, when a German officer, Police Captain Heufeldt, assumed command. Heufeldt led the battalion until 30 January 1943, when it was disbanded and its men incorporated into the Latvian SS Legion as the II. Battalion of Armed Grenadier Regiment of the SS 32 (Latvian No. 3). From December 1941 until May 1942 the unit remained in Latvia. In May 1942 it was sent to Krasnoye Selo and remained there performing guard duty and occasionally taking part in front-line service until January 1943.

19E Latvian Self-Defence Battalion

Assigned Field Post No. 15205, this battalion was raised on 18 March 1942 from Latvian customs and border guard personnel. On 18 May 1942 it was redesignated the 269th Latvian Self-Defence Battalion. It operated in the Baltic coast region for most of its existence. In July 1942 it became part of SS Battlegroup Jeckeln, and between 7 January and 20 February 1943 it operated under the 2nd SS Infantry Brigade (motorized) of 18th Army.[2] It then performed frontier guard duty in Latvia until the summer of 1943, when it was disbanded and its men incorporated into the forming II. Battalion of Armed Grenadier Regiment of the SS 42 (Latvian No. 4).

20th Latvian Self-Defence Battalion

This battalion was raised in Riga on 4 September 1941. The initial commander was Captain K. Porietis, who led it until 4 December 1941. Then Captain Karlis Bems assumed control of the unit, remaining in post until 14 January 1942, when Captain K. Porietis resumed command. He led the formation again until late 1942, when Major Oskars Tiltins assumed command. Tiltins led the battalion until early 1943, when Lieutenant Colonel Peteris Uzans assumed control. In October 1944 the battalion found itself in Danzig. Uzans commanded the unit until November 1944, when the battalion was disbanded and its men transferred *en masse* to the 15th Armed Grenadier Division of the SS (Latvian No. 1). At this time, this Latvian SS division was stationed in Lyck, West Prussia.

20E Latvian Self-Defence Battalion

The battalion was formed on 9 May 1942 in Abrene, Latvia, and on 18 May 1942 it was redesignated the 270th Latvian Self-Defence Battalion. Captain P. Saulite led the battalion from 9 May 1942 until 18 February 1943. Between May 1942 and February 1943 it trained continuously as an engineer unit. It was listed as part of the 281st Security Division (under Army Group North) between 12 September 1942 and 22 February 1943. On 12 September two companies of the battalion were said to be operating under II. Army Corps. The 270th Latvian Self-Defence Battalion served under the control of the Commander of the Order Police in Ukraine and South Russia from September 1942. It was redesignated the 672nd Latvian Eastern Engineer Battalion in July 1944, at which time the German Army Field Post Number assigned to it was No. 47162.

21st Latvian Self-Defence Battalion

This battalion was formed on 25 February 1942 in Lipeja (Libau) and was assigned Field Post No. 45849. According to German records, the formation was not raised until April 1942. Between 25 February and 20 August 1942 the battalion commander was Lieutenant Colonel Teodors Rutulis, and in April 1942 it apparently came under the control of the Commander of the Order Police Riga. In July 1942 it was listed as part of SS Battlegroup Jeckeln and served in the region of Krasnoye Selo until January 1943. In the summer of 1943 the battalion was absorbed into the Latvian SS Legion. From 1 to 20 July the unit fought under the 2nd SS Infantry Brigade (motorized) of the 18th Army on an emergency basis. Police Captain Jakob assumed command of the battalion from 20 August 1943 until 30 January 1944.

22nd Latvian Self-Defence Battalion

This battalion was formed on 25 February 1942 in Riga and Bolderaja and assigned Field Post No. 19620 (later, 09939). The first commander was Lieutenant Colonel Gerbers, who led the unit from its inception until October 1942, when Captain H. Vanags assumed command. In July 1942 the battalion was sent to Warsaw, Poland, where it performed guard duty until October of that same year. In October it was sent to Stalino, in Ukraine. Captain Vanags led the unit until 7 February 1943. In March and again in June 1943 the battalion was sent to Maevsk and Zaporozhe (Zaporizhzhia), along the banks of the Dnipro river, in southeastern Ukraine. It then moved on to Zhitomir, where it operated as a police battalion and performed anti-partisan duty. Between August and December 1943 it was performing security tasks around Luck (Lutsk). Between December 1943 and February 1944 it returned to Latvia. On 7 February 1944 the formation was absorbed into the 2nd Latvian Police Regiment. This unit was a mixed bag of older men, some without much combat experience, and some only partially armed. Command of the regiment was given to Lieutenant Colonel of the SS Nikolajs Rusmanis. The unit was ordered to be withdrawn to Germany in late 1944 but by the time the men arrived at the embarkation point, nearly 40 per cent had deserted. The remnants were eventually merged with the 15th Armed Grenadier Division of the SS (Latvian No. 1) in West Prussia.

23rd Latvian Self-Defence Battalion

This battalion was formed on 25 February 1942 in Riga and Bolderaja and was assigned Field Post No. 15576. Captain Kristaps Brigaders led the battalion from the unit's inception until the end of the war. In March 1942 the unit was sent to Ukraine. In July 1942 and July 1943 it was stationed in Dnepropetrovsk, and assigned to guard Prisoner of War Transition Camp No. IV. In June 1943 the unit had returned to Riga, where it was reformed and reorganized as a police battalion. One source states that the battalion was stationed in Kerch, in eastern Crimea, in late 1943. Between 26 January and 5 February 1944 the battalion was part of an emergency front-line combat formation under SS Battlegroup Prützmann. This combat group was under the control of the XIII Army Corps of 4th Panzer Army. It incurred heavy losses between March and July 1944, making a fighting withdrawal through Kremianetz, Podkamien, Brody and other western Ukrainian towns. The battalion returned to the Baltic States and next served under the 215th Infantry Division of I Army Corps, 16th Army, from 1 August to 15 September 1944. It continued to fight under the 215th Infantry Division, but as part of XLIII Army Corps, 16th Army. The unit was apparently withdrawn from the Courland pocket in Latvia in the autumn of 1944. German reports place the formation in Danzig in October 1944, where it was apparently reformed as a police battalion and assigned a new field post number (No. 56833). However, one Latvian source claims that the battalion spent the rest of the war in the region of Bauska, Courland, in Latvia.

24th Latvian Self-Defence Battalion

The battalion was formed on 1 March 1942 in Lipaja (Libau) and assigned Field Post No. 48276 (later, 40019). In April 1942 the Germans listed the battalion as a formation available to the Commander of the Order Police Riga. Between 1 March 1942 and 9 February 1943 Colonel Alfreds Veveris led the battalion. Between May and October 1942 the unit was stationed in Minsk, Belarus. In July 1942, however, the battalion was transferred to Stankov where, under German orders, it took part in numerous anti-guerrilla operations. In October 1942 it was sent to the Leningrad front, where it served under the 2nd SS Infantry Brigade (motorized). Major Alfons Skrauja led the battalion from 9 February until 18 April 1943. In March 1943 the unit was once again under the KdO Riga,[3] but by April it was no longer in the Latvian capital. On 18 April 1943 it was fighting on the Leningrad front. There the unit was disbanded and its personnel used to form the Latvian Legion's I. Battalion of the Armed Grenadier Regiment of the SS 33 (Latvian No. 4).

25th Latvian Self-Defence Battalion

This battalion was formed on 6 March 1942 in Liepaja and assigned Field Post No. 41246. It was initially under the command of Captain R. Aluts, who led it from 6 March until June 1942, when Lieutenant Colonel Karlis Plikausis assumed control. He led the battalion until 7 February 1944, when the unit was disbanded and its men absorbed into the 2nd Latvian Police Regiment. In July 1942 the unit was sent to Ukraine, where it was assigned to help collect and guard the grain harvest in the region of Korosten and Ovruch, near Zhitomir. The unit was withdrawn from Russia and returned to Latvia in the beginning of 1944.

26th Latvian Self-Defence Battalion

This battalion was formed on 6 March 1942 in Tuckums and assigned Field Post No. 42181. In April 1942 the battalion came under the control of the Commander of the Order Police Riga. The first commander, Lieutenant Colonel Gredzens, led the unit from 6 March until 31 August 1942. In July 1942 the battalion was sent to Begoml in Belarus, where it came under the control of the Commander of the Order Police Minsk. One report states that the battalion was stationed in and around the Belarusian capital. The unit was employed in numerous anti-guerrilla drives. Colonel Alfreds Veveris assumed control of the battalion on 1 September 1942 and led it until 9 February 1943, when Lieutenant Colonel Karlis Aperats assumed command, remaining in post until 23 April 1943. The formation operated in the Novgorod region as a front-line unit from December 1942,[4] and was attached to the 1st Luftwaffe Field Division under the 18th Army from 7 January until 27 March 1943. The battalion then served in the 2nd SS Infantry Brigade (motorized), then operating under 18th Army (1 April to 6 May 1943). In June the unit was disbanded and its men were incorporated into the Latvian SS Legion as the II. Battalion of Armed Grenadier Regiment of the SS 33 (Latvian No. 4).[5]

27th Latvian Self-Defence Battalion

This battalion was formed in Riga and Mangalsala (Magnisholm) on 14 March 1942. The first commander was Captain Karlis Rems, who led the unit until 20 July 1942. The battalion was transferred to Ukraine in March 1942 and placed in the front lines in the region of Grishino. In July 1942 the unit was sent to Krivoi-Rog, where it performed guard duty for Prisoner of War Transit Camp No. IV. Shortly thereafter the formation was returned to the front lines, but in January 1943 it was once again sent to Krivoi-Rog. Between February and March 1943 the unit was assigned to the Bela Gora region, where it was attached to the 19th Panzer Division of Battlegroup Lieutenant General Schmidt, then operating under 1st Panzer Army. The unit remained with the 19th Panzer Division from 13 February until 5 March 1943. Colonel Karlis Ziverts assumed control of the battalion from July 1942 and led it until April 1943. This was probably the most trying period for the men in the battalion. On 23 March 1943 (until 27 March) the unit was attached to the 3rd Panzer Division of 1st Panzer Army. At the beginning of April 1943 the battalion was still in the Bela Gora region but had sustained such heavy losses that it was disbanded. It wasn't until June, however, that the battalion was finally removed from the German field post rolls.

28th Latvian Self-Defence Battalion

This battalion was formed on 9 March 1942 in Liepaja (Libau) and assigned Field Post No. 43965. The initial commander was Lieutenant Colonel Gramatins, who led the unit until 6 June 1942, when Major Ernests Smits assumed command, leading the unit until 13 July 1943. In July 1942 the battalion was sent to Krivoi-Rog in Ukraine, where it helped to guard Prisoner of War Transit Camp No. IV. It remained in the Krivoi-Rog region, performing guard duty and occasional anti-partisan sweeps, until July 1943, when it was recalled to Latvia and disbanded. The men of the battalion were absorbed into the Latvian SS Legion.

271st Latvian Self-Defence Battalion

This battalion began forming in Libau in July 1942 but was not ready until 15 January 1943. It was shifted to Belarus in the late summer of 1942 and stationed at Hansevicze, near Minsk. Captain J. Avotins was the initial battalion commander, and led the unit until 13 August 1944. The battalion spent all of 1943 in Belarusia performing anti-partisan operations. In March and April 1943 the battalion was posted to Uretschye and Sluzk.[6] In Belarus, the unit came under the control of the Commander of the Order Police White Ruthenia. In January 1944 the unit listed a roster of only 304 officers, non-commissioned officers and men. At this time the unit was quartered in Dokschyze.[7] Most of 1944 was spent performing the same type of duty.

A German roster of the available anti-partisan forces for April 1944 listed the 271st Latvian Self-Defence Battalion as currently performing an anti-guerrilla operation in Belarusia.[8] May 1944 found the unit operating in the region of Minsk. In June the unit took part in Operation Cottbus, which proved to be the largest German anti-guerrilla drive of the war. The battalion had been stationed at Slutsk when the operation began.[9] Between July and November 1944, the main period in which Army Group Centre was pushed out of Belarusia and into Poland and Prussia, the battalion was employed on the front lines, operating in the Sigulda and Dobele regions of Latvia. Trapped in the Courland pocket in Latvia, the battalion was assigned to the VI SS Army Corps.

The commander of the battalion between 13 August and November 1944 was Lieutenant Colonel Birzulis. According to survivors of the battalion, it was through his good leadership that the battalion survived the trying summer and autumn months of 1944. On 11 October 1944 VI SS Army Corps was located in the region of Dzukste. The battalion was part of a reserve which on 15 October helped to repel a Soviet attack around Nabadzini and Puces. This marked the battalion's last independent action. Later that month it was disbanded and the remnants absorbed into the Armed Grenadier Regiment of the SS 43 (Latvian No. 5). One German source lists the 271st Latvian Self-Defence Battalion as being located in Danzig in October 1944, but this seems highly unlikely.

272nd Latvian Self-Defence Battalion

This battalion was formed in Riga and Bolderaja on 1 July 1942. Lieutenant Colonel Gustavs Mangulis became its commanding officer and held that post until August 1942. In October 1942 one company from the battalion was detached and became the core of a new battalion, the 274th Latvian Self-Defence Battalion. The 272nd remained in Warsaw performing guard duty until the end of April 1943 and took part in the liquidation of the Jewish ghetto in Warsaw. In May 1943 the battalion was sent to Dnepropetrovsk in Ukraine. During this time Lieutenant Colonel Julijs Taube led the unit. It was disbanded in late 1943 and absorbed into the Latvian SS Legion.

273rd Latvian Self-Defence Battalion

This battalion was formed in Ludza (Lüdzen) on 1 July 1942, and between its formation and 15 July 1943 it was led by Lieutenant Colonel Birzulis. In March 1943 the battalion was attached to Operational Staff Schröder. This was a special formation under the command of SS Brigadier General and Major General of the Police Walther Schröder, who held the post of SS and Police Leader Latvia.[10] The battlegroup was formed in March 1943 and was employed against the partisans in the region around the town of Ludza in the Latgale region of eastern Latvia. It was part of a planned employment of the SS and police forces, and auxiliary police units. On 15 July 1943 the battalion was completely absorbed by the 276th Latvian Self-Defence Battalion.

274th Latvian Self-Defence Battalion

This battalion was formed on 1 October 1942 in Warsaw. In November a company of the 272nd Latvian Self-Defence Battalion was used to help form the battalion. It was intended that this company would be the core of a new battalion but circumstances prevented this. The battalion was shifted from Warsaw to Bobruisk in Belarus in late October 1942, where it remained until 30 September 1944. In that month it was ordered to be disbanded. During its life span the battalion was little more than a company in size. Nevertheless, it took part in anti-partisan sweeps in Belarus. The commander of the unit during its entire history was Lieutenant Brummers. The formation was stationed in Bobruisk, Belarus, between October 1942 and October 1943. It then served in the front lines in the Polocka (Polotsk) region between October 1943 and March 1944 under SS Battlegroup Jeckeln. From March until September 1944 the formation was on guard duty in Riga, Latvia.

275th Latvian Self-Defence Battalion

This 'battalion' was in reality a reinforced rifle company (just as the 272nd Latvian Self-Defence Battalion was only one reinforced company). It performed guard duty in Riga from mid-October until early December 1942. The Commander of the Order Police Riga raised this unit on 16 October 1942 and the formation was assigned to Captain Kuginieks, who led the unit from inception until 7 December 1942, when it was disbanded. Its men were absorbed into another self-defence formation. One Latvian source states that this reinforced company was absorbed by the 276th Latvian Self-Defence Battalion, while a German reference claims that the company was absorbed into the ranks of the 278th Latvian Self-Defence Battalion. Whichever is the case, the men served in Battlegroup Knecht, an emergency anti-guerrilla force that was organized in early February 1943 under the command of Police Colonel Max Knecht.[11] This combat group was raised in conjunction with

SS Police Battlegroup Schröder (two to three battalions) and was to perform operations against the growing partisan menace on the Latvian/Russian frontier. The battlegroups were to operate independently of each other, but were to coordinate their drives.[12] German and Latvian language sources regarding the history of the 275th Latvian Self-Defence Battalion concur that the men from this company-sized battalion ended up serving in the 1st Latvian Police Regiment. Records state that both the 276th and the 278th Latvian Self-Defence Battalions were absorbed into the 1st Latvian Police Regiment when it was formed in August 1943. Prior to that they both saw service under Police Battlegroup Knecht.

276th Latvian Self-Defence Battalion

This battalion was raised on 7 December 1942 in Kuldiga, Latvia, although unconfirmed German records say it was not raised until February 1943. It was common practice for a formation to be raised in one month, but for its Field Post Number not to appear until several months later. This may explain the apparent discrepancy with regard to the unit's formation. Lieutenant Colonel Osvalds Meija led the battalion from December 1942 until 15 July 1943, and Lieutenant Colonel Birzulis from 15 July until 11 August 1943. The battalion was disbanded on that date and its men used to create the IV. Battalion of the 1st Latvian Police Regiment. Between December 1942 and August 1943 the unit had served as guards for rear area installations in Vilaka, Latvia. The only period when the battalion was not on guard duty was in February 1943 when it was attached to SS Police Battlegroup Knecht. The entire battlegroup of four Schuma battalions and three independent support platoons numbered 2,500 men.

277th Latvian Self-Defence Battalion

This unit was also formed in Riga on 7 December 1942. Lieutenant Colonel Julijs Taube took charge of it from December 1942 until 11 August 1943, when it was absorbed into the Latvian SS Legion. This battalion also took part in anti-partisan operations under SS Police Battlegroup Knecht in February 1943 and again in the autumn, when it was deployed between the towns of Pustina, Asune and Pizani. In March 1943 the battalion was once again back in Riga. It performed guard duty in the Indra region until absorbed into the Latvian SS Legion in August 1943. One month before, in July 1943, it had taken into its ranks the remnants of the 282nd Latvian Self-Defence Battalion, which had suffered heavy losses and was ordered to be disbanded.

278th Latvian Self-Defence Battalion

This battalion, formed from men recruited in Riga and Bolderaja, was also raised on 7 December 1942 and was led from inception until 11 August 1943 by Lieutenant Colonel Gredzens. The first actions of the unit included security duties in the Ludza region of Latvia. In February 1943 the battalion was part of SS Police Battlegroup Knecht. After the battlegroup was disbanded in late March 1943, the unit went back to guard duty in the Ludza region.[13] In August 1943 the battalion was disbanded and its men used to form the II. Battalion of the 1st Latvian Police Regiment under the command of Colonel of the SS Roberts Osis. This police regiment was officially given the title 'Riga'. The 1st Latvian Police Regiment Riga eventually found itself in Danzig, East Prussia, and soon afterwards was absorbed into the 15th Armed Grenadier Division of the SS (Latvian No. 1).

279th Latvian Self-Defence Battalion

This battalion was raised on 4 January 1943 in Riga and Bolderaja. Initially command of the battalion fell on Major Oskars Tiltins, but by 15 July 1943 it was under the control of Lieutenant Colonel Alberts Kleinbergs.[14] The main responsibility of this unit between January and July 1943 was the protection of rear area facilities in the area of Zilupe, Latvia. In February 1943 the unit formed part of SS Police Battlegroup Knecht. Latvian records indicate that in mid-July 1943 the 279th Latvian Self-Defence Battalion was disbanded and its men used to replenish the 278th Latvian Self-Defence Battalion.

280th Latvian Self-Defence Battalion

The 280th Latvian Self-Defence Battalion was organized and raised in Riga and Bolderaja on 23 January 1943. Colonel Karlis Lobe was its only commanding officer,[15] holding this post until 9 April 1943, when the battalion was disbanded. The battalion's main region of responsibility was Zilupe, Latvia, where it performed numerous anti-partisan sweeps between March and July 1943. In March 1943 the battalion was assigned to SS Police Battlegroup Schröder. This was the second SS and police combat group raised in February 1943 to help combat the guerrilla menace in the Latvian-Russian border region. This battlegroup was under the command and control of SS Brigadier General and Major General of the Police Walther Schröder and his staff.[16]

281st Latvian Self-Defence Battalion

According to German records, the existence of the 281st, 282nd and 283rd Latvian Self-Defence Battalions is questionable. This is quite puzzling. The 281st Latvian Self-Defence Battalion was said to have been raised in Riga and Bolderaja on 23 January 1943, and its area of activity was the Zilupe region of Latvia, mainly performing guard duty. The battalion was supposed to have served under SS Police Battlegroup Schröder in March 1943. Colonel Voldemars Veiss was said to have led the unit from 23 January until 9 April 1943, when the battalion was finally disbanded. Born in 1897, the 46-year-old Veiss would later reach the rank of SS Oberführer and obtain the post of deputy commander of the 19th Armed Grenadier Division of the SS (Latvian No. 2) in 1944.

282nd Latvian Self-Defence Battalion

The battalion was said to have been raised on 5 March 1943 in Riga and Bolderaja. The commanding officer throughout its brief existence was Captain J. Zilvers. This unit was also posted to the region of Zilupe, Latvia, where it undertook numerous anti-guerrilla drives, being heavily engaged. On 15 July 1943 the remnants were absorbed into the 277th Latvian Self-Defence Battalion.

311th Latvian Self-Defence Battalion[17]

Official German military records state that the 311th and 312th Latvian Self-Defence Battalions were never really formed. However, Latvian sources state that in fact they were created, although they existed very briefly. Therein lies the confusion. The 311th Latvian Self-Defence Battalion was organized and raised in Valmeira on 12 May 1943 and performed railway security duty guarding the railway line between the Meitene and Valka regions of Latvia until 2 July 1943, when the battalion was officially disbanded. The commander of this battalion was Colonel Eduards Ozolins.

312th Latvian Self-Defence Battalion

Although German records list this Schuma battalion as never having been formed, it in fact did briefly exist before it became the III. Battalion of the 1st Latvian Police Regiment. The confusion comes from the fact that the Germans did not employ the unit at all when it was raised on 15 May 1943 in the city of Daugavpils. When the Germans asked for the unit to be employed as part of the 1st Latvian Police Regiment, the battalion was simply redesignated as that regiment's III. Battalion on 11 August. Between 15 May and 11 August 1943 the formation was in training and was led by Lieutenant Colonel Karlis Mikelsons.[18]

313th Latvian Self-Defence Battalion

This battalion was assigned Field Post No. 39428. German records list this unit as having been raised in November 1943 as a police battalion, but Latvian sources state that it was actually established on 2 August 1943 in Riga. The first commanding officer was Police Major Jumis, under whom the battalion performed various anti-partisan operations in the Vilnius (Lithuania) and Molodechno (Belarus) regions between August and October 1943. From October 1943 to 30 January 1944 the battalion saw further action against the guerrillas and even some front-line service in the Sebezha and Nevel regions.

At this time the formation was under SS Police Battlegroup Jeckeln.[19] By 7 February 1944 command of the unit had been assigned to Captain K. Blitte. This occurred when the battalion became part of the 2nd Latvian Police Regiment, whose commander was Colonel of the SS Janis Grosbergs.

The 2nd Latvian Police Regiment saw action against Soviet guerrillas in the area along the Daugava river from February 1944. Apparently, the 313th Latvian Self-Defence Battalion, now part of the 2nd Latvian Police Regiment, came under the control of the 263rd Infantry Division of VIII Army Corps, 16th Army. The battalion remained under this division from 16 January to 10 February 1944. From 14 to 19 February the unit fought under the battlegroup of the 83rd Infantry Division of VIII Army Corps, 16th Army. This period of time involved front-line fighting. The battalion was lost in September 1944 when the 2nd Latvian Police Regiment was destroyed. In the same month a replacement 2nd Latvian Police Regiment was ordered to be formed in order to replace the one that had been destroyed. This new regiment was to be named 'Kurzeme' (Courland). It began to assemble at SS Military Training Area Seelager (near Dundaga) on 21 September 1944. The initial formation date of the new regiment was 16 September 1944 in Riga. The new 2nd Latvian Police Regiment was a mixed bag of older men with few arms and little training.

314th Latvian Self-Defence Battalion

This battalion began forming in May 1944 and was assigned Field Post No. 27288. From the beginning there was difficulty in obtaining enough weapons, so a decision was made to form this unit into an engineer construction battalion. By July 1944, when the formation was redesignated, it was attached to Army Group North as an army group support formation. It ended the war trapped in Courland, Latvia. The unit was lost in December 1944 when its personnel were used to replenish Latvian ground combat units.

315th Latvian Self-Defence Battalion

Assigned Field Post No. 56540, this battalion was raised in January 1944 and from the very beginning was intended to become a construction unit. It served in the region of Army Group North and was trapped in Courland. It was disbanded in April 1945.

316th Latvian Self-Defence Battalion

According to Latvian records, this battalion was formed on 2 August 1943 in Riga and Bolderaja. Between August and October 1943 the battalion was used against the Lithuanian and Russian communist guerrillas in the Vilnius region of Lithuania. In November 1943 the German Field Post Records finally gave the unit a number (No. 36570). Colonel Eduards Ozolins initially led the formation, but by 7 February 1944 Major Arturs Bergs was in command. When the unit was incorporated into the 2nd Latvian Police Regiment, Major Natins assumed control. From 17 to 31 December 1943 the battalion formed part of emergency SS Police Battlegroup Jeckeln, then under VIII Army Corps, 16th Army. The unit saw front-line service under this combat group in the Nevel and Sebezha areas. The battalion was once again under the control of SS Police Battlegroup Jeckeln from 5 to 11 January 1944. Thereafter it served with the 263rd Infantry Division between 16 January and 10 February 1944. It then saw employment under the remnant battlegroup of the 83rd Infantry Division from 14 to 19 February 1944. The battalion again saw service with SS Police Battlegroup Jeckeln between 19 July and 8 August 1944. This last employment was the largest that SS General Friedrich Jeckeln had ever organized. There were so many native auxiliary and German units that Jeckeln's ad-hoc divisional headquarters staff was upgraded to corps level. The 316th Latvian Self-Defence Battalion was disbanded in September 1944, when the 2nd Latvian Police Regiment was lost.

317th Latvian Self-Defence Battalion

This battalion was formed on 18 October 1943 in Riga and Bolderaja and was assigned Field Post No. 09505. Its first commander, until 14 February 1944, was Captain Z. Krummins. Between October 1943 and February 1944 the battalion was employed against the guerrillas in the Zilupe and Olaine regions of Latvia. On 14 February 1944 the unit became part of the 3rd Latvian Police Regiment, led by Lieutenant Colonel of the SS Alberts Kleinbergs. The battalion was employed in the front lines under this police regiment until September 1944, when the unit was disbanded.

318th Latvian Self-Defence Battalion

This battalion was formed on 25 October 1943 in Riga and Bolderaja and assigned Field Post No. 11441. Captain Rudolfs Abeltins led this unit until 14 February 1944. Between October 1943 and February 1944 the battalion was employed in rear area security duty in the Vecslabada region of Latvia. On 14 February 1944 it was incorporated into the 3rd Latvian Police Regiment. Like the 317th Latvian Self-Defence Battalion, the 318th Latvian Self-Defence Battalion was employed in the front lines until September 1944, when the 3rd Latvian Police Regiment was destroyed. From 6 to 15 July 1944 the 3rd Latvian Police Regiment was attached to the 290th Infantry Division, then under II Army Corps, 16th Army.

319th Latvian Self-Defence Battalion

This battalion was formed on 25 October 1943 in Riga and the Germans placed it on their rolls as a police battalion in March 1944. Major Oskars

Tiltins commanded the unit from 25 October 1943 until 8 May 1944. The battalion spent October and half of November 1943 in Riga. Between November 1943 and March 1944 the unit was performing guard duty in the Sebezha and Indra regions of Latvia. On 16 January 1944 a German order of battle roster listed the 319th Latvian Self-Defence Battalion as a battalion attached directly to VIII Army Corps command. German records listed the battalion in March 1944 as a police battalion but by December 1944 its designation had changed to that of a 'front' battalion. March and April 1944 were spent on furlough in Olaine, Latvia. Between April and July 1944 the unit was performing rear area security duties in the Aluske and Gulbene regions of Latvia. On 17 September 1944 the battalion was attached to the 215th Infantry Division of XLIII Army Corps, 16th Army. It served in Battlegroup Kleffel from 27 to 29 October 1944, working directly under the control of 16th Army headquarters. Between 30 October 30 and 4 November 1944 the battalion was assigned to Battlegroup General von Mellenthin (16th Army). The unit was pushed out of Latvia and thus evaded the fate of Army Group North, which would become trapped in Courland.[20] According to German records, the battalion was stationed in Danzig in October 1944.

320th Latvian Self-Defence Battalion

This battalion was formed on 21 December 1943 in Riga, Latvia. Captain Levings led it throughout its existence and it performed guard duty in the Jelgava, Kegums, Liepaja and Salaspils regions of Latvia. The formation was disbanded on 20 September 1944. According to German records this battalion was never formed.

321st Latvian Self-Defence Battalion

This battalion was formed on 22 December 1943 at Daugavpils, Latvia, and assigned Field Post No. 10865. The first commander of the unit was Lieutenant Colonel Jekabs Zeltins. On 14 February 1944 the battalion became the III. Battalion of the 3rd Latvian Police Regiment. That same day Captain Fridichsons was made the new battalion commander. Between December 1943 and February 1944 the unit performed rear area security duties in the Abrene area. On 14 February 1944 the formation was assigned to the 3rd Latvian Police Regiment, and between 19 July and 3 August 1944 the battalion was attached to SS Police Battlegroup Jeckeln as that regiment's III. Battalion.

322nd Latvian Self-Defence Battalion

This unit was raised on 23 July 1944 in Riga and Bauska, and its commander until 8 May 1945 was Captain A. Kikuts. Between 1 August and 15 September 1944 it was attached to the 215th Infantry Division, then operating under I Army Corps, 16th Army. On 17 September 1944 the unit was still under the

215th Infantry Division, but was attached to XLIII Army Corps, 16th Army. Between 27 and 29 October 1944 the unit was attached to Battlegroup Kleffel, which formed part of the 16th Army. By 30 October the 322nd Latvian Self-Defence Battalion was placed under Battlegroup von Mellenthin (16th Army) and remained with it until 4 November 1944. In October 1944 the formation was located in Danzig. In December 1944 the unit was designated as a front battalion. The German field post system assigned a number to this unit only late in the war, in February 1945, when it was renamed as a police battalion. By 30 March 1945 the battalion was trapped in Courland and serving under the 19th Armed Grenadier Division of the SS (Latvian No. 2). This Latvian SS division was a part of VI SS Army Corps, 16th Army.

Glossary of German military and political terms

Abschnitt – Sector, district.
Abteilung – Battalion. It could also mean Section or Department.
Abwehr – The Intelligence and Clandestine Warfare Service of the German Armed Forces High Command.
Abzeichen – Insignia, badge of rank, appointment or distinction.
Adlerhorst – Eagle's nest. The name given by British intelligence to Hitler's mountain-top retreat located in Berchtesgaden in the Bavarian Alps.
Afrika Korps – The German military force led by Erwin Rommel that fought in North Africa, 1941–1943.
Amt – Office, Bureau or Department.
Angriff – Attack.
Angriffspunkt – Attack point.
Anwärter – Cadet or candidate.
AOK – see *Armee-Oberkommando*.
Arbeit – Work.
Arbeitsdienst – The literal translation is 'work service' but it meant a labour service.
Arbeitskommando – Work commando or work group.
Arbeitslager – Work camp.
Armee – Army.
Armeegebiet – Army region or district.
Armeekorps – Army corps.
Armee-Oberkommando (*AOK*) – Army headquarters.
Artillerie – Artillery.
Aufklärung – Reconnaissance.
Ausbildung – Training.
Bahnlinie – Rail line.
Bahnschutzpolizei – Railway security police.
Bandengebiet – Bandit region (partisan-controlled region).
Banditen – Bandits. The Germans referred to the partisans behind the front lines as bandits.
Barbarossa – Codename for the German invasion of the USSR.

Bataillon – Battalion.
Bataillonsführer – Battalion commander.
Bataillonskommandeur – Battalion commander.
Batterie – Battery.
Bau – Construction.
Baudienst – The national labour service of the Reich.
Baupionier – Construction engineer.
BDO – see *Befehlshaber der Ordnungspolizei.*
BdS – see *Befehlshaber der Sicherheitspolizei.*
Befehl – Command. The plural form of the word is Befehle.
Befehlshaber – Commander.
Befehlshaber der Ordnungspolizei (BdO) – Supreme Commander of the Order Police.
Befehlshaber der Sicherheitspolizei (BdS) – Supreme Commander of the Security Police.
Begleit – Escort, usually denoting an elite unit.
Belarus – White Russia.
Beobachter – Artillery or air observer.
Beutepanzer – Captured tank or armoured vehicle.
Bewachungsmannschaft – The literal translation is security crew, but in Third Reich era terminology it referred to an SS guard detachment in a concentration camp.
Bezirk – A district or administrative unit of the German civilian government.
Brigade – A brigade of troops.
Brigadeführer – Generalmajor in either the SS or Police.
Brücke – Bridge.
Brücken – Bridging.
Bürgermeister – The mayor of a town or community.
Chef – Commander of a unit or sub-unit.
Chef des Generalstabes – Chief of the General Staff.
der SS – Belonging to the SS. Usually a Germanic SS unit was prefixed with the title 'SS' while non-Germanic formations were referred to as '*der SS*' (of the SS).
Dienst – Service.
Dienstgrad – Rank.
Dienststelle – An administrative department or administrative office.
Division – A division-sized military unit.
Dnjepr – German spelling for Dnieper.
Dorpat – German spelling for the town of Tartu in Estonia.

Drang nach Osten – Spread to the East, or Push to the East. It was the nineteenth-century German nationalist *zeitgeist* for a desire to expand German territory into eastern European lands.
Eingeschlossen – Surrounded, trapped, encircled.
Eingreifgruppe – The literal translation is 'response group', but in military terms it meant 'assault group'.
Einheit – A detachment or a unit.
Einsatz – Mission, action.
Einsatzgruppen – An operational group made up of the *Sipo* (Security Police), *SD* (Security Service) and Order Police units used for special missions, initially for liquidation of the Jewish population, communist commissars, etc., but later used to fight the partisans. One Einsatzgruppe could have as many as six *Einsatzkommandos*.
Einsatzkommando – A sub-group detachment of the *Einsatzgruppen*.
Ersatz – Replacement.
Ersatzheer – Replacement army.
Estland – Estonia.
Estnische (*Est.*) – Estonian.
Fallschirmjäger – Paratrooper.
Feind – Enemy.
Feldausbildungs – Field training.
Feldheer – Field army.
Feldkommandantur – Field command: a German Army military administration headquarters.
Feldwebel – Sergeant.
Feldzug – Military campaign.
Fellin – German spelling for the Estonian town of Viljandi.
Festung – Fortress.
Feuerpolizei – Fire Police.
Finnische – Finnish.
Flak – Anti-aircraft.
Fluss – River.
Frankreich – France.
Freiwilliger (*pl. Freiwillige*) – Volunteer.
Front – Referring to the front line or a front-line unit. Example: *(estnische) Front Bataillon 38*.
Frontkämpfer – Front-line soldier.
Führer – Leader; specifically, in the Second World War, referring to Adolf Hitler.
Führungshauptamt – Leadership Head Office.

Gau – The main territorial division of the Nazi Party. Germany was divided into forty-two *Gau*. The conquered territories also had this system.

Gauleiter – The highest-ranking Nazi Party official in a *Gau*. The *Gauleiter* was responsible for all political and economic activity, mobilization of labour and civil defence in his area.

Gefreiter – Enlisted rank, senior to the rank of private, but not considered an NCO.

Geheimfeldpolizei – Secret Field Police of the *Heer* (Army).

Geheimstaatspolizei (*Gestapo*) – State Secret Police. Formerly *Amt IV* (Department IV) of the *Reichssicherheitshauptamt* (*RSHA*), the Reich Main Security Office.

Gemeindepolizei – Municipal police.

Gendarmerie – The rural police, including motorized units for traffic control.

Generalgouvernement – The General Government, i.e., German-occupied Poland administered by a German civilian governor with its headquarters in the city of Cracow. It was classed as an appended territory (*Nebenland*, meaning outlying) of the Reich.

Generalkommando – General command. Refers to a corps-sized unit in the military.

Generalleutnant – Lieutenant general.

Genesenden – Convalescent. Example: *Genesendenbataillon* (convalescent battalion).

Gestapo – see *Geheimstaatspolizei*.

Goldfassanen Golden Pheasants. Pejorative reference to the representatives of Alfred Rosenberg's Office for the Eastern Occupied Territories, who wore the Nazi Party brown uniform with gold epaulets (shoulder insignia). The term was derogatory and implied Nazi opportunists who sought their fortune by exploiting the captured eastern territories, with no regard for the people they ruled.

Grenadier – Elite infantrymen of the seventeenth and eighteenth centuries. In 1943 Hitler redesignated most of his infantry units as 'Grenadier', thus elevating them to the status of elite troops, if only in name.

Grenzpolizei – Border police.

Grenzschutz – Frontier or border.

Gruppenführer – The SS equivalent to *Generalleutnant* (lieutenant general).

Gulag – Soviet penal camp for political dissidents and others considered to be enemies of the state. Such camps were usually located in Siberia. Very few ever left these camps. For example, when the German 6th Army surrendered at Stalingrad, the Red Army captured approximately 91,000 soldiers. They were force-marched to Siberian gulags and many died along the way. From these camps only about 3,000 survived to return to Germany between 1953 and 1956.

Hauptamt – Main office.

Hauptmann – Captain.

Hauptmann der Polizei – Captain of the police.

Hauptsturmführer – The SS rank equivalent to captain.

Heer – Army.

Heeresgebiet – Army region. It usually referred to an army's rear area.

Heeresgruppe – Army group.

Heimat – Homeland.

Heimatwehr – The uncapitalized version of home guard.

Heimwehr – Home Guard.

Hilfsdienst – Auxiliary service.

Hilfswilliger – Helper or assistant.

Höhere SS und Polizeiführer (*HSSPF*) – Higher SS and Police Commander. Also referred to as Senior SS and Police Commander. These staffs represented *Reichsführer SS* Heinrich Himmler's personal representatives in the Reich military districts and in the occupied territories.

Hundertschaft – Century, equivalent to a company or more of men.

im Dienst – In service.

Infanterie – Infantry.

Inspekteur – Inspector.

Iwan – Ivan, German slang term used to denote a Red Army soldier.

Jagdkommando – Hunting commando. In Second World War terms, a German anti-partisan unit between a platoon and company in size.

Jagdpanzer Tank destroyer.

Jäger – Hunter; in military terms it meant light infantry.

Kaukasische – Caucasian. In the Second World War the Germans recruited Caucasian volunteers from the Caucasus mountains in southern Russia.

Kavallerie – Cavalry.

KdO – see *Kommandeur der Ordnungspolizei.*

KdS – see *Kommandeur der Sicherheitspolizei.*

kollektive Gewaltmassnahmen – Collective violence, but meaning 'collective punishment'.

Kommandeur – Commander.

Kommandeur der Ordnungspolizei (*KdO*) – Commander of the uniformed police. A subordinate command to the *BdO.*

Kommandeur der Sicherheitspolizei (*KdS*) – Commander of the security police. A subordinate command to the *BdS.*

Kommandeur des Rückwartige Heeresgebiete (*Korück*) – Commander of the Army Rear Area.

Kommissarbefehl – Commissar Order, the infamous command which ordered that all Red Army political officers were to be shot, even if they surrendered.
Kompanieführer – Company commander.
Konzentrationslager (*KZL*) – Concentration camp.
Korporal – Corporal.
Korps – Corps.
Korpsabteilung – Army detachment.
Kriegsgefangener (*pl. Kriegsgefangene*) – Prisoner of war (POW).
Kriegsmarine – The German Navy, as it was referred to between 1935 and 1945 (the Third Reich era).
Krim – Crimea.
Kriminalpolizei – Criminal police.
Krimtatar – Crimean Tartar. A Turkic people that live in the Crimea.
Landesschützen – The literal translation is 'provincial shooters', but in the Nazi period it meant older-age men who were members of regional defence battalions. Like the Army security forces, these battalions were employed behind the German lines. They guarded important geographical structures, like bridges and rail lines, and physical structures vital to the war effort. They also took part in anti-partisan drives.
Landkreis – A rural administrative district.
Landrat – A district administrator.
Lebensraum – Living space. The Nazi belief that Germans needed land upon which to grow and expand.
Lebensunwertes Leben – Life unworthy of life. In Nazi thinking, a person who does not deserve to exist.
Leichte – Light.
Lettische (*lett.*) – Latvian.
Leutnant – Lieutenant.
Litauische (*lit.*) – Lithuanian.
Luftwaffe – The German Air Force, as it was referred to between 1935 and 1945 (the Third Reich era).
Major – Major, a rank between captain and colonel.
Massenmörder – Mass murder.
Militär – Military.
Mitte – Centre, as in *Heeresgruppe Mitte* (Army Group Centre).
Mörser – Mortar.
Nachricht or *Nachrichten* – Communication, signals or even intelligence.
Nachrichtendienst – Intelligence service.
Nachschub – Supply.
Nationalsozialisten Kraftfahrkorps (*NSKK*) – National Socialist Motor Corps.
Nebelwerfer – Rocket artillery.

Nord – North.
NSKK – see *Nationalsozialisten Kraftfahrkorps*.
Oberbaustab – The higher military construction staff. This headquarters usually controlled several construction regiments.
Oberbürgermeister – Lord mayor.
Oberführer – SS rank below *Brigadeführer*. There was no equivalent rank in the British or US Armies.
Obergruppenführer – SS rank equivalent to lieutenant general.
Oberkommando der Wehrmacht – Armed Forces High Command.
Oberkommando des Heeres – Army High Command.
Oberstgruppenführer – Like *Obergruppenführer*, the SS rank equivalent to lieutenant general.
Oberstleutnant Lieutenant colonel. Example: Oberstleutnant der Polizei (Lieutenant Colonel of the Police).
Obersturmbannführer SS rank equivalent to lieutenant colonel.
OKH – see *Oberkommando des Heeres*.
OKW – see *Oberkommando der Wehrmacht*.
Omakaitse – Estonian term meaning 'self-defence'.
Ordnungsdienst – Auxiliary service, made up of foreign volunteers, that assisted the German police.
Ordnungspolizei – Order police.
Organization Todt – This was a semi-military Nazi government agency established in 1933 and used mainly for the construction of strategic highways and military fortifications and installations.
Ortskommandantur – Local command: local army headquarters below the *Feldkommandantur*.
Ost – East.
Ostbataillon – A battalion of foreign volunteers from eastern Europe, including the USSR.
Ostfront – Eastern Front.
Ostheer – 'Eastern Army': the German Army fighting on the Eastern Front.
Ostland – German name for the Baltic region encompassing the Baltic countries of Lithuania, Latvia and Estonia, and part of Belarus (Belarusia, or White Russia).
Ostministerium – The (Nazi) Ministry for the Occupied Eastern Territories.
Osttruppen – Eastern troops who served in either the *Heer*, SS or Police forces of the Third Reich.
Ostvolker – Eastern people.
Panzer – Armoured.
Panzerfaust – Literally 'armoured fist'. It was a disposable, hand-held, one-shot, anti-tank weapon.

Panzerschreck – German name for Bazooka, a hand-held, reusable, anti-tank weapon.
Partisan (*pl. Partisanen*) – Partisan.
Partisanenjäger – Partisan hunter.
Partisanhelfer – Partisan helper.
Pferd – Horse.
Pionier – Engineer.
Pleskau – German spelling for the Russian city of Pskov.
Polizei – Police.
Prepjet-Sümpfe – German spelling for the Pinsk (Pripyat) Marshes. In English the spelling is Pripet.
Putsch – An internal uprising against an existing government, like a *coup d'etat*.
Quartiermeister – Quartermaster.
RAD – see *Reichsarbeitsdienst*.
Radfahr – Bicycle.
Regiment – Regiment.
Reich – Nation.
Reichsarbeitsdienst (*RAD*) – (Nazi) National Labour Service.
Reichsführer SS – National Leader of the SS.
Reichskommissar – National Commissioner.
Reichskommissariat Ostland – The civilian occupation government in the Baltic states, led by Hinrich Lohse.
Reichskommissariat Ukraine – The civilian occupation government in Ukraine, headed by Erich Koch.
Reichsministerium für die besetzten Ostgebiete – Reich Ministry for the Occupied Eastern Territories.
Reichssicherheitshauptamt – Reich Security Main Office.
Reiter – Horse, cavalryman.
Reserve – Reserve.
Reval – German spelling for the Estonian capital of Tallinn.
RSHA – see *Reichssicherheitshauptamt*.
Rückwärtig – Behind, as in the rear of the front lines.
Russische (*russ.*) – Russian.
SA – see *Sturmabteilung*.
Schlachtfliegerstaffel – Attack squadron.
Schule – School.
Schutzmannschaft (*Schuma*) – Self Defence Guard. These men, organized into battalions, assisted the SS and Police.
Schutzstaffel – The SS originated as a small core of bodyguards for Adolf Hitler, while he travelled the countryside giving speeches. This paramilitary branch of the Nazi Party expanded exponentially beginning

in 1933, creating numerous separate departments, in much the same way that an octopus has many tentacles. They included such branches as the *Allgemeine SS*, *Waffen SS* and *SS Totenkopfverbände*.

Selbstschutz – Self-defence. Referring to eastern-raised militia units of volunteers from the USSR and other eastern countries. It was originally to have consisted of ethnic Germans from these territories, but also included large numbers of non-ethnic German people.

Sicherheitsdienst – SS Security Service.

Sicherheitspolizei – Security Police.

Sicherung – Security.

Sipo – see *Sicherheitspolizei*.

Sonder – Special. In Third Reich terminology, it could refer to a special detachment or even a penal formation.

Sonderdienst – Special Service. This organization was part of the German occupation force in Poland. It was made up of ethnic German Poles serving as guards.

Sonderkommando – Sub-group detachment of the *Einsatzkommando*.

Sonderstab – Special staff.

SS – see *Schutzstaffel*.

SS und Polizeiführer (*SSPF*) – SS and Police Leader.

SSPF – see *SS und Polizeiführer*.

SS Waffengruppe – An armed group, usually of regimental or brigade size, serving in the *Waffen SS*.

Stabsoffizier – Staff officer.

Staffeln Flieger Gruppe – Squadron Air Group.

Stamm – Cadre.

Standarte – Basically another way to say regiment. The formation so named was equivalent to a regiment in size.

Standartenführer – SS colonel.

Strafe – Penal, referring to a penal (punishment) formation, such as *Strafbataillon* (penal battalion).

Sturmabteilung – Storm detachment. The militarized members of the Nazi Party.

Sturmbannführer – SS major.

Sturmkompanie – Assault company.

Süd – South.

Technische Nothilfe (*TN*) – The Technical Emergency Corps, an auxiliary police force of the ORPO consisting of engineers, technicians and specialists concerned with communications, construction work, public utilities, salvage and recovery, etc. Each police regiment that entered the USSR in 1941 had one TN company attached. Later on, these companies were detached and expanded into battalions.

Teilkommando – A sub-unit of a special force, such as a *Teilkommando* of an *SS Sonderkommando*.
Totenkopfstandarte – Any one of a series of SS Death's Head (*Totenkopfstandarte*) regiments.
Truppenübungslager – Troop Training Camp.
Truppenübungsplatz – Troop Training Ground.
Ukrainische (*ukr.*) – Ukrainian.
Und (*u.*) – And.
Verband – Formation. Could also mean a military unit of brigade size.
Verbindungsoffizier – Liaison officer.
Vernichtungskrieg – War of extermination.
Vernichtungslager – Extermination camp.
V1 / V2 – Designations for two types of rocket-propelled jet bombs used by the Nazis, mainly against the city of London.
Wach – Guard.
Wachbataillon – Guard battalion.
Waffen SS – Armed SS. SS ground combat formations that fought in the field.
Wehrkreis – A German military district.
Wehrmachtbefehlshaber – The Armed Forces Commander for a military region or area. Example: *Wehrmachtbefehlshaber der Rückwärtig Heeresgebiet* (Armed Forces Commander of the Army Rear Area).
Weissruthenische – White Russian. Properly spelled using the *eszett*: *Weißruthenische*. It refers to Belarus.
Weltanschauungskrieg – Ideological war.
Wolga – Volga.
zbV – see *zur besondere Verwendung*.
Zug – Platoon.
Zugführer – Platoon leader.
zur besondere Verwendung (*zbV*) – For special use, or special employment.

Notes

Author's note

1. https://freedomhouse.org/report/freedom-world/2022/global-expansion-authoritarian-rule (accessed 13 June 2022).
2. Sebastian Ullrich, *Der Weimar-Komplex. Das Scheitern der ersten deutschen Demokratie und die politische Kultur der fruhen Bundesrepublik 1945–1959*. Göttingen: Wallstein Verlag, 2009, p. 120.
3. In 1926 Marshal Józef Pilsudski established a dictatorship in Poland. Pilsudski claimed that he was doing this for the good of the nation. However, it is no coincidence that the political party he helped to create won all four of the next national elections (1928, 1930, 1935 and 1938). Most historians agree that the elections were rigged. Therefore, Czechoslovakia was the only nation in central Europe which remained a true democracy by 1938.
4. There were many instances between 1934 and September 1938 when Hitler broke the Treaty of Versailles and the democracies of the West did nothing.
5. Putin wanted this *Oblast*, which belonged to Georgia, because it has vast deposits of oil.

Introduction

1. The term literally translates as 'collective violence', but it meant 'collective punishment'.
2. Christopher Browning, *Ordinary Men: Reserve Police Battalion 101 and the Final Solution in Poland*. New York: Harper Collins, 1992, p. 182.
3. Christian Streit, 'Wehrmacht, Einsatzgruppen, Soviet POWs and Anti-Bolshevism in the Emergence of the Final Solution', *The Final Solution. Origins and Implementation*, ed. David Cesarani. London: Routledge, 1994, p. 110.
4. For our purposes, the term USSR refers to those lands that in 1941 encompassed the Baltic States, European Russia, Belarus (White Russia) and Ukraine. European Russia covers an area roughly 3,960,000km^2. Its eastern border is defined by the Ural Mountains, and in the south by the border with Kazakhstan. The Caucasus mountains and the region bordering Turkey and Persia define the southernmost boundary, while the northern edge covers the border area with Finland and Norway.
5. *Ostheer*: Eastern Army, the German military forces fighting on the Russian Front.
6. International Military Tribunal, *Trial of the Major War Criminals before the International Military Tribunal*, 42 vols. Nuremberg: Secretary of the Tribunal, vol. 7, p. 59.
7. Matthew Cooper, *The Nazi War Against Soviet Partisans 1941–1944*. New York: Stein & Day, 1979, pp. 171–2.
8. Ben Shepperd, *War in the Wild East: The German Army and Partisans*. Cambridge: Harvard University Press, 2004, p. 130.
9. Shepperd, *War in the Wild East*, p. 233.
10. The American edition of this book was released a year later, in 1957.
11. Although a bit dated, the book is still considered essential reading for anyone interested in the topic of the German occupation of the East.

12. Alexander Dallin, *German Rule in Russia 1941–1945: A Study of Occupation Policies*. London: MacMillan & Co. Ltd, 1957, p. 30.
13. Yitzhak Arad, 'The Holocaust of Soviet Jewry in the Occupied Territories of the Soviet Union', *Yad Vashem Studies XXI*, No. 21 (1991), p. 6.
14. Gerald Reitlinger, *The House Built on Sand: The Conflicts of German Policy in Russia*. New York: Viking Press, 1960, p. 81.
15. Ibid.
16. *Landser* is the German equivalent of G.I.
17. Omer Bartov, *The Eastern Front 1941–45: German Troops and the Barbarization of Warfare*. New York: St Martin's Press, 1986, p. 68.
18. Theo J. Schulte, *The German Army and Nazi Policies in Occupied Russia*. Oxford: Berg Publishers, 1989, p. 284.
19. Michael Geyer, 'Traditional Elites and National Socialist Leadership', in Charles S. Maier and Andrew Gould, eds, *The Rise of the Nazi Regime: Historical Reassessments*. Boulder: Westview Press, 1986, p. 71.
20. Edward Davies and Ronald Smelser, *The Myth of the Eastern Front: The Nazi-Soviet War in American Popular Culture*. New York: Cambridge University Press, 2007, pp. 22–4.
21. Davies & Smelser, *The Myth of the Eastern Front*, p. 24.
22. Paul Kohl, *Der Krieg der deutschen Wehrmacht und der Polizei 1941–1944*. Frankfurt am Main: Fischer Taschenbuch Verlag, 1995, p. 333.
23. Walter Manoschek, ed., *Die Wehrmacht im Rassenkrieg: Der Vernichtungskrieg Hinter der Front*. Vienna: Picus Verlag, 1996, p. 142.
24. Willi Dreßen, 'The Role of the Wehrmacht and the Police in the Annihilation of the Jews, the Prosecution of Postwar Careers of Perpetrators in the Police Force of the Federal Republic of Germany', *Yad Vashem Studies XXIII* (1993), pp. 295–319.
25. 'War of Annihilation: Crimes of the [German] Armed Forces 1941 to 1944'.
26. Hannes Heer and Klaus Naumann, *Vernichtungskrieg: Verbrechen der Wehrmacht 1941 bis 1944*. Hamburg: Hamburger Edition, 1995, p. 14.
27. Hannes Heer and Klaus Naumann, *War of Extermination: The German Military in World War II, 1941–1944*. New York: Berghahn Books, 2000, p. 4.
28. Wolfram Wette, *The Wehrmacht: History, Myth, Reality*. Cambridge: Harvard University Press, 2006, p. 296.
29. 'Crimes of the Armed Forces: Dimensions of the War of Extermination'.
30. Hamburg Institute for Social Research.
31. Wolfram Wette, *Die Wehrmacht: Feindbilder, Vernichtungskrieg, Legenden*. Frankfurt am Main: S. Fischer Verlag, 2002.
32. Wette, *The Wehrmacht*, p. 296.
33. Ibid., p. 297.
34. Daniel J. Goldhagen, *Hitler's Willing Executioners: Ordinary Germans and the Holocaust*. New York: Alfred A. Knopf, 1996, pp. 23–4.
35. Julius Schoeps, ed., *Ein Volk von Mordern? Die Dokumentation zur Goldhagen-Kontroverse um die Rolle der Deutschen im Holocaust*. Hamburg: Hoffmann & Campe, 1996, pp. 1–5.
36. Dr Fritz Stern, 'Book Review: *Hitler's Willing Executioners: Ordinary Germans and the Holocaust*', *Foreign Affairs*, vol. 75, no. 6 (November–December 1996), pp. 640–4.
37. Geoffrey P. Megargee, *War of Annihilation: Combat and Genocide on the Eastern Front, 1941*. New York: Rowman & Littlefield Publishers Inc., 2006, p. 151.
38. S.R.G.G. 1203 (c) v. 6. Mai 1945, PRO WO 208/4170 *Generalleutnant* SIRY171 (Comd., 347ID), Captured Friedrichsroda 10 April 1945 *Generalstabsintendant* PAUER172 (Formerly of the OKH), Captured Kleinrinderfeld, 7 April 1945.

39. Sönke Neitzel, *Abgehort: Deutsche Generale in britischer Kriegsgefangenschaft 1942–1945*. Berlin: List-Ullstein Verlag, 2007, p. 231.
40. Timothy Snyder, *Bloodlands: Europe Between Hitler and Stalin*. New York: Basic Books, 2010.
41. Mark Mazower, *Hitler's Empire: How the Nazis Ruled Europe*. New York: Penguin Books, 2008.

Chapter 1: Police reinforcements and the war behind the lines

1. Regenberg, Werner, *Panzerfahrzeuge und Panzereinheiten der Ordnungspolizei 1936–1945*. Friedberg: Podzun Pallas Verlag, 1996, p. 58.
2. George Fischer, *Soviet Opposition to Stalin: A Case Study in World War II*. Cambridge: Harvard University Press, 1952, p. 43.
3. Martin Dean, *Collaboration in the Holocaust: Crimes of the Local Police in Belarusia and Ukraine, 1941–1944*. New York: St. Martin's Press, 2000, p. 211.
4. Leonid Rein, *The Kings and the Pawns: Collaboration in Belorussia during World War II*. New York: Berghahn Books, 2011, p. 237.
5. Shepperd, *War in the Wild East*, pp. 130–4.
6. Ben Shepperd, *German Army Security Units in Russia, 1941–1943: A Case Study*. A thesis submitted to the Faculty of Social Science and Commerce of the University of Birmingham for the degree of Doctor of Philosophy. Institute for German Studies, Faculty of Social Science and Commerce, University of Birmingham, June 2000, p. 111.
7. This battalion had been organized in the Baltic states in August 1941, and was composed mostly of Baltic volunteers. The 1st Company was created using ethnic German Estonians. The title of the battalion was originally Police Battalion Eastland. The title was changed in October 1941, when the unit was transferred to Ukraine and stationed in Rovno.
8. BA MA RH 22/231, pp. 84–90.
9. From 1941 to 1942 Police Major Barkhold led Police Training Battalion Cologne, which was renamed the 309th Police Battalion. The 65th Reserve Police Battalion was led by Police Major Ernst Weis from 1941 to 1942. In 1942 the 65th Reserve Police Battalion was renamed I. Battalion of Police Regiment 25.
10. John A. Armstrong, ed., *Soviet Partisans in World War II*. Madison: University of Wisconsin Press, 1964, p. 342.
11. Erich Hesse, *Der Sowietrussische Partisanenkrieg 1941 bis 1944*. Göttingen: Musterschmidt Verlag, 1969, p. 170n.
12. *Meldung vom 06.06.1943 über die Personalstärke der landeseigenen Verbände (BA-MA, RH 21-2/509, Bl. 78 und 78r). Vgl. Tabelle im Anhang auf Seite 405f. Der Arbeit.*
13. Wolf Keilig, *Rangliste Des Deutschen Heeres 1944/45*. Friedberg: Podzun Pallas Verlag, n.d., p. 48.
14. Peter Schmitz, Klaus-Jürgen Thies, Günther Wegmann and Christian Zweng, *Die Deutschen Divisionen 1939–1945*. Osnabrück: Biblio Verlag, 2000, vol. 4, p. 22.
15. Georg Tessin, *Verbände und Truppen der deutschen Wehrmacht und Waffen SS 1939–1945*. Osnabrück: Biblio Verlag, 1975–2002, 18 vols, vol. 13, p. 26., vol. 4, p. 64.
16. Rolf Michaelis, *Die russische Volksbefreiungsarmee 'RONA' 1941–1944*. Erlangen: Selbstpubliziert, 1992, p. 16.
17. Antonio J. Muñoz, *The Druzhina SS Brigade: A History, 1941–1943*. New York: Europa Books, 2000, p. 39.
18. Horst Scheibert, *Die Träger des Deutschen Kreuzes in Gold: Kriegsmarine, Luftwaffe, Waffen SS und Des Deutschen Kreuzes in Silber*. Friedberg: Podzun Pallas Verlag, n.d., p. 459.
19. Rolf Michaelis, *Der Weg zur 36. Waffen-Grenadier-Division der SS*. Rodgau: Verlag für Militärhistorische Zeitgeschichte, 1991, p. 51.
20. Ibid., p. 50.

21. On 27 November 1942 the entire *1. Kompanie* of *Batáillon Rodjanoff* (Rodionov) defected to the partisans, taking all its equipment: *Kräfteübersichten nach dem Stand vom 31. März und 30. Apr. 1943. Befehle der Abteilungen Ia, Ib (Besondere Anordnungen für die Versorgung) und Ic, mit Regimentsbefehl Nr. 1–4 des Polizeiregiment Mitte; Merkblatt für die Behandlung sowjetischer Kriegsgefangener.*
22. French L. MacLean, *The Cruel Hunters. SS Sonderkommando Dirlewanger. Hitler's Most Notorious Anti-Partisan Unit.* Atglen: Schiffer Publishers, 1998, p. 98.
23. Georg Tessin, Norbert Kannapin and Brün Meyer. *Waffen-SS und Ordnungspolizei im Kriegseinsatz 1939–1945.* Biblio Verlag: Osnabrück, 2000, p. 620.
24. *Bandenlagekarte, vom 15.1.43–15.2.43, WFSt Op (H).* United States Holocaust Memorial Museum Collection.
25. MacLean, *The Cruel Hunters*, p. 280.
26. Withdrawn from the regiment in May 1944.
27. Existed from September 1943 to March 1944.
28. Becoming the regiment's I., II. and III. Battalions respectively.
29. Shepperd, *German Army Security Units in Russia*, p. 167.
30. Ibid.
31. Hesse, *Der Sowietrussische Partisanenkrieg*, p. 280.
32. Kletnya lies 60 miles west of the city of Bryansk.
33. Matveev's overview of the damage inflicted on the Orel region by the Germans (October 1943), (RGASPI, Fond 17, Opis' 122, Delo 54, List 64).
34. Bernhard led this headquarters from 13 April 1942 to 8 May 1945.
35. Cooper, *Nazi War Against Soviet Partisans*, p. 153.
36. BA MA RH 21-2/501, RH 26-707.
37. Ben Shepperd, 'Wehrmacht Security Regiments in the Soviet Partisan War, 1943', *European History Quarterly*, 33(4):512.

Chapter 2: Partisan warfare in the region of Army Group North

1. Rudolf Aschenauer, *Krieg Ohne Grenzen: Der Partisanenkampf gegen Deutschland 1939–1945.* Leoni am Starnberger See: Druffel Verlag, 1982, p. 252.
2. David M. Glantz, *The Battle for Leningrad, 1941–1944.* Lawrence: University Press of Kansas, 2002, p. 147.
3. Ibid.
4. Brigadier C. Aubrey Dixon and Otto Heilbrunn. *Communist Guerrilla Warfare.* London: George Allen & Unwin, 1954, p. 53.
5. *Bandenlagekarten: Anti-partisan Warfare Maps, 1941–1944.* Thirty-nine full colour detailed maps from Records Group RG-30.004; Accession 1999.A.0080. United States Holocaust Memorial Museum.
6. Although Narva was an Estonian border town, the Germans made it part of Korück 583's region of control.
7. Tessin, *Verbände und Truppen*, vol. 13, p. 26.
8. This headquarters was redesignated as Garrison Commander Pskov on 20 January 1942. It returned to its previous designation in 1944.
9. Antonio Muñoz, *Hitler's Eastern Legions, vol. 2 – The Osttruppen, 1941–1945*, 3rd revised and expanded edition. New York: Europa Books Inc., 2003, pp. 71–2.
10. Oleg Romanko and Antonio J. Muñoz, *Hitler's White Russians: Collaboration, Extermination and Anti-Partisan Warfare in White Russia, 1941–1944.* New York: Europa Books, 2002, p. 189.
11. Earl F. Ziemke, *Stalingrad to Berlin: The German Defeat in the East.* Washington DC: Centre of Military History, United States Army, 1986, p. 113.

12. Muñoz, *Forgotten Legions: Obscure Combat Formations of the Waffen SS, 1943–1945*. Boulder: Paladin Press, 1991, p. 181. This SS recruit depot operated from 1942 to 1944.
13. The regiment had difficulty both in forming and in cohesion, given the language barrier that needed to be overcome by many of the *Volksdeutsche* recruits. In addition, there was a lack of proper arms and equipment because there weren't enough German weapons. As a result, the German command had to resort to Czechoslovak rifles and other foreign stock.
14. Philip Blood, *Hitler's Bandit Hunters: The SS and the Nazi Occupation of Europe*. Lawrence: Potomac Books, 2008, p. 163.
15. Soviet Government Pamphlet. *The Case Against General Heusinger. Documents Illustrating the Charges of the USSR Against Former Lieutenant-General Adolf Heusinger, Former Operations Chief of the Wehrmacht High Command*. Soviet Government. New York: Translation World Publishers, 1961, p. 105.
16. Ibid., p. 107; Shalom Cholawsky, *The Jews of Belorussia during World War II*. Amsterdam: Harwood Academic Publishers, 1998, p. 191.
17. BA-MA, *Chef der Sicherungstruppen Rückwärtigen Heeresgebiet 102, Operationsabteilung Nr.272/43, 25.1.43*.
18. Ibid.
19. https://www.forum-der-wehrmacht.de/index.php?user-post-list/15971-sinclair/&p.No=21 (accessed: 13 November 2019).
20. At this time, Police Regiment 9 was split up amongst three security divisions: I. Battalion was attached to the 285th Security Division, II. Battalion to the 207th Security Division and III. Battalion to the 281st Security Division.
21. Formed on 12 April 1942 from elements of XXIII Army Corps, Army Group Centre.
22. https://www.forum-der-wehrmacht.de/index.php?user-post-list/15971-sinclair/&p.No=21 (accessed on 13 November 2019).
23. Mart Laar, *War in the Woods: Estonia's Struggle for Survival, 1944–1956*. Washington DC: Compass Press, 1992, p. 9.
24. Wolfgang Benz, Johannes Houwink ten Cate and Gerhard Otto, *Anpassung, Kollabouration, Widerstand: Kollektive Reaktion auf die Okkupation*. Berlin: Metropol Verlag, 1996, p. 171.
25. Cooper, *Nazi War Against Soviet Partisans*, pp. 15–16, 61.
26. Werner Haupt, *Army Group North. The Wehrmacht in Russia 1941–1945*. Atglen: Schiffer Publishers, 1997, p. 307.
27. Hans-Heinrich Wilhelm, *Die Einsatzgruppe A: der Sicherheitspolizei und des SD 1941/42*. Frankfurt am Main: Peter Lang Verlag GmbH, 1996, p. 264.
28. Lester Eckman and Chaim Lazar, *The Jewish Resistance: The history of Jewish partisans in Lithuania and White Russia during the Nazi occupation*. New York: Shengold Publishers, Inc., 1977, pp. 12–13.
29. Leonid Grenkevich, *The Soviet Partisan Movement 1941–1944*. London: Frank Cass Ltd, 1999, p. 151.
30. Laar, *War in the Woods*, p. 10.
31. The Forest Brothers – *Metsavennad* in Estonian – were nationalist guerrillas opposed to the Soviet occupation of their country.
32. Laar, *War in the Woods*, p. 11.
33. Eckman and Lazar, *The Jewish Resistance*, p. 13.
34. Ibid., p. 23.
35. Romanko and Muñoz, *Hitler's White Russians*, p. 166.
36. This number included ghettos in Belarussia.
37. Cholawsky, *The Jews of Belorussia*, p. 296.
38. Eckman and Lazar, *The Jewish Resistance*, p. 41.

39. The Polish regions of Novogrudok and Lida were part of Belarus during the German occupation of Belarusia.
40. The Germans referred to this region as *Weissruthenien* (White Ruthenia).
41. Colonel of the Municipal Police.
42. Led by SS Brigadier General and Major General of the Police Walther Schröder.
43. The 275th Battalion contained only 4 officers, 14 NCOs and 148 enlisted men. It was disbanded on 7 December 1942 and merged into the 276th Latvian Self-Defence Battalion, which was itself then absorbed into the 1st Latvian Police Regiment.
44. *BA RH 26-123/240, Geschichte der 123. Infanterie Division.*

Chapter 3: The war against the Jews and partisans in Belarus, 1942

1. David J. Hogan, editor-in-chief, *The Holocaust Chronicle: A History in Words and Pictures*. Lincolnwood: Publications International Ltd, 2002, p. 303.
2. Cholawsky, *The Jews of Belorussia*, p. 191.
3. Dean, *Collaboration in the Holocaust*, pp. 151, 182.
4. F.H. Hinsley, *British Intelligence in the Second World War*. London: HMSO, 1984, vol. 3, pt I, p. 671.
5. Cholawsky, *The Jews of Belorussia*, p. 74.
6. Letter from Wilhelm Kube, dated 31 July 1942 and addressed to Heinrich Lohse, *Reichskommissar* for the Ostland region. The letter quoted figures of Jews killed during the first half of 1942. Yad Vashem Archives, G507/42 g.
7. Dean, *Collaboration in the Holocaust*, p. 86
8. Werner Haupt, *Army Group Centre. The Wehrmacht in Russia, 1941–1945*. Atglen: Schiffer Publishing, Ltd, p. 245.
9. Hans Becker, *Devil on My Shoulder*. London: Jarrolds Publishers, 1955, pp. 35–6.
10. Cooper, *Nazi War Against Soviet Partisans*, pp. 82–3.
11. Armstrong, *Soviet Partisans*, p. 154.
12. Martin Gilbert, *Atlas of the Holocaust*. London: Lester Publishing Ltd, 1988; rev. edn, 1993, p. 129.
13. Nechama Tec, *The Bielski Partisans*. Oxford: Oxford University Press, 1993, pp. 196–7.
14. MacLean, *The Cruel Hunters*, pp. 167–9.
15. Antonio Muñoz, *Hitler's Eastern Legions, vol. I: The Baltic Schutzmannschaft 1941–1945*. New York: Europa Books, 1998, p. 19.
16. Werner Haupt, *Die Schlachten Der Heeresgruppe Mitte 1941–1944*. Friedberg: Podzun Pallas Verlag, 1983, pp. 359–62.
17. Tessin, *Verbände und Truppen*, vol. 9, pp. 17–18.
18. Cooper, *Nazi War Against Soviet Partisans*, p. 122.
19. Tessin, *Verbände und Truppen*, vol. 8, pp. 2–3.
20. BA MA – GMDS, Wi/ID 2.779. *Wi. Kdo. Witebsk, 'Monatsbericht', 23 Nov. 1942.*
21. Antonio Muñoz, ed., *The German Police*. Supreme Allied Headquarters, G-2 Section, prepared jointly with British MI-14(d). US Army War Office: Washington, April 1945. Reprinted in revised and expanded format. New York: Europa Books, 1997, section M, p. 16.
22. Ruth Bettina Birn, *Die Höheren SS und Polizeiführer. Himmlers Vertreter im Reich und in den besetzten Gebieten*. Dusseldorf: Droste Verlag, 1986, p. 331.
23. *Gendarmerie*: a term to denote the rural police used outside large city areas.
24. *Dienstalterliste, Stand vom 1. Juli 1944*, p. 8.
25. Birn, *Die Höheren SS*, p. 331.
26. Heinz Höhne, *The Order of the Death's Head*. New York: Coward McCann, 1970, p. 369.

27. John Erickson, *The Road to Berlin. Stalin's War with Germany*. London: Weidenfeld & Nicolson, 1983, p. 95.
28. Dallin, *German Rule in Russia*, p. 27.
29. MacLean, *The Cruel Hunters*, pp. 13–16.
30. One member of the SS Sonderkommando Dirlewanger, Friedrich Walter, who was 21 years old in 1942, claims that the unit did not transfer to the region of Mogilev until the late summer of that year. It is possible that part of the formation transferred earlier and the rest of the unit moved later in the summer as Walter claims.
31. The figures vary, depending on the source referenced. These figures were given by Rolf Michaelis.
32. Michaelis, *Der Weg zur 36*, pp. 41–2.
33. Christian Gerlach, *Kalkulierte Morde: Die deutsche Wirtschafts- und Vernichtungspolitik in Weißrußland 1941 bis 1944*. Hamburg: Hamburger Edition HIS, 2013, pp. 919–21.
34. National Archives, International Military Tribunal, 1113-PS. This is a partial translation of a report organized by the Higher SS and Police Leader Riga on the operation. The equipment obtained during the successful drive against what the Germans called 'bandits' was detailed in the report. In terms of casualties, 389 partisans were shot, while 1,274 people labelled as 'suspicious individuals' were captured, found guilty of colluding with the guerrillas, and murdered. In addition, 8,350 Jews were also put to death.
35. The only person higher in the Secret Field Police than Cuno Schmidt was his boss, Wilhelm Krichbaum, who was head of the entire secret field police organization.
36. Robert Winter, *Die Geheime Feldpolizei*. Wolfenbütte: Melchior Verlag, 2013, p. 44.
37. There's a dispute as to whether Kaintzig left this post in January or in May 1942.
38. In July 1942 the 403rd Security Division was transferred to the region of Army Group South.
39. The *339. Infanterie Division* (including GFP-709) was involved in the murder of approximately 7,000–8,000 Jews in Mogilev from October 1941. While the men of the 339th Static Infantry Division cordoned off the Jewish ghetto in Mogilev, GFP-709 provided security at the murder site while the SS and SS security service provided the killing units. For a full detail of this massacre, see Dieter Pohl, *Die Herrschaft der Wehrmacht: Deutsche Militärbesatzung und einheimische Bevölkerung in der Sowjetunion 1941–1944*. München: R. Oldenbourg Verlag, 2008, pp. 269–70. In 1944 the 339th Static Infantry Division was reorganized as a '1944' infantry division and employed at the front.
40. This armoured group was transferred to the region of Army Group South in the spring of 1942.
41. GFP-716 was employed under the 286th Security Division in the central sector of the Russian front until March 1944 when the unit was withdrawn and sent to the West to take charge of security for the V-1 and V-2 weapons under the German LXV Army Corps in Belgium and the Netherlands.
42. GFP: an abbreviation for the German words *Geheime Feldpolizei* (Secret Field Police). Thus, GFP-716 would be the 716th Secret Field Police Group.
43. GFP-709 began its operations in Russia under the 286th Security Division (Bialystok/Orsha), and was later shifted to the 339th Static Infantry Division (Vitebsk/Bobruisk).
44. Heinz Kuhnrich, *Der Partisanenkrieg in Europa 1939–1945*. Berlin: Dietz Verlag, 1968, pp. 537–38; Muñoz, *Hitler's Eastern Legions*, vol. I, p. 32.
45. Cooper, *Nazi War Against Soviet Partisans*, p. 122.
46. Dallin, *German Rule in Russia*, p. 28.
47. Cooper, *Nazi War Against Soviet Partisans*, p. 123.

48. This figure is for 1 August 1943. According to Soviet sources, these men were split up into five partisan detachments and one guerrilla regiment operating behind the lines of Army Group North.
49. This figure is for April 1943 and included the major partisan units there: Kovpak's 1,929 men split up into seven battalions; Saburov's 3,333 men in nineteen battalions; and Fyodorov's 1,777 men in eight guerrilla battalions. According to another, more reliable source, the strength figures for the Saburov, Fyodorov and Kovpak formations are a Soviet overestimation. The actual number should be 5,568 men for the Ukraine region. The true figures (dated 25 August 1943) should be 1,728 men for Kovpak, 1,862 for Saburov and 1,978 for Fyodorov.
50. Dallin, *German Rule in Russia*, p. 29.
51. Actually a part of Poland, although absorbed into Belarusia in early 1944.
52. This headquarters served in Berezino in 1944.
53. This headquarters served in Mogilev, then Smolensk in 1942 and Gomel in 1943.
54. This command was stationed in Gorki in 1942.
55. Actually a part of Poland, although absorbed into Belarusia in early 1944.
56. This unit was stationed in Dobryn in 1943.
57. This command was located in Vitebsk in 1941.
58. This town was decreed a part of Belarusia in early 1944.
59. This headquarters was officially disbanded in 1942.
60. In early 1944 this town was officially assigned to Belarusia.
61. This town bordering Belarusia was located in February 1944 in the General District of White Ruthenia.
62. Part of the Bialystok District.
63. Actually part of Poland, although 'absorbed' into Belarusia in early 1944 by German decree.
64. From the 354th Local Command.
65. This headquarters was stationed in Kurzenice in 1944.
66. Raul Hilberg, *The Destruction of the European Jews*. New Haven: Yale University Press, 2003, 3 vols, vol. 1, p. 385.
67. Only 439 were said to have been sent to work in Germany from this operation.
68. Hesse, *Der Sowietrussische Partisanenkrieg*, p. 280.
69. Hermann Franz, *Gebirgsjäger der Polizei: Polizei Gebirgsjäger Regiment 18 und Polizei Gebirgs Artillerieabteilung 1942 bis 1945*. Bad Nauheim: Verlag Hans Henning Podzun, 1963, p. 52.
70. Regenberg, *Panzerfahrzeuge und Panzereinheiten*, p. 60.
71. Rolf Michaelis, *Russen in der Waffen SS*. Berlin: Michaelis-Verlag, 2002, p. 64.
72. MacLean, *The Cruel Hunters*, p. 110.
73. Reitlinger, *The House Built on Sand*, p. 239.
74. Hesse, *Der Sowietrussische Partisanenkrieg*, p. 280.
75. MacLean, *The Cruel Hunters*, p. 106.
76. Michaelis, *Der Weg zur 36*, p. 48.
77. A month later, in February 1943, members of the 57th Belarusian Self-Defence Battalion led by Police Major Hans Siegling were involved in the massacre of guerrillas and Jewish civilians in the village of Salihorsk, Belarus. The victims were herded together into a cowshed that was then set on fire.
78. Later redesignated as the 56th Belarusian Self-Defence Artillery Battalion.
79. Regenberg, *Panzerfahrzeuge und Panzereinheiten*, p. 84.
80. Ibid., p. 85.
81. *The Case Against General Heusinger*, p. 106.
82. Tessin, *Verbände und Truppen*, vol. 11, p. 156.
83. Regenberg, *Panzerfahrzeuge und Panzereinheiten*, p. 76.

84. Tessin et al., *Waffen SS und Ordnungspolizei*, p. 643.
85. Ziemke, *Stalingrad to Berlin*, p. 115.
86. Hesse, *Der Sowietrussische Partisanenkrieg*, p. 281.
87. Muñoz, *Göring's Grenadiers*, p. 41.
88. Tessin, *Verbände und Truppen*, vol. 13, p. 32.
89. Hesse, *Der Sowietrussische Partisanenkrieg*, p. 204.
90. Adolf Reinicke, *Die 5. Jäger Division 1939–1945*. Friedberg: Podzun Pallas Verlag, p. 257. Hachtel assumed command of the 56th Jäger Regiment on 1 February 1943. In late June he was seriously wounded, requiring his transfer to Germany, where he died from his wounds on 20 July 1943.
91. Ziemke, *Stalingrad to Berlin*, p. 115.
92. Kevin Conley Ruffner, *Luftwaffe Field Divisions 1941–45*. London: Osprey Publishing, 1990, p. 13.
93. Armstrong, *Soviet Partisans*, pp. 370, 539. General Ponomarenko's full name was Panteleimon Kondratyevich Ponomarenko.

Chapter 4: Collaboration in 1942

1. The Graukopf Brigade was named after its commander, Colonel Kromiadi, who had greying hair.
2. Muñoz, *The Druzhina SS Brigade*, p. 29.
3. Colonel Aimé Costantini, *L'Union Soviétique En Guerre (1941–1945)*. Paris: Imprimerie Nationale, 1968, 3 vols, vol. II, p. 255.
4. Muñoz, *The Druzhina SS Brigade*, p. 65.
5. Antonio Muñoz, 'Losing World War II: Nazi Racial and Recruitment Policies in the East', in *Command Magazine*, XTR Corporation: San Luis Obispo, November 1995, 35:66–7.
6. Nicholas P. Vakar, *Belorussia: The Making of a Nation. A Case Study*. Cambridge: Harvard University Press, 1956, p. 197.
7. The word *Hilfswilligern* literally translates as 'those willing to help', but in this case it means 'volunteer'.
8. Hilberg, *Destruction*, vol. 1, p. 288.
9. Dean, *Collaboration in the Holocaust*, p. 211n.
10. Muñoz, *Hitler's Eastern Legions*, vol. 2, p. 26.
11. Waitman W. Beorn, 'A Calculus of Complicity: The Wehrmacht, the Anti-Partisan War, and the Final Solution in White Russia, 1941–1942', in *Central European History*, 2011, 44:308–37.
12. *Sonderanweisungen zum Kampf gegen Partisanenbanden*. Berlin: *Gedruckt in der Reichsdruckerei*, 1941, p. 7.
13. Kushel was responsible for inspecting and supervising the creation of all local self-defence battalions.
14. *Sonderanweisungen zum Kampf gegen Partisanenbanden*, p. 7.
15. The literal translation of *Schutzmannschaft* is 'protection team', but in Nazi terminology it meant 'self-defence'. In May 1944 this unit was renamed *Schutzmannschaft Sicherungs Abteilung 64* (64th Self-Defence Security Battalion). '*Schuma*' is an abbreviation of *Schutzmannschaft*.
16. Muñoz, *Hitler's Eastern Legions*, vol. I, p. 29.
17. Romanko and Muñoz, *Hitler's White Russians*, p. 293.

Chapter 5: The war against the Jews and partisans in Ukraine ...

1. Piryatin is located in the Poltava Oblast, roughly between Kiev and Poltava, in Ukraine.
2. NARA Microfilm T-315, Roll 2214, Frame 1057.

3. Gilbert, *Atlas of the Holocaust*, p. 97.
4. *Umgesiedelt* means 'relocated', but in this particular case, 'resettled' is more appropriate.
5. Tessin, *Verbände und Truppen*, vol. 12, p. 298.
6. NARA Microfilm T-315, Roll 2214, Frame 1156.
7. Gilbert, *Atlas of the Holocaust*, p. 64.
8. Andrej Angrick, *Besatzungspolitik und Massenmord: Die Einsatzgruppe D in der Sowjetunion 1941–1943*. Hamburg: Hamburger Edition, 2003, p. 231n.
9. Angrick, *Besatzungspolitik und Massenmord*, p. 236.
10. NARA Microfilm T-315, Roll 2214, Frame 1163.
11. Ibid., Frames 1167–68.
12. Ibid., Frame 1168.
13. Snyder, *Bloodlands*, p. 319.
14. NARA Microfilm T-315, Roll 2213, Frame 924.
15. Ibid., Frame 960.
16. Ibid., Frame 923.
17. NARA Microfilm T-315, Roll 2214, Frame 904.
18. The 1929 Geneva Convention was updated in 1949.
19. International Committee of the Red Cross.
20. The German word *landser* is the German equivalent to the American GI.
21. On 3 May 1942 GFP-720 was ordered to Genitschesk, while GFP-711 was sent to Sinelnikovo and GFP-726 to Zaporozhye. On 13 May the 444th Security Division received a substantial reinforcement when *Sicherungs Regiment 4* was attached to the division. This unit had two bicycle-borne battalions: the 613th and 614th Bicycle Guard Battalions. By 18 May 1942 the headquarters, together with the 1st and 2nd Companies of the 694th Military Field Police Battalion (Commander: Major Marschall), were located in Stalino. Together with the 617th Guard Battalion (Commander: Captain Österreich), these two formations became part of the *Standort Kommandantur Stalino* (Local Command Stalino). In general, the 444th Security Division was at this time located in and around the Stalino-Makeyevka areas.
22. NARA Microfilm T-315, Roll 2213, Frame 998.
23. Andris J. Kursietis, *The Wehrmacht at War 1939–1945*. Soesterberg: Aspekt Verlag, 1999, p. 209.
24. Winter, *Die Geheime Feldpolizei*, p. 60.
25. Not to be confused with Cuno Schmidt.
26. BA-MA, RH 22/199 u. RH 22/200.
27. NARA Microfilm T-315, Roll 2213, Frame 931.
28. Ibid., Frame 1014.
29. Ibid., Frame 1136.
30. Ibid., Frame 1031; *The Case Against General Heusinger*, p. ix.
31. The document stated that these hunter units would conceal themselves by day and operate at night; marching by night and disappearing inconspicuously into the forests by day so that none of the inhabitants of the nearby village would be aware of them. The Hunter Commandos are to operate in the same manner as the enemy bands ... to destroy all enemy bands that would fall into their ambush. They were to avoid battle with superior forces and do reconnaissance until larger forces could arrive.
32. NARA Microfilm T-315, Roll 2213, Frame 1136.
33. Ibid., Frame 1036.
34. Paul Carell, *Hitler Moves East, 1941–1943*. Boston: Little Brown & Co., 1964, p. 502.
35. NARA Microfilm T-315, Roll 2213, Frame 1136.
36. Ibid., Frame 1050.

37. Formerly the 1st and 2nd Companies of the 311th Police Battalion.
38. NARA Microfilm T-315, Roll 2213, Frame 1140.
39. Valdis Redelis, *Partisanenkrieg: Entstehung und Bekämpfung der Partisanen und Untergrundbewegung im Mittelabschnitt der Ostfront 1941 bis 1943*. Heidelberg: Scharnhorst Buchkameradenschaft, 1958, p. 40.
40. The city of Chernigov is bordered to the southwest and west by the Pripyat Marshes and is located about 90 miles north-northeast of Kiev.
41. Armstrong, *Soviet Partisans*, p. 115.
42. The German word 'Hornung' may be a nickname for someone with a relationship to the month of February, or can be used as a term for a person born out of wedlock. If the latter is the case, then the word is derived from Middle Low German.
43. The commander of this police mountain artillery battalion was *SS Sturmbannführer und Major der Gendarmerie* Wilhelm Braun.
44. Translation: 'Mine Clearing and Bridge Building Emergency Technical Battalion No. 2'.
45. *Schutzmannschaft Bataillon 103* was attached to *Polizeiregiment 11*.
46. Hannes Heer and Klaus Naumann, eds, *The German Army and Genocide: Crimes Against War Prisoners, Jews, and Other Civilians in the East, 1939–1944*. New York: New Press, 1999, p. 162.
47. Regenberg, *Panzerfahrzeuge und Panzereinheiten*, p. 66.

Chapter 6: Stalingrad and its consequences

1. NARA Microfilm T-315, Roll 2213, Frame 936.
2. Klaus Gebner, *Geheime Feldpolizei: Die Gestapo der Wehrmacht*. Berlin: Militärverlag, 2010, p. 72.
3. NARA Microfilm T-315, Roll 2214, Frames 826–8.
4. Kiril Feferman, 'The Food Factor as a Possible Catalyst for Holocaust-Related Decisions: The Crimea and the North Caucasus', *War In History*, 2008, 15(1):91.
5. NARA Microfilm T-315, Roll 2213, Frame 939.
6. Keith E. Bonn, ed., *Slaughterhouse: The Handbook of the Eastern Front*. Bedford: Aberjona Press, 2005, p. 211.
7. Tessin, *Verbände und Truppen*, vol. 10, p. 27.
8. NARA Microfilm T-315, Roll 2213, Frame 942.
9. Ibid.
10. Eduard Abramian and Antonio Muñoz, *Forgotten Legion: Sonderverbänd Bergmann in World War II, 1941–1945*. New York: Europa Books Inc., 2007, p. 90.
11. NARA Microfilm T-315, Roll 2214, Frame 339.
12. The division consisted of the following forces: *Infantry*: 360th Grenadier Regiment, III. Battalion of the 375th Grenadier Regiment, 46th Security Regiment. *Artillery*: II. Battalion of the 221st Artillery Regiment. *Anti-Tank*: 94th Anti-Tank Battalion, 445th Heavy Weapons Company. *Engineer*: 666th Engineer Battalion (motorized), 444th Engineer Company. *Cavalry*: I. and II. Cavalry Battalions of the 444th Eastern Cavalry Battalion (actually a regiment), Kalmuck Cavalry Battalion Dr Doll (attached 18 January 1943). *Special Troops*: 3rd Company of the 698th Field Gendarmerie Battalion, GFP-711 (attached 18 January 1943), II. Battalion of Police Regiment 6 (attached 7 January 1943), I. Battalion of Police Regiment 6 (attached 12 January 1943).
13. NARA Microfilm T-315, Roll 2214, Frame 305.
14. Dallin, *German Rule in Russia*, pp. 549–50.
15. NARA and RFSS papers, *Chef des Generalstabes des Heeres, Auszug: aus einem Bericht des Ia der 365 JD über die Kämpfe bei der 8. italienischen Armee, 23 Marz 1943*.

16. Joachim Hoffmann, *Die Ostlegionen 1941–1943*. Friedberg: Verlag Rombach GmbH, 1986, pp. 38–9.
17. NARA Microfilm T-315, Roll 2214, Frame 364.
18. Ibid., Frame 365.
19. Joachim Hoffmann, *Kaukasien 1942/43: Das deutsche Heer und die Orientvölker der Sowjetunion*. Friedberg: Verlag Rombach GmbH, 1991, pp. 17–18.
20. Paul Carell's history of the Nazi invasion of the USSR spanned two volumes. In spite of this, he did not complete the history of that conflict. Instead, his second volume ends with the destruction of Army Group Centre in the summer of 1944. Thus, he failed to write a description of the end of the war in the East. In spite of this, his two-volume history on the Russo-German conflict (*Hitler Moves East, 1941–1943* and *Scorched Earth, 1943–1944*) is considered a classic and a 'must read' for any serious student of the war. Not many people know that Paul Carell's real name was Paul Schmidt, and that during the war he was Adolf Hitler's press secretary. In spite of this, his narration of the war in the East is fairly well balanced.
21. Carell, *Hitler Moves East*, p. 140.
22. NARA Microfilm T-315, Roll 2214, Frame 310.
23. Abramian and Muñoz, *Forgotten Legion*, p. 90.
24. NARA Microfilm T-315, Roll 2214, Frame 312.
25. Ibid., Frame 387.
26. Ibid., Frame 401.
27. Up until late 1943, Adolf Hitler had forbidden the creation of foreign volunteer units larger than a battalion in size. In order to get around this rule, the regiment-sized cavalry formation composed of Russian and Cossack volunteers was divided into two battalions and employed as the I. and II. Battalions of the 444th Eastern Cavalry Battalion.
28. NARA Microfilm T-315, Roll 2214, Frame 405.
29. Ibid., Frame 324
30. NARA Microfilm T-501, Roll 349, Frame 250.
31. Paul B. Brown, 'The Senior Leadership Cadre of the Geheime Feldpolizei, 1939–1945', *Holocaust and Genocide Studies*, 2003, 17(2):281.
32. *The Case Against General Heusinger*, pp. 142–3.
33. Kitzinger had been *Befehlshaber des Luftgau Norwegen* until 26 June 1941, when he was transferred to Ukraine and placed in charge of combating the partisan movement behind the lines of Army Group South. He held this post until 1 August 1944.
34. NARA Microfilm T-315, Roll 2216, Frames 335–8.
35. Krisztlán Ungváry, 'Ungarische Besatzungskräfte in der Ukraine 1941–1942', *Ungarn Jahrbuch*, no. 26, Budapest (2002/2003), p. 126.
36. The original title was Commander Army Group South but it changed to Commander of the Rear Area Army Group South 103 on 5 July 1941. On 15 March 1942 it changed again to Commanding General of Security Troops and Commander in the Southern Army Area. On 9 July 1942, when Army Group South was divided into Army Groups A and B, this title was again redesignated as Commanding General of the Security Forces and Commander in Army Area B.
37. NARA Microfilm T-315, Roll 2215, Frame 489.
38. The 4th Security Regiment was transferred to Commanding General of the Security Forces and Commander in Army Area A in May 1942. It was also redesignated as 4th Bicycle Regiment at this time.
39. The unit was being organized in the 8th Military District, forming into a security division.
40. By April 1943 the division was down to a cadre staff.

41. The division formed part of Battlegroup Dostler. In addition, the division served under the VIII Army Corps from April to May 1942.
42. The division was reduced to a cadre staff, but was later replenished, partly through the infusion of troops from the shattered 444th Security Division.

Conclusion

1. This quotation is attributed to Henry Kissinger but it is important to note that there is no specific date associated with when he said, or perhaps wrote, it. Kissinger, who was Secretary of State for President Richard M. Nixon, is known for his writings and speeches on foreign policy and military strategy. This quotation encapsulates his perspective on the challenges posed by unconventional warfare and insurgency tactics. While the exact context in which he made this statement is not certain, it reflects his views on the dynamics of asymmetric warfare and the difficulties faced by conventional forces when confronting guerrilla or insurgent movements.
2. Paul Carell, *Scorched Earth. The Russo-German War 1943–1944*. Boston: Little, Brown & Co., 1970, p. 270.

Appendix I: Russian volunteer formations, March 1942–April 1943

1. For a complete listing of volunteer forces created between June 1941 and April 1942, please see Antonio J. Munoz, *Hitler's War Against the Partisans During Operation Barbarossa, June 1941 to the Spring of 1942* (Barnsley: Pen & Sword Military, 2024).
2. White Ruthenia, White Russia and Belarus all refer to the same territorial land mass that today comprises the nation of Belarus.
3. At the beginning of February 1943 the German 6th Army surrendered at Stalingrad.

Appendix II: Lithuanian volunteer formations, 1941–1945

1. Tadeusz Piotrowski, *Poland's Holocaust: Ethnic Strife, Collaboration with Occupying Forces and Genocide in the Second Republic, 1918–1947*. Jefferson: MacFarland & Co., 1998, p. 164.
2. Later sent to perform guard duty for a while in Maydanek concentration camp in Poland.
3. Performing guard duty in the Vilnius region.
4. 'Lithuanian Battalions of National Work'.
5. Antonio Muñoz, 'Lithuania's Volunteer Police Battalions', *Europa Magazine* (New York: Europa Books), summer 1998, 14:38.
6. Piotrowski, *Poland's Holocaust*, p. 165.
7. The initial first five battalions were created from the Lithuanian Home Guard, which included a good number of Lithuanian Nationalist Party members.
8. Tessin et al., *Waffen SS und Ordnungspolizei*, p. 585.
9. Muñoz, *Hitler's Eastern Legions*, vol. I, p. 35.
10. Carlos Caballero-Jurado and Nigel Thomas, *Germany's Eastern Front Allies (2) Baltic Forces*. London: Osprey Men-at-Arms Series, Osprey Publishing, 2002, p. 36.
11. Muñoz, *Hitler's Eastern Legions*, vol. I, p. 156.
12. Hinze, *Rückzugskämpfe in der Ukraine*, p. 161.

Appendix III: Latvian volunteer formations, 1941–1945

1. One unconfirmed report says that the battalion was established on 21 December 1941.
2. In its capacity as part of SS Battlegroup Jeckeln.
3. KdO: abbreviation for *Kommandeur der Ordnungspolizei* (Commander of the Order Police).
4. Just north of Lake Ilmen in the area of Army Group North.
5. Which later became the 19th Latvian SS Division.
6. NARS Microfilm T-175, Roll 225, Frame 2764109.

7. Ibid., Frame 2764393.
8. NARS Microfilm T-175, Roll 174, Frame 2709404.
9. Muñoz, *The Druzhina SS Brigade*, p. 42.
10. Schröder held this position until October 1944.
11. Please see the section of this book covering Battlegroup Knecht.
12. Led by SS Brigadier General and Major General of the Police Walther Schröder. The battlegroup contained the 280th and 281st Latvian Self-Defence Battalions.
13. Like all other SS and police battlegroups, SS Police Battlegroup Knecht would be formed numerous times.
14. Kleinbergs would eventually become the commander of the 3rd Latvian Volunteer Police Regiment. His rank would reach that of a Lieutenant Colonel of the SS.
15. Lobe would later win the German Cross in Gold while leading a unit of the Latvian SS.
16. Basically, the staff and personnel of the SS and Police Leader Latvia were used to form the temporary anti-partisan headquarters combat group. SS Brigadier General Hinrich Möller was the head of the SS and Police Leader Estonia command from 4 August 1941 to 1 April 1944. SS Brigadier General and Major General of the Police Walther Schröder assumed control from 1 April to 19 October 1944.
17. It is possible that many of these '300' series numbered Latvian battalions were created from the Latvian Depot Brigade.
18. On 11 August 1943 the battalion officially became the III. Battalion of the Latvian 1st Police Regiment.
19. The specific time periods for its employment under SS Police Battlegroup Jeckeln were 17–31 December 1943 and 5–11 January 1944.
20. Army Group North was redesignated Army Group Courland.

Bibliography

Primary Source Material

Belarus Central State Archives, Minsk, Records 1941–1949

Belarusian State Minsk Archives, USHMM RG-53.002M (1993.A.0082), Folder 1262 and 1265.

Grodno Oblast Archive Records, 1940–1944. Records Group RG-53.004M, Reel 5.

Grodno Oblast Archive Records, 1940–1944. RG-53.004M. Reel No. 2, Fond 1, Section 100 – Grodno Amtskommissar correspondence.

Records Group RG-53.002M, Reels 3, 5, 11, and 13.

Military Historical Institute (Prague), Records 1941–1944

Records Group RG-48.004M, Reels 1, 2, 3, 4, and 6.

RG-48.004M (1993.A.0019), Reel No. 3 – *1. SS Infanterie-Brigade (mot.)–29.11.42, 'Aufmarsch Glebokie'.*

Bundesarchiv, Koblenz

BAK-N756/214a, *SS Kampfgruppe von Gottberg: Band Zwei. Vgl. BArch Bestand RS 4 Brigaden, Legionen, Standarten sowie Kampfgruppen und Einheiten der Waffen SS; Verschiedene Sperrverbände und Eingreifgruppen Fotografie von SS Hauptsturmführer Robert Ancans.*

BAK-NS19-03, *Reichssicherheitshauptamt Nachrichten Uebermittlung*, NR 162/42 (G) AUS 160 ZWEI/42. Pp. 12–13.

BAK-NS19-11. 470.

BAK-NS19-13, Reichsführer-SS Meldung an der Führer über Bandenbekämpfung. Feldkommandostelle, 8.10.1942. Neldung Nr. 23.

Bandenkampf Unternehmen – Folio: NS19/1, 1500, 1671, 1463, 2661, 2835, 3140, and 3695.

Meldung vom 06.06.1943 über die Personalstärke der landeseigenen Verbände (BA-MA, RH 21-2/509, Bl. 78 und 78r). Vgl. Tabelle im Anhang auf Seite 405f. Der Arbeit. Operations Abteilung, NO. 5645/42, Heeresgruppe Mitte. 15.07.42.

RH 22-229. Berück, Kriegstagebuch 07.04.42.

Bundesarchiv, Freiburg

Heeresgruppe Mitte, Ia. Nr.14550/43 g.Kdos., 8.XII.43., Anlage zur Kriegstagebuch, Heeresgruppe Mitte, Führungsabteilung, Akte XXIII, Heft 12, 1.X.-31.XII.43. 65002/24. Bundesarchiv, Frieburg. Chef der Sicherungstruppen–Rückwartigen Heeresgebiet 102, Operationsabteilung Nr.272/43, 25.1.43. 23.

Reichssicherheitshauptamt. Höhere SS und Polizeiführer Ostland. 7.8.42. BAF, NS–19/1, 1500, 1671, 1463, 2661, 2835, 3140 and 3645.

Bundesarchiv/Militärarchiv Berlin-Lichterfelde

BA-MA RH 19 VII/2, Bl. 2.

BA-MA RH 19 XI/37, *Bericht des GFP-Angehörigen Georg Koch*, 37.

BA-MA RH 22/31, *Meldung Direktor GFP, Mai 1942.*

BA-MA RH 22/60, *Bericht GFP für Heeresgebiet B, August 1942.*

BA-MA RH 22/86, 27.

BA-MA RH 22/173, *Meldung Direktor GFP, Juli 1942.*

BA-MA RH 22/199 *Befehlshaber rückwärtiger Heeresgebiete Tätigkeitsberichte der Geheimen Feldpolizeigruppen 1, 708, 719, 725, 730, 739, 721. - Stärkemeldungen Laufzeit: Jan.–Aug. 1942.*

BA-MA RH 22/200 *Befehlshaber rückwärtiger Heeresgebiete Tätigkeitsberichte der Geheimen Feldpolizeigruppen 1, 708, 719, 725, 730, 739, 721. - Stärkemeldungen Laufzeit: Sept.–Dez. 1942.*

BA-MA RH 23-25, '*Befehl Nr. 1 für Unternehmen 'Dreieck', 11 September 1942*'.

BA-MA RH 23-25, 'Gefechtsbericht über Unternehmen 'Dreieck' und 'Viereck' vom 17.9-2.10.1942, 19 October 1942'.

BA/MA RH 24-22/21, folio 88–9.

BA-MA RH 24-22/23, *Jäger - Gen.Kdo.22 AK, 14 May 1944, Ic - Aussenstelle Korfu - Korpsgruppe Joannina / Ic, 25 April 1944.*

BA-MA RH 24-23/24.

BA-MA RH 26, 117/16.

BA-MA RH 48 *Dienststellen und Einheiten der Ordnungstruppen, der Geheimen Feldpolizei, der Betreuungs und Streifendienste des Heeres. RW 40/170: Fester Platz Kreta, Sept. 1944 RW 40/172: Tätigkeitsbericht, Juli–Aug. 1944; Bundesarchiv.*

BA-MA RH 40, 10.

BA-MA RH 40, 11.

BA-MA WF 01/2151, Bl. 816.

BA-MA WF 03/15831, *Feldpolizeidirektor beim Befehlshaber Heeresgebiet 103.*

National Archives, College Park, Maryland

NARS Microfilm T-78 Rolls 413, 645.

NARS Microfilm T-175 Rolls 16, 111, 129, 140, 141, 174, 191, 225, 233.

NARS Microfilm T-315, Rolls 1665, 1687, 2213, 2214, 2215, 2216.

NARS Microfilm T-580 Roll 88.

NARA RG-238 Working Conference on 23 April 1940, Service Diary of Governor General Hans Frank, vol. 9.

National Archives, Kew, Richmond, Surrey, United Kingdom

CSDIC (UK) SIR (Special Interrogation Report) 730 (8 Aug 1944) 'Geheime Feldpolizei Gruppe 644'.

CSDIC (UK) SIR (Special Interrogation Report) 818 (20 Aug 1944) 'Geheime Feldpolizei in Greece 1942'.

CSDIC (UK) SIR (Special Interrogation Report) 1675 (24 May 1945) 'Notes on the GFP and Other Security Services in the Area of Army Group Nord (Later Kurland) 1942–1 Jan 45'.

CSDIC (UK) SIR (Special Interrogation Report) 1676 (24 May 1945) 'Notes on the GFP and Other Security Services in the West 1939–42'. CAB/129/28, *Kommandobefehl, den 18 Okt. 1942.*

German Armed Forces War Diary

Schramm, Percy. *Kriegstagebuch Des Oberkommandos Der Wehrmacht 1939–1945*, 8 vols. Herrsching: Manfred Pawlak, 1982.

Supreme Headquarters Allied Expeditionary Force, Office of Assistant Chief of Staff G-2, Counterintelligence Sub-Division Evaluation and Dissemination Section

EDS Report No. 15 – *Geheime Feldpolizei* (Secret Field Police) January 8, 1945, Supreme Headquarters Allied Expeditionary Force, Office of Assistant Chief of Staff G-2, Counterintelligence Sub-Division Evaluation and Dissemination Section.

Geheime Feldpolizei (GFP) Vol. I XE 019650 Par 43, SR 380-20-10. General Staff, U.S. Army G2 Central Records Facility, Fort Holabird, Baltimore 19, Maryland.

Geheime Feldpolizei – EI (GFP) G-2 Department of the Army, Volume II, XE 019650.

Office of Strategic Services Research and Analysis Branch, R and A N, 2500.15, 'German Military Government Over Europe: Economic Controls in Occupied Europe', Washington DC, 28 August 1945.

Records of the Army Staff (Record Group 319) – CIC Collection - Declassified Files

Box No. 4 – No. XE003923 German Police System in Occupied Czechoslovakia.

Box No. 5 – NND 881019, File No. XE019650 *Geheime Feldpolizei* (GFP) vols I and II.

Military Intelligence Service Centre / US Forces European Theater CI

Final Interrogation Report No. 98 (14 Mar 1946) 'Reg.-u.Krim.Dir. Philipp GREINER, Leitender FP Direktor, Mil.Befh. Frankreich'.

7th Army Interrogation Centre

Final Interrogation Report No. 20 (8 Aug 1945) 'Secret Military Police Unit 712'.

French Army Military Archive, Paris

Ordre De Bataille II – A – Etat-Major de la 30ème Division d'Infanterie des Waffen-SS (Russe Nr. 2) (plustard): Stab Waffen Grenadier Brigade der SS (Weissruthenien).

Legal Court Cases

Innsbruck Court Case: GG Innsbruck 10 Nr. 415170-23 10 H 7170: 1–43.

Nuremberg Trial: NOKW 1382, Directive of the Quartermaster of the *Kommandant rückwärtiges Armeegebiet* 560 (Army Groups A, Twelfth Army, 560th Army Rear Area Security Command), 21 May 1941.

The Minister of Canadian Citizenship and Immigration vs. Vladimir Katriuk Court transcripts, Docket No.: T-2409-96. Date: 1999/01/29.

Court transcripts: *The Canadian Government vs. Vladimir Katriuk*. Docket No.: T-2409-96, Date: 1999.01.29.

Nazi Conspiracy and Aggression (Washington, DC: Government Printing Office, 1946), 8:205–8. R-135.

Trials of War Criminals before the Nuremberg Military Tribunals under Control Council Law No. 10, October 1946–April 1949 (Washington, DC: Government Printing Office, 1949), 13:516-22. NO-3028.

Court Trial Testimonials

Testimony of Heinz Hermann Schubert, Office of Chief of Counsel for War Crimes. APO 696 A, US Army, Document No. 4816, pp. 3–4, 18).

Testimony of Private Albert Rodenbusch, Grenadier (Feldausbildungs) Regiment 635, given during court proceedings of the Minsk war crimes trials held in 1946 and 1947. Belarusian SSR, 15–19 January 1946 (Minsk Trial), Minsk (1947), pp. 262–3.

Testimony of Erich von dem Bach-Zelewski at the Nuremberg War Crimes Trials: The Trial of German Major War Criminals. London: HMSO, 1946–1952. 24 volumes.

Other Primary Sources

Krüger to Gunst, 14 November 1939, W. Gunst SS Officer file (formerly Berlin Document Centre), RGp-242, A3343/SSO/043A/321, NARA; judgment in proceedings against Friedrich Paulus, 26 May 1977, p. 6, file 4 Ks 1/74, State Prosecutor's Office in Frankfurt am Main.

Meyer, Brünn. *Dienstalterliste der Waffen-SS: SS Obergruppenführer bis SS Hauptsturmführer; Stand vom 1 Juli 1944*. Osnabrück Biblio Verlag: 1987.

Telex: General Löhr to the *Befehlshaber Südost*, dated October 1, 1944-RH 19 VII/37, Part 1, Annex 12.

'*Generalkommando LIV.A.K., Abt.Ic/A.O. vom 2.8.41, An den Führer des Sonderkommandos XIa Herrn SS Sturmbannführer Zapp*'., MAP, microfilm 56748, fr. 954; '*Geheime Feldpolizei 647, Koat II beim LIV.A.K., Tgb.-Nr. 77/41 vom 2.8.1941, An den Stab der Geheimen Feldpolizei 647 beim A.O.K. 11*'., Ibid., fr. 945.

'*Der Beauftragte des Chefs der Sicherheitspolizei und des SD beim Befehlshaber des rückwartigen Heeresgebiet Süd, Sonderkommando 11a, Tgb. 83/41 vom4.8.1941, Betrifft: Bericht über die Tätigkeit des Sonderkommandos in der Zeit vom 17. Juli bis 3. August und die Einsatzplanung für die erste Augusthalfte 1941*'. On the concentration of Jews in labour camps in Bessarabia, see '*Die Gesandschaft in Bukarest an das Auswartige Amt*', 6 August 1941, Nuremberg Doc. NO-2067, reproduced in ADAP, Series D, vol. XIII/1, 238–9.

Roosevelt, Franklin D. 'No Peace with Hitler: Eight Common Principles for a Better World', in *Vital Speeches of the Day*. vol. 7, issue 22 (1 September 1941).

'Central Registry of War Criminals and Security Suspects' (CROCASS Allied Control Authority, Parts 1 and 2, US Army, APO 742, 1947).

Publications by the Third Reich Printing Office, Berlin

Der Reichsführer SS und Chef der Deutschen Polizei, Banden-bekämpfung. Berlin: Gedruckt im Reichssicherheitshauptamt, 1. Ausgabe, September 1942.

Dienstalterliste der Schutzstafel der NSDAP (SS Obergruppenführer bis SS Standartenführer) Stand vom 30. Januar 1942. Herausgegeben vom Personalhauptamt. Berlin: Gedruckt in der Reichsdruckerei, 1942.

Dienstalterliste der Schutzstafel der NSDAP (SS Obersturmbannführer und SS Sturmbannführer) Stand vom 1. Oktober 1944. Herausgegeben vom Personalhauptamt. Berlin: Gedruckt in der Reichsdruckerei, 1944.

Dienstalterliste der Schutzstafel der NSDAP (SS Obergruppenführer bis SS Standartenführer) Stand vom 1. Oktober 1944. Herausgegeben vom Personalhauptamt. Berlin: Gedruckt in der Reichsdruckerei, 1944.

Befehlsblatt des Chefs der Sicherheitspolizei und der SD, Nr. 14/44 Berlin, 1. April 1944. Herausgegeben vom Reichssicherheitshaupt-amt. Berlin: Gedruckt in der Reichsdruckerei, 1944.

Dienstalterliste der Schutzstaffel der NSDAP, Stand vom 1. Oktober 1934. Berlin: Gedruckt in der Reichsdruckerei, 1934.

Dienstalterliste der Schutzstafel der NSDAP, stand vom 30 Januar 1942. Berlin: Gedruckt in der Reichsdruckerei, 1942.

Dienstalterliste der Schutzstafel der NSDAP, stand vom Oktober/November 1944. Berlin: Gedruckt in der Reichsdruckerei, 1944. *Wi. Kdo. Witebsk, 'Monatsbericht', 23 November 1942 (GMDS, Wi/ID 2.779)*

Dienstalterliste der Schutzstafel der NSDAP, stand vom 1 Juli 1944. Berlin: Gedruckt in der Reichsdruckerei, 1944.

Secondary source material

Doctorate of Philosophy Works Cited

Birn, Ruth Bettina. *Die Höheren SS und Polizeiführer: Himmlers Vertreter im Reichs und in den besetzten Gebieten*. Droste Verlag, 1986.

Gordon, Gary Howard. *Soviet Partisan Warfare, 1941–1944. The German Perspective*. University Microfilms: Ann Arbor, 1972.

Porter, Jack Nusam. *Jewish Partisans: A Documentary of Jewish Resistance in the Soviet Union during World War II*. Volume II. University Press of America, Inc.: Washington DC, 1982.

Pronin, Alexander. *Guerrilla Warfare in the German Occupied Soviet Territories 1941–1945*. Georgetown: Georgetown University Graduate School, 1965.

Sheppard, Ben. *German Army Security Units in Russia, 1941–1943: A Case Study.* A thesis submitted to the Faculty of Social Science and Commerce of the University of Birmingham for the degree of Doctor of Philosophy, Institute for German Studies Faculty of Social Science and Commerce: University of Birmingham, June 2000.

Pamphlets and journals

German Anti-Guerrilla Operations in the Balkans, 1941–1944. DA Pamphlet 20-243, August 1954, Washington, DC: Centre of Military History, US Army.

Krichbaum, Wilhelm. *The Secret Field Police.* MS # C-029, ed. George Vanderstadt, trans. M. Franke. Washington, DC: Centre for Military History, US Army Historical Division, 18 May 1947.

The Case Against General Heusinger. Documents Illustrating the Charges of the USSR Against Former Lieutenant General Adolf Heusinger, Former Operations Chief of the Wehrmacht High Command. Soviet Government. New York: TransWorld Publishers, 1961.

Kowalska, Magdalena. *A Polish heart in a feldgrau uniform – complicated journeys from the Wehrmacht to the Polish Army in Exile* in 'Polish Scientific Society Abroad in London'. Poznań: Adam Mickiewicz University, Humanities Education No. 2 (33), 2015.

Internet

Grabowski, Jan. *The Polish Police: Collaboration in the Holocaust.* US Holocaust Memorial Museum: Washington, DC. https://www.ushmm.org/m/pdfs/20170502-Grabowski_OP.pdf (2017).

Published works

Adair, Paul. *Hitler's Greatest Defeat. The Collapse of Army Group Centre.* New York: Sterling Publishing, 1994.

Albrecht-Carrié, René. *A Diplomatic History of Europe Since the Congress of Vienna.* New York: Harper & Row, 1958.

Anders, Wladyslaw. *Hitler's Defeat in Russia.* Chicago: Henry Regnery Company, 1953.

Anders, Wladyslaw. *Russian Volunteers in Hitler's Army, 1941–1945.* New York: Europa Books. 1997.

Andrew, Christopher. *Defend the Realm: The Authorized History of MI5.* New York: Knopf Doubleday, 2009.

Andreyev, Catherine. *Vlasov and the Russian Liberation Movement. Soviet Reality and Émigré Theories.* Cambridge: Cambridge University Press, 1987.

Angolia, Lieutenant Colonel J.R. *Cloth Insignia of the SS.* San Jose: R. James Bender Publishing, 1983. 2nd (updated) edn.

Angrick, Andrej. *Besatzungspolitik und Massenmord: Die Einsatzgruppe D in der Sowjetunion 1941–1943.* Hamburg: Hamburger Edition, 2003.

Applebaum, Ann. *Red Famine: Stalin's War on Ukraine.* New York: Doubleday, 2018.

Arad, Yitzhak. 'The Holocaust of Soviet Jewry in the Occupied Territories of the Soviet Union', in Aharon Weiss (ed.), *Yad Vashem Studies XXI*, Jerusalem: The Holocaust Martyrs' and Heroes' Remembrance Authority, 1991.

Arico, Massimo. *Ordnungspolizei Volume 1: Encyclopedia of the German Police Battalions September 1939–July 1942.* Stockholm: Leandoer & Co. Forlag, 2016.

Armstrong, John A. (ed.) *Soviet Partisans in World War II.* Madison: University of Wisconsin Press, 1964.

Armstrong, John A. *Ukrainian Nationalism.* Englewood: Ukrainian Academic Press, 1990.

Aschenauer, Rudolf. *Abgehört. Deutsche Generäle in britischer Kriegsgefangenschaft 1941–1945.* Munich: Druffel-Verlag, 1982.

Axworthy, Mark W.A. *Axis Slovakia: Hitler's Slavic Wedge, 1938–1945*. New York: Europa Books, 2002.

Baker, Gabriel. *Spare No One: Mass Violence in Roman Warfare*. New York: Rowman & Littlefield, 2021.

Banach, Jens. *Heydrichs Elite: Das Führerkorps der Sicherheitspolizei und des SD 1936–1945*. Paderborn: Ferdinand Schöningh, 1998.

Bartov, Omer. *The Eastern Front 1941–1945: German Troops and the Barbarization of Warfare*. New York: St. Martin's Press, 1986.

Bartov, Omer, *Hitler's Army: Soldiers, Nazis, and War in the Third Reichs*. Oxford: Oxford University Press, 1992.

Bartov, Omer. *Mirrors of Destruction: War, Genocide, and Modern Identity*. Oxford: Oxford University Press, 2000.

Bartov, Omer. *Germany's War and the Holocaust: Disputed Histories*. Cornell: Cornell University Press, 2003.

Bauer, Eddy. *The History of World War II*. London: Galley Press, 1984.

Bayer, Hanns. *Die Kavallerie Der Waffen SS*. Heidelberg: Selbstverlag der Truppenkameradenschaft der SS Kavallerie Divisionen, 1980.

Bayer, Hanns. *Kavallerie Divisionen der Waffen-SS im Bild*. Osnabrück: Munin Verlag, 1982.

Becker, Hans. *Devil on My Shoulder*. London: Jarrolds Publishers, 1955.

Beevor, Anthony. *Crete: The Battle and the Resistance*. New York: Penguin Books, 2014.

Bennett, Rab. *Under the Shadow of the Swastika: The Moral Dilemmas of Resistance and Collaboration in Hitler's Europe*. New York: New York University Press, 1999.

Bergen, Doris L. *War and Genocide: A Concise History of the Holocaust*. New York: Rowman & Littlefield, 2009.

Berthel, Hans Dieter. *Die Feldgendarmerie im Zweiten Weltkrieg und ihre Teilnahme an völkerrechtswidrigen Aktionen 1939–1945*. Norderstedt: Herstellung & Verlag, 2006.

Bethell, Nicholas. *The Last Secret. The Delivery to Stalin of Over Two Million Russians by Britain and the United States*. New York: Basic Books Inc., 1974.

Birn, Ruth Bettina. *Die Sicherheitspolizei in Estland, 1941–1944: Eine Studie zur Kollaboration im Osten*. Paderborn: Ferdinand Schöningh, 2006.

Bischof, Günther, Plasser, Fritz and Maltschnig, Eva (eds). *Austrian Lives: Contemporary Austrian Studies Vol. 21*. New Orleans: University of New Orleans Press, 2012.

Blood, Philip W. *Hitler's Bandit Hunters: The SS and the Nazi Occupation of Europe*. Washington DC: Potomak Books Inc., 2006.

Bonn, Keith E. (ed.) *Slaughterhouse: The Handbook of the Eastern Front*. Bedford: Aberjona Press, 2005.

Boog, Horst et al. *Germany and the Second World War. Vol. IV, the Attack on the Soviet Union* Oxford: Clarenden Press, 1998.

Boshyk, Yury (ed.) *Ukraine during World War II: History and its Aftermath*. Edmonton: Canadian Institute of Ukrainian Studies, 1986.

Brandon, Ray and Lower, Wendy. *Shoah in Ukraine: History, Testimony, Memorialization*. Bloomington: Indiana University Press, 2008.

Browning, Christopher. *Ordinary Men: Reserve Police Battalion 101 and the Final Solution in Poland*. New York: Harper Collins, 1992.

Browning, Christopher. *The Origins of the Final Solution: The Evolution of Nazi Jewish Policy, September 1939–March 1942*. Lincoln: University of Nebraska Press, 2004.

Browning, Christopher R. *Project Muse. Nikolaev and Dnepropetrovsk Regions*. The United States Holocaust Memorial Museum Encyclopedia of Camps and Ghettos, 1933–1945, vol. II: Ghettos in German-Occupied Eastern Europe. Indiana University Press, 2012.

Bruns, Friedrich. *Die Brücke von Neuenburg: Eine Dokumentation über den Endkampf der 19 Armee in Elsaß 1945*. Celle: Self Published, 1990.

Buchanan, Patrick J. *Churchill, Hitler, and The Unnecessary War: How Britain Lost Its Empire and the West Lost the World*. New York: Crown Press, 2008.

Buchner, Alex. *Ostfront: The German Defensive Battles on the Russian Front 1944*. West Chester: Schiffer Military History, 1991.

Campbell, Bruce. *The SA Generals and the Rise of Nazism*. Lexington: University Press of Kentucky, 1998.

Campbell, Stephen. *Police Battalions of the Third Reichs*. Atglen: Schiffer Publishers, 2007.

Carell, Paul. *Hitler Moves East, 1941–1943*. Boston: Little, Brown & Company, 1964.

Carell, Paul. *Scorched Earth. The Russo-German War 1943–1944*. Boston: Little, Brown & Company, 1970.

Carnier, Pier Arrigo. *L'Armata Cosaca in Italia 1944–1945*. Milan: Mursia Editoriale, 1990.

Caroe, Olaf. *Soviet Empire. The Turks of Central Asia and Stalinism*. New York: MacMillan & Co. Ltd, 1954.

Chiari, Bernhard. *Alltag Hinter Der Front: Besatzung, Kollaboration und Widerstand in Weissrussland, 1941–1944*. Düsseldorf: Droste Verlag, 1998.

Cholawsky, Shalom. *The Jews of Belarusia during World War II*. Amsterdam: Harwood Academic Publishers, 1998.

Citino, Robert M. *The German Way of War: From the Thirty Years' War to the Third Reichs*. Lawrence: University Press of Kansas, 2005.

Clark, Alan. *Barbarossa. The Russo-German Conflict, 1941–45*. New York: William Morrow & Co., 1965.

Clarke, Jeffrey J. and Ross Smith, Robert. *United States Army in World War II. The European Theater of Operations: Riviera to the Rhine*. Washington DC: Centre of Military History, 1993.

Cooper, Matthew. *The Nazi War Against Soviet Partisans, 1941–1944*. New York: Stein & Day, 1979.

Conquest, Robert. *Harvest of Sorrow: Soviet Collectivization Methods and the Terror-Famine*. New York: Oxford, 1986.

Costantini, Colonel Aimé. *L'Union Soviétique En Guerre (1941–1945)*. Paris: Imprimerie Nationale, 1968, 3 vols.

Coudry, Georges. *Les Camps Sovietiques Les Russes Livres a Stalin en 1945*. Paris: Albin Michel, 1997.

Crankshaw, Edward. *Gestapo: Instrument of Tyranny*. London: Greenhill Books, 1990.

Cüppers, Martin. *Wegbereiter der Shoah: Die Waffen SS, der Kommandostab Reichsführer-SS und die Judenvernichtung 1939–1945*. Darmstadt: Wissenschaftliche Buchgesellschaft, 2005.

Curilla, Wolfgang. *Die deutsche Ordnungspolizei und der Holocaust im Baltikum und im Weißrußla, 1941–1944*. Paderborn: Verlag Ferdinand Schöningh GmbH, 2006.

Dallin, Alexander. *German Rule in Russia 1941–1945, A study of Occupation Policies*. London: MacMillan & Co. Ltd, 1957.

Dasnoy, Philippe and Leon Charles, Jean. *Les dossiers secrets de la police allemande en Belgique. La Geheime Feldpolizei en Belgique et dans le Nord de la France, Vols 1 and 2*. Brüssel: Arts et Voyages/Lucien De Meyer, 1972.

Dawidowicz, Lucy S. *The War against the Jews 1933–1945*. New York: Holt, Reinhart & Winston, 1975.

Dean, Martin. *Collaboration in the Holocaust: Crimes of the Local Police in Belarusia and Ukraine, 1941–1944*. New York: St. Martin's Press, 2000.

Dixon, Brigadier C. Aubrey and Heilbrunn, Otto. *Communist Guerrilla Warfare*. New York: Frederick A. Praeger, 1954.

Dorril, Stephen. *M.I.6*. London: Fourth Estate, 2000.

Dreßen, Willi. 'The Role of the Wehrmacht and the Police in the Annihilation of the Jews; the Prosecution of Postwar Careers of Perpetrators in the Police Force of the Federal Republic of Germany'. *Yad Vashem Studies XXIII*, 1993: 295–319.

Drum, D. Karl et al. *Airpower in Russian Partisan Warfare*. USAF Historical Study No. 177. New York: Arno Press, 1968.

Dunnigan, James F. et al. (eds). *War in the East: The Russo-German Conflict, 1941–45*. New York: Simulations, 1977.

Eckmann, Lester, and Lazar, Chaim. *The Jewish Resistance: The History of the Jewish Partisans in Lithuania and White Russia during the Nazi Occupation 1940–1945*. New York: Shengold Publishers, 1977.

Ehrenburg, Ilya, and Grossman, Vasily. *The Black Book*. New York: Holocaust Library, 1981.

Erickson, John. *The Road to Berlin. Stalin's War with Germany*. London: Weidenfeld & Nicolson, 1983.

Evans, Richard J. *The Third Reichs in Power*. New York: Penguin, 2005.

Evans, Richard J. *The Third Reichs at War*. London: Penguin Books Ltd., 2008.

Ezergailis, Andrew. *The Holocaust in Latvia 1941–44*. Washington DC: United States Holocaust Memorial Museum, 1996.

Faber, David. *Munich 1938: Appeasement and World War Two*. New York: Simon & Schuster, 2010.

Federov, Alexander. *partisans d'Ukraine – 2. operations contre la Wehrmacht*. Paris: Editions J'ai Lu, 1951.

Fischer, George. *Soviet Opposition to Stalin: A Case Study in World War II*. Cambridge: Harvard University Press, 1952.

Fontaine, Thomas. 'Chronology of Repression and Persecution in Occupied France, 1940–44', in *The Encyclopedia of Mass Violence* (Philadelphia: Running Press, 2004).

Förster, Jürgen. 'The German Army and the Ideological War against the Soviet Union', in *The Policies of Genocide: Jews and Soviet Prisoners of War in Nazi Germany*, 15–29, ed. Gerhard Hirschfeld (London: Allen & Unwin, 1986).

Franz, Hermann. *Gebirgsjäger der Polizei: Polizei-Gebirgsjäger-Regiment 18 und Polizei-Gebirgs-Artillerieabteilung 1942*. Bad Nauheim: Verlag Hans Henning, 1963.

Frei, Norbert. *Vergangenheitspolotik*. Einbeck: AHA-Buch GmbH, 1996.

Geldmacher, Thomas. *Wir als Wiener waren ja bei der Bevölkerung beliebt: Östtereichsische Schutzpolizisten und die Judenvernichtung in Ostgalizien 1941–1944*. Vienna: Mandelbaum Verlag, 2002.

Gellermann, Guenther W. *Moskau ruft Heeresgruppe Mitte. Was nicht im Wehrmachtbericht stand: Die Einsätze des geheimen Kampfgeschwaders 200 im Zweiten Weltkrieg*. Koblenz: Bernard & Graefe Verlag, 1988.

Gerlach, Christian. *Kalkulierte Morde: Die deutsche Wirtschafts- und Vernichtungspolitik in Weißrußland, 1941 bis 1944*. Hamburg: Hamburger Edition HIS, 2013.

Gerlach, Christian. 'Men of 20 July and the War in the Soviet Union', in *War of Extermination: The German Military in World War Two 1941–1944*, ed. Hannes Heer and Klaus Naumann. New York: Berghahn Books, 2000.

Gebner, Klaus. *Geheime Feldpolizei*. Berlin: Militarverlag der Deutschen Demokratische Republik, 1986.

Gebner, Klaus. *Geheime Feldpolizei: Die Gestapo der Wehrmacht*. Berlin: Militärverlag, 2010.

Geyer, Michael, Maier, Charles S and Gould, Andrew (eds). 'Traditional Elites and National Socialist Leadership', 77–133, in *The Rise of the Nazi Regime: Historical Reassessments* (Boulder: Westview Press, 1986).

Gibson, Hugh, and Welles, Sumner (eds). *Ciano Diaries 1939–1943, Complete, Unabridged Diaries of Count Galeazzo. Italian Minister for Foreign Affairs 1936–1943.* New York: Doubleday & Co., 1946.

Gilbert, Dr Martin. *Atlas of the Holocaust.* London: Lester Publishing, 1988; rev. edn, 1993.

Gilbert, Dr Martin. *The Holocaust: A History of the Jews of Europe During the Second World War.* New York: Henry Holt & Co., 1985.

Gildea, Robert, Warring, Anette and Wieviorka, Olivier (eds). *Surviving Hitler and Mussolini: Daily Life in Occupied Europe.* New York: Bloomsbury Academic, 2006.

Glantz, David M. and Orenstein, Harold S. *Belarusia 1944: The Soviet General Staff Study.* London: Frank Cass, 2001.

Gogun, Alexander. *Stalin's Commandos. Ukrainian Partisan Forces on the Eastern Front.* London: I.B. Tauris, 2016.

Goldhagen, Daniel Jonah. *Hitler's Willing Executioners: Ordinary Germans and the Holocaust.* New York: Alfred A. Knopf, 1996.

Gooch, John. *Mussolini and His Generals: The Armed Forces and Fascist Foreign Policy, 1922–1940.* Cambridge: Cambridge University Press, 2007.

Görlitz, Walter, and David Irving (eds). *In the Service of the Reich.* New York: Stein & Day, 1979.

Grenkevich, Leonid. *The Soviet Partisan Movement 1941–1944.* London: Frank Cass, 1999.

Grundmann, Siegfried. *Die V-Leute des Gestapo-Kommissars Sattler.* Berlin: Hentrich & Hentrich Verlag, 2010.

Hamburger Institut für Sozialforschung (ed.) *Verbrechen der Wehrmacht: Dimensionen des Vernichtungskrieges 1941–1944.* Hamburg: Hamburger Edition HIS, 2002.

Hanusiak, Michael. *Lest We Forget.* Toronto: Progress Books, 1976.

Hartmann, Christian, Hürter, Johannes and Jureit, Ulrike. *Verbrechen der Wehrmacht: Bilanz einer Debatte.* Munich: Verlag C.H. Beck, 2005.

Hartmann, Christian et al. *Der deutsche Krieg in Osten 1941–1944: Faceten einer Grenzüberschreitung.* Oldenbourg: Wissentschaftsverlag, 2009.

Haupt, Werner. *Leningrad: Die 900 Tage Schlacht 1941–1944.* Friedberg: Podzun Pallas Verlag, 1980.

Haupt, Werner. *Die Schlachten Der Heeresgruppe Mitte 1941–1944.* Friedberg: Podzun Pallas Verlag, 1983.

Haupt, Werner. *Die Schlachten Der Heeresgruppe Süd. Aus der Sicht der Divisionen.* Friedberg: Podzun Pallas Verlag, 1985.

Haupt, Werner. *Die 8. Panzer Division im 2. Weltkrieg.* Friedberg: Podzun Pallas Verlag, 1987.

Haupt, Werner. *Die Deutschen Infanterie-Divisionen.* Friedberg: Podzun Pallas Verlag, 1991. 3 vols.

Haupt, Werner. *Army Group North. The Wehrmacht in Russia 1941–1945.* Atglen: Schiffer Publishers, 1997.

Haupt, Werner. *Army Group Centre. The Wehrmacht in Russia 1941–1945.* Atglen: Schiffer Publishing, 1997.

Haupt, Werner. *Army Group South. The Wehrmacht in Russia 1941–1945.* Atglen: Schiffer Publishers, 1997.

Hausser, Paul. *Soldaten Wie Andere Auch. Der Weg der Waffen SS.* Osnabrück: Munin Verlag GmbH, 1966.

Hechelhammer, Bodo, and Meinl, Susanne. *Geheimobjekt Pullach: Von der NS-Mustersiedlung zur Zentrale des BND.* Berlin: Christoph Links Verlag, 2014.

Heer, Hannes, and Naumann, Klaus. *Vernichtungskrieg: Verbrechen der Wehrmacht 1941–1944.* Hamburg: Hamburger Edition, 1995.

Heer, Hannes and Naumann, Klaus (eds). *The German Army and Genocide: Crimes Against War Prisoners, Jews, and Other Civilians in the East, 1939–1944.* New York: New Press, 1999.

Heer, Hannes and Naumann, Klaus (eds). *War of Extermination: the German Military in World War II – 1944*. New York: Berghan Books, 2000.
Heer, Hannes and Naumann, Klaus (eds). *Verbrechen der Wehrmacht: Dimensionen des Vernichtungskrieges 1941–1944*. Hamburg: Hamburger Institut für Sozialforschung, 2002.
Herbert, Ulrich (ed.) *National Socialist Extermination Policies: Contemporary German Perspectives and Controversies*. New York: Berghan Books, 2000.
Herf, Jeffrey. *Reactionary Modernism: Technology, Culture, and Politics in the Third Reich*. New York: Cambridge University Press, 1984.
Hesse, Erich. *Der Sowietrussische Partisanenkrieg 1941 bis 1944*. Göttingen: Musterschmidt Verlag, 1969.
Hilberg, Raul. *Perpetrators, Victims, Bystanders: The Jewish Catastrophe 1933–1945*. New York: Harper Collins, 1992.
Hilberg, Raul. *The Destruction of the European Jews*. New Haven: Yale University Press, 2003, 3rd edn.
Hill, Alexander. *The War Behind the Eastern Front: The Soviet Partisan Movement in North-West Russia, 1941–44*. New York: Frank Cass, 2005, 3 vols.
Hinsley, F.H. *British Intelligence in the Second World War*. London: HMSO, 1984. vol. 3, pt I.
Hinze, Rolf. *Der Zusammenbruch Der Heeresgruppe Mitte Im Osten 1944*. Stuttgart: Motorbuch Verlag, 1980.
Hinze, Rolf. *Das Ostfront-Drama 1944*. Stuttgart: Motorbuch Verlag, 1988.
Hinze, Rolf. *Rückzugskämpfe in der Ukraine 1943/44*. Meerbusch: Verlag Dr Rolf Hinze, 1991.
Hinze, Rolf. *East Front Drama 1944. The Withdrawal Battle of Army Group Centre*. Winnipeg: J.J. Fedorowicz, 1996.
Hoffmann, Joachim. *Die Geschichte Der Wlassow-Armee*. Frieburg: Rombach Verlag, 1986.
Hoffmann, Joachim. *Deutsche und Kalmyken 1942 bis 1945*. Frieburg: Rombach Verlag, 1986.
Hoffmann, Joachim. *Die Ostlegionen 1941–1943*. Frieburg: Rombach Verlag, 1986.
Hoffmann, Joachim. *Kaukasien 1942/43. Das deutsche Heer und die Orientvölker der Sowjetunion*. Frieburg: Rombach Verlag, 1991.
Hogan, David J. (ed.) *The Holocaust Chronicle: A History in Words and Pictures*. Lincolnwood: Publications International Ltd, 2002.
Höhne, Heinz. *Der Orden unter dem Totenkopf. Die Geschichte der SS*. Frankfurt am Main: Fischer Bücherei, 1969.
Höhne, Heinz. *The Order of the Death's Head. The Story of Hitler's SS*. New York: Coward McCann, Inc., 1970.
Höttl, Wilhelm. *The Secret Front: The Story of Nazi Political Espionage*. New York: Praeger, 1954.
Howell, Edgar M. et al. *The Soviet Partisan Movement 1941–1944*. Washington DC: Centre of Military History, US Army, 1956.
Hull, Isabel V. *Absolute Destruction: Military Culture and the Practices of War in Imperial Germany*. Ithaca: Cornell University Press, 2005.
Huxley-Blythe, Peter J. *The East Came West*. Caldwell: Caxton Printers Ltd, 1968.
Ignatov, P.K. *Partisans of the Kuban*. New York: Hutchinson & Co., 1944.
Ioanid, Radu. *The Holocaust in Romania: The Destruction of Jews and Gypsies under the Antonescu Regime, 1940–1944*. Chicago: Ivan R. Dee, 2008.
Jackson, Robert H. *Tyranny on Trial: The Evidence at Nuremberg*. Dallas: Southern Methodist University Press, 1954.
Jörgensen, Christer. *Hitler's Espionage Machine: The True Story Behind One of the World's Most Ruthless Spy Networks*. Guilford: Lyons Press, 2004.
Jurado, Carlos Caballero. *Rompiendo Las Cadenas: La Division Ucraniana De Las Waffen-SS*. Granada: Garcia Hispan, 1992.

Jurado, Carlos Caballero. *Commandos En El Caucaso: La Unidad Especial Bergmann, Voluntarios Caucasianos En El Ejercito Aleman, 1941–45*. Granada: Garcia Hispan, 1995.

Jurado, Carlos Caballero. *Breaking the Chains. 14. Waffen Grenadier Division der SS and Other Ukrainian Volunteer Formations, Eastern front, 1942–1945*. London: Shelf Books, 1998.

Jurado, Carlos Caballero and Thomas, Nigel. *Germany's Eastern Front Allies (2) Baltic Forces*. London: Osprey Men-at-Arms Series, Osprey Publishing, 2002.

Jurs, August (ed.) *Estonian Freedom Fighters in World War II*. Printed with a grant from the 'New Horizons Program'. Onatrio: Vôitleja Relief Foundation, n.d.

Kamenetsky, Ihor. *Hitler's Occupation of Ukraine (1941–1944). A Study of Totalitarian Imperialism*. Milwaukee: Marquette University Press, 1956.

Kampe, Norbert, Schleffler, Wolfgang and Schoenberger, Gerhard (eds). *Die Einsatzgruppen in der besetzten Sowjetunion 1941/42. Die Tätigkeits und Lageberichte des Chefs der Sicherheitspolizei und des SD*. Berlin: Edition Hentrich, 1997.

Karashuk, A. (ed.) *Russkiya Osvobodetelnya Armia 1939–1945* (Russian Liberation Army, 1939–1945). Moscow: Act Publishers, 1999.

Keegan, John. *The Second World War*. Toronto: Key Porter Books, 1989.

Keilig, Wolf. *Rangliste Des Deutschen Heeres 1944/45*. Friedberg: Podzun Pallas Verlag, n.d.

Kershaw, Ian. *Fateful Choices: Ten Decisions That Changed the World, 1940–1941*. New York: Penguin Press, 2007.

Kirchubel, Robert. *Operation Barbarossa 1941: Army Group South*. Westport: Praeger Illustrated Military History Series, 2004.

Kirchubel, Robert. *Hitler's Panzer Armies on the Eastern Front*. London: Pen & Sword, 2009.

Klausch, Hans Peter. *Antifaschisten in SS-Uniform*. Bremen: Edition Temmen, 1993.

Klee, Ernst, Dressen, Willi and Riess, Volker. *The Good Old Days*. Old Saybrook: Konecky & Konecky, 1991.

Kleitmann, Dr K.G. *Die Waffen SS: eine Dokumentation*. Osnabrück: Verlag 'Der Freiwillige' GmbH, 1965.

Kliment, Charles and Nakladal, Bretislav. *Germany's First Ally: Armed Forces of the Slovak State 1939–1945*. Atglen: Schiffer Publishing Ltd, 1997.

Knopp, Guido. *Die Wehrmacht – Eine Bilanz*. Munich: Wilhelm Goldmann Verlag, 2009.

Kohl, Paul. *Der Krieg der deutschen Wehrmacht und der Polizei 1941–1944*. Frankfurt am Main: Fischer Taschenbuch Verlag, 1995.

Krätschmer, Ernst-Günther. *Die Ritterkreuzträger der Waffen-SS*. Preussich Oldendorf: Verlag K.W. Schütz KG, 1955.

Krausnick, Helmut. *Hitlers Einsatzgruppen. Die Truppen des Weltanschauungskrieges 1938–1942*. Frankfurt am Main: Fischer Taschenbuch Verlag, 1985.

Krausnick, Helmut (ed.) *Anatomy of the SS State*. New York: Walker & Co., 1965.

Künrich, Heinz. *Der Partisanenkrieg in Europa 1939–1945*. Berlin: Dietz Verlag, 1968.

Kurowski, Franz. *Deadlock before Moscow: Army Group Centre 1942–1943*. Atglen: Schiffer Publishers, 1992.

Kurowski, Franz. *The Brandenburgers – Global Mission*. Winnipeg: J.J. Fedorowicz Publishing, 1997.

Kurowski, Franz. *The Brandenburger Commandos: Germany's Elite Warrior Spies in WWII*. Mechanicsburg: Stackpole Books, 2005.

Kursietis, Andris J. *The Fallen Generals: The Destruction of the German Officer Corps in World War II and Its Aftermath*. Osceola: Ark Publications Co., 1994.

Kursietis, Andris J. *The Wehrmacht at War 1939–1945. The Units and Commanders of the German Ground Forces during World War II*. Soesterberg: Aspekt, 1999.

Laar, Mart, *War in the Woods: Estonia's Struggle for Survival, 1944–1956*. Washington DC: Compass Press, 1992.

Landwehr, Richard. *Fighting for Freedom: The Ukrainian Volunteer Division of the Waffen SS*. Silver Spring: Bibliophile Legion Books, 1985.

Laqueur, Walter. *The Holocaust Encyclopedia*. New Haven: Yale University Press, 2001.

Laub, Thomas J. *After the Fall: German Policy in Occupied France, 1940–1944*. New York: Oxford University Press, 2010.

Leide, Henry. *NS-Verbrecher und Staatssicherheit: Die geheime Vergangenheitspolitik der DDR*. Göttingen: Vandenhoeck and Ruprecht GmbH and Co., 2007.

Lemkin, Raphael. *Axis Rule in Occupied Europe: Laws of Occupation, Analysis of Government. Proposals for Redress*. Washington DC: Carnegie Endowment for International Peace, 1944.

Le Tissier, Tony. *Zhukov at the Oder: The Decisive Battle for Berlin*. Westport: Praeger Publishing, 1996.

Le Tissier, Tony. *The Battle of Berlin 1945*. New York: St Martins Press, 1988.

Leumi, Vaad (ed.) *The Black Book: The Nazi Crime Against the Jewish People*. New York: The Jewish Black Book Committee, 1946.

Lichtenstein, Heiner. *Himmlers grüne Helfer: Die Schutz-und-Ordnungspolizei im Dritten Reichs*. Bund Verlag: Berlin, 1996.

Lieb, Peter. *Konventioneller Krieg oder NS-Weltanschauungskrieg? Kriegfürung und Partisanenbekämpfung in FrankReichs 1943/44*. Munich: R. Oldenbourg Verlag, 2007.

Lieb Peter: 'Täter aus Überzeugung? Oberst Carl von Andrian und die Judenmorde der 707. Infanteriedivision 1941/42', in Hartmann/Hürter/Lieb/Pohl, *Der deutsche Krieg im Osten 1941–1944*. Oldenbourg: De Gruyter, 2009.

Linck, Stephan. *Der Ordnung verpflichtet: Deutsche Polizei 1933–1949*. Paderborn: Ferdinand Schöningh Verlag, 2000.

Littlejohn, David. *The Patriotic Traitors: The History of Collaboration in German Occupied Europe, 1940–45*. Garden City: Doubleday & Co., 1972.

Littlejohn, David. *Foreign Legions of the Third Reichs, Vol. IV – Poland, Ukraine, Bulgaria, Rumania, Free India, Estonia, Latvia, Lithuania, Finland and Russia*. San Jose: R. James Bender Publishing, 1987.

Littman, Sol. *Pure Soldiers or Sinister Legion: The Ukrainian 14th Waffen-SS Division*. Montreal: Black Rose Books, 2003.

Loftus, John. *The Belarus Secret*. New York: Alfred A. Knopf, 1982.

Logusz, Michael O. *Galicia Division: The Waffen SS 14th Grenadier Division 1943–1945*. Atglen: Schiffer Publishing Ltd, 1997.

Longhardt-Söntgen, Rainer. *Partisanen, Spione und Banditen: Abwehrtätigkeit in Oberitalien 1943–1945*. Neckargemünd: Kurt Vowinckel Verlag, 1961.

Lower, Wendy. *Nazi Empire-Building and the Holocaust in Ukraine*. Chapel Hill: University of North Carolina Press, 2005.

Lower, Wendy and Ray Brandon (eds). *The Shoah in Ukraine: History, Testimony, Memorialization*. Bloomington: Indiana University Press, 2008.

Lukas, Richard C. *The Forgotten Holocaust: The Poles under German Occupation 1939–1944*. Lexington: University Press of Kentucky, 1986.

Lumans, Valdis O. *Himmler's Auxiliaries: The Volksdeutsche Mittelstelle and the German National Minorities of Europe, 1933–1945*. Chapel Hill: University of North Carolina Press, 1993.

MacLean, French L. *The Cruel Hunters. SS Sonderkommando Dirlewanger. Hitler's Most Notorious Anti-Partisan Unit*. Atglen: Schiffer Publishers, 1998.

MacLean, French L. *The Field Men. The SS Officers Who Led the Einsatzkommandos – the Nazi Mobile Killing Units*. Atglen: Schiffer Publishers, 1999.

MacLean, French L. *The Camp Men: The SS Officers Who Ran the Nazi Concentration Camp System*. Atglen: Schiffer Military History, 1999.

Mallmann, Klaus-Michael, Rieb, Volker and Pyta, Wolfram. *Deutscher Osten 1939–1945: Der Weltanschauungskrieg in Photos und Texten*. Darmstadt: Wissenschaftliche Buchgesellschaft, 2003.

Malthäus, Jürgen. *War, Pacification, and Mass Murder, 1939: The Einsatzgruppen in Poland*. Lanham: Rowman & Littlefield, 2014.

Manoschek, Walter. *Die Wehrmacht Im Rassenkrieg: Der Vernichtungskrieg Hinter der Front*. Vienna: Picus Verlag, 1996.

Mayer, Hermann Frank. *Blutiges Edelweib: die 1. Gebirgsdivision im Zweiten Weltkrieg*. Berlin: Christoph Links Verlag GmbH, 2008.

Megargee, Geoffrey P. *War of Annihilation: Combat and Genocide on the Eastern Front, 1941*. New York: Rowman & Littlefield, 2006.

Mehner, Kurt. *Die Geheimen Tagesberichte Der Deutschen Wehrmachtführung Im Zweiten Weltkrieg 1939–1945*. Biblio Verlag: Osnabrück, 12 vol., 1989–1994.

Mehner, Kurt. *Die Waffen-SS und Polizei 1939–1945*. Norderstedt: Militair-Verlag Klaus D. Patzwall, 1995.

Mendelsohn, John (ed.) *The Holocaust. Selected Documents in Eighteen Volumes*. New York: Garland Publishing, 1982, 18 vols.

Mendelsohn, John (ed.) *Covert Warfare: Intelligence, Counterintelligence and Military Deception during the World War II Era*, 18 vols. Vol. 13: *The Final Solution of the Abwehr*. New York: Garland Publishing, Inc., 1988.

Messenger, David A. and Paehler, Katrin (eds). *A Nazi Past: Recasting German Identity in Postwar Europe*. Lexington: University Press of Kentucky, 2015.

Messerschmidt, Manfred. *Die Wehrmachtjustiz 1933–1945*. Paderborn: Ferdinand Schöningh Verlag, 2005.

Michaelis, Rolf. *Der Weg zur 36. Waffen Grenadier Division der SS*. Rodgau: Verlag fuer Militaerhistorische Zeitgeschichte, 1991.

Michaelis, Rolf. *Die Russische Volksbefreiungsarmee 'RONA' 1941–1944*. Erlangen: Selbstspubliziert, 1992.

Michaelis, Rolf. *Die Kavallerie Divisionen der Waffen SS*. Erlangen: Selbstpubliziert, 1993.

Michaelis, Rolf. *Ukrainer in der Waffen SS: Die 14. Waffen Grenadier Division der SS (ukrainische Nr. 1). Berlin: Michaelis Verlag, 2000.*

Michaelis, Rolf. *Russen in der Waffen SS*. Berlin: Michaelis Verlag, 2002.

Miller, Norbert. *Deutsche Besatzungspolitik in der UdSSR 1941–1944*. Köln: Pahl-Rugenstein, 1980.

Milton, Sybil, transl. *The Stroop Report*. New York: Pantheon Books, 1979.

Mitcham, Samuel W. *Hitler's Legions: the German Army Order of Battle, World War II*. New York: Dorset Press, 1985.

Mitcham, Samuel W. *Crumbling Empire: The German Defeat in the East, 1944*. Westport: Praeger Publishers, 2001.

Mitcham, Samuel W. *German Order of Battle, Vol. One: 1st–290th Infantry Divisions in WWII*. Mechanicsburg: Stackpole Books, 2007.

Mollo, Andrew. *Uniforms of the SS. Volume 5: Sicherheitsdienst und Sicherheitspolizei 1931–1945*. London: Windrow & Greene, 1992.

Müller, Norbert. *Deutsche Besatzungspolitik in der UdSSR 1941–1944*. Köln: Pahl-Rugenstein Verlag, 1980.

Müller, Rolf-Dieter and Ueberschaer, Gerd R. *Hitler's War in the East 1941–1945. A Critical Assessment*. Providence: Berghahn Books, 1997.

Müller, Rolf-Dieter, and Volkmann, Hans Erik. *Die Wehrmacht: Mythos und Realität*. Oldenbourg: Wissenschaftsverlag, 1999.

Mulligan, Patrick Timothy. *The Politics of Illusion and Empire. German Occupation Policy in the Soviet Union, 1942–1943*. New York: Praeger Publishers, 1988.
Muñoz, Antonio. *Forgotten Legions: Obscure Combat Formations of the Waffen SS, 1943–1945*. Boulder: Paladin Press, 1991.
Muñoz, Antonio. *Forgotten Legions Companion Booklet*. New York: Europa Books, 1995.
Muñoz, Antonio. *Hitler's Eastern Legions, Vol. I – The Baltic Schutzmannschaft 1941–1945*. New York: Europa Books, 1996.
Muñoz, Antonio. *The Kaminski Brigade: A History, 1941–1945*. New York: Europa Books, 1996.
Muñoz, Antonio. *For Croatia and Christ: The Croatian Army in World War II, 1941–1945*. New York: Europa Books, 1996.
Muñoz, Antonio. *Hitler's Eastern Legions, Vol. II – The Osttruppen*. New York: Europa Books, 1997.
Muñoz, Antonio (ed.) *The German Police*. Supreme Allied Headquarters, G-2 Section, prepared jointly with British MI-14(d). Washington DC: US Army War Office, April 1945. Reprinted in rev. and exp. format. New York: Europa Books, 1997.
Muñoz, Antonio. *The last Levy: Waffen SS Officer Roster, March 1st 1945*. New York: Europa Books, 2000.
Muñoz, Antonio. *The Druzhina SS Brigade: A History, 1941–1943*. New York: Europa Books, 2000.
Muñoz, Antonio (ed.) *The East Came West: Muslim, Hindu, and Buddhist Volunteers in the German Armed Forces, 1941–1945*. New York: Europa Books, 2002.
Muñoz, Antonio. *Göring's Grenadiers: The Luftwaffe Field Divisions 1942–1945*. New York: Europa Books, 2002.
Muñoz, Antonio. *The Kaminski Brigade: A History, 1941–1945*. New York: Europa Books, 2003, 2nd rev. and exp. edn.
Nafziger, George F. *The German Order of Battle. Waffen SS and Other Units in World War II*. Conshohocken: Combined Publishing, 2001.
Neufeldt, H.-J., Huck, J. and Tessin, Georg. *Zur Geschichte der Ordnungspolizei: Die Stabe und Truppeneinheiten der Ordnungspolizei, 1936–1945*. Koblenz: Als Manuskript gedruckt. Bundesarchiv, 1957.
Neulen, Hans Werner. *An Deutscher Seite: Internationale Freiwillige von Wehrmacht und Waffen SS*. München: Universitas Verlag, 1985.
Newland, Samuel J. *Cossacks in the German Army, 1941–1945*. London: Frank Cass & Co. Ltd, 1991.
Newton, Steven H. *German Battle Tactics on the Russian Front*. Atglen: Schiffer Publishing, 1994.
Newton, Steven H. *Retreat from Leningrad. Army Group North, 1944/1945*. Atglen: Schiffer Publishing, 1995.
Niehorster, Leo W.G. *The Royal Hungarian Army, 1920–1945*. New York: Europa Books, 1998.
Niepold, Gerd. *Battle for White Russia: The Destruction of Army Group Centre June 1944*. New York: Brassey's Defence Publishers, 1987.
Nirenstein, Albert. *A Tower from the Enemy: Contributions to a History of Jewish Resistance in Poland*. New York: Orion Press, 1959.
Overmans, Rüdiger. *Deutsche militärische Verluste im Zweiten Weltkrieg*. München: R. Oldenbourg Verlag, 1999.
Overy, Richard. *Russia's War: A History of the Soviet War Effort, 1941–1945*. New York: Penguin Putnam Inc., 1998.
Padfield, Peter. *Himmler*. New York: Henry Holt & Co., 1990.
Perro, Oskars. *Fortress Cholm*. Toronto: Kurland Publishing, 1981.
Person, Katarzyna. *Warsaw Ghetto Police: The Jewish Order Service during the Nazi Occupation*. Ithaca: Cornell University Press, 2021.

Piotrowski, Tadeusz. *Poland's Holocaust: Ethnic Strife, Collaboration with Occupying Forces and Genocide in the Second Republic, 1918–1947*. Jefferson: MacFarland & Co., 1998.

Pohl, Dieter et al., *Der deutsche Krieg im Osten 1941–1944*. Munich: De Gruytyer, 2009.

Pohl, Otto J. *Ethnic Cleansing in the USSR, 1937–1949*. Westport: Greenwood Press, 1999.

Poirier, Robert G. and Conner, Albert Z. *The Red Army Order of Battle in the Great Patriotic War*. Novato: Presidio Press, 1985.

Porter, Jack Nusan (ed.) *Jewish Partisans: A Documentary of Jewish Resistance in the Soviet Union During World War II*. Washington DC: University Press of America, 1982.

Pottgeiser, Hans. *Die Reichsbahn in Ostfeldzug*. Neckargemünd: Kurt Vowinckel Verlag, 1960.

Präg, Werner and Jacobson, Wolfgang. *Das Dienstagebuch des deutschen Generalgouverneurs in Polen 1939–1945*. Stuttgart: Deutsche Verlag Anstalt, 1975.

Prechtl, G.M. *Unsere Ehre Heisst Treue: Kriegstagebuch des Kommandostabes Reichsführer SS; Tätigkeitsberichte der 1. und 2. SS Infanterie-Brigade und von Sonderkommandos der SS*. Zürich: Europa Verlag, 1965.

Preradovich, Nikolaus von. *Die Generale der Waffen-SS*. Berg Am See: Kurt Vowinckel Verlag, 1985.

Ramme, Alwin. *Der Sicherheitsdienst Der SS*. Berlin: Deutscher Militärverlag der DDR, 1970.

Ready, J. Lee. *The Forgotten Axis: Germany's Partners and Foreign Volunteers in World War II*. Jefferson: MacFarland & Co., 1987.

Redcliffe, Alexander. *Lessons Learned from the Partisan War in Russia*. MS No. P055C, Washington DC: Office of the Chief of Military History, Department of the Army, 1947.

Redelis, Valdis. *Partisanenkrieg: Entstehung und Bekämpfung der Partisanen und Untergrundbewegung im Mittelabschnitt der Ostfront 1941 bis 1943*. Heidelberg: Scharnhorst Buchkameradenschaft, 1958.

Regenberg, Werner. *Panzerfahrzeuge und Panzereinheiten der Ordnungspolizei 1936–1945*. Friedberg: Podzun Pallas Verlag, 1996.

Regenberg, Werner. *Armored Vehicles and Units of the German Order Police (Ordnungspolizei) 1936–1945*. Atglen: Schiffer Military History, 2002.

Reinicke, Adolf. *Die 5. Jäger-Division 1939–1945*. Friedberg: Podzun Pallas Verlag GmbH, n.d.

Reitlinger, Gerald. *The SS, Alibi of a Nation, 1922–1945*. London: William Heinemann Ltd, 1956.

Reitlinger, Gerald. *The House Built on Sand: The Conflicts of German Policy in Russia, 1939–1945*. New York: Viking Press, 1960.

Reitlinger, Gerald. *The Final Solution. The Attempt to Exterminate the Jews of Europe 1939–1945*. South Brunswick: Thomas Yoseloff, 1961.

Richter, Hans. *Einsatz der Polizei bei den Polizei Bataillonen im Ost, Nord, und West*. Berlin: Zentralverlag der NSDAP, 1943.

Romanko, Oleg and Antonio Muñoz. *Hitler's White Russians: Collaboration, Extermination and Anti-Partisan Warfare in White Russia, 1941–1944*. New York: Europa Books, 2002.

Rossino, Alexander B. *Hitler Strikes Poland: Blitzkrieg, Ideology, and Atrocity* (Modern War Studies) Lawrence: University Press of Kansas, 2003.

Rürup, Dr Reinhard and Jahn, Dr Peter (eds). *Der Krieg gegen die Sowjetunion 1941–1945*. Berlin: Berliner Festspiele GmbH, 1991.

Ryan, Cornelius. *The Last Battle*. New York: Simon & Schuster, 1966.

Scheibert, Horst. *Die Träger Der Deutschen Kreuzes In Gold: Kriegsmarine, Luftwaffe, Waffen SS*. Friedberg: Podzun Pallas Verlag, n.d.

Scheibert, Horst. *Die Träger Der Ehrenblattspange Des Heeres Und Der Waffen SS*. Friedberg: Podzun Pallas Verlag, 1986.

Schellenberg, Walter. *The Labyrinth. The Memoirs of Hitler's Secret Service Chief*. New York: Harper & Brothers, 1956.

Schmitz, Peter and Thies, Klaus-Jürgen. *Die Truppenkennzeichen der Verbände und Einheiten der Deutschen Wehrmacht und Waffen SS und ihre Einsätze im Zweiten Weltkrieg 1939–1945*. Osnabrück: Biblio Verlag, 1987-1994. 4 vols.

Schneider, Jost W. *Verleihung Genehmigt! Eine Bild und Dokumentargeschichte Der Ritterkreuzträger Der Waffen SS und Polizei 1940–1945*. San Jose: R. James Bender Publishing, 1993.

Schülte, Theo. *The German Army and Nazi Policies In Occupied Russia 1941–1944*. New York: Berg Publishers, 1989.

Schumann, Wolfgang and Ludwig Nestler. *Nacht über Europa: Band II: Die faschistische Okkupationspolitik in Polen (1939–1945). Köln: Pahl-Rugenstein Verlag GmbH, 1989.*

Schuster, Peter and Tiede, Harald. *Die Uniformen und Abzeichen der Kosaken in der Deutschen Wehrmacht*. Norderstedt: Verlag Klaus D. Patzwall, 1999.

Seaton, Albert. *The Russo-German War 1941–45*. New York: Praeger Publishers, 1970.

Seewald, Dr Heinrich. *Das toenende Erz: Deutsche Propaganda gegen die Rote Armee im Zweiten Weltkrieg*. Stuttgart: Seewald Verlag, 1978.

Seidler, Franz W. *Deutscher Volkssturm: Das letzte Aufgebot, 1944–1945*. München: F.A. Herbig Verlag, 1989.

Seidler, Franz W. *Die Militaergerichtsbarfeit der Deutschen Wehrmacht 1939–1945*. Munich: Herbig Verlag, 1991.

Seidler, Franz W. *Die Kollaboration 1939–1945*. München: F.A. Herbig Verlagsbuchhandlung, 1995.

Silgailis, Arthur. *Latvian Legion*. San Jose: R. James Bender Publishing, 1986.

Snyder, Timothy. *Into the Bloodlands: Europe Between Hitler and Stalin*. New York: Basic Books, 2022.

Steenberg, Sven. *Vlasov*. New York: Alfred A. Knopf, 1970.

Stein, George H. *The Waffen SS: Hitler's Elite Guard at War 1939–1945*. Ithaca: Cornell University Press, 1966.

Stöber, Hans. *Die Flugabwehrverbände der Waffen SS*. Preussiche Oldendorf: Verlag K.W. Schütz KG, 1984.

Stöber, Hans. *Die 22. Panzer Division; 25. Panzer Division; 27. Panzer Division; und die 233. Reserve Panzer Division*. Friedberg: Podzun Pallas Verlag, 1985.

Stockhorst, Erich. *5000 Köpfe: Wer War Was Im Dritten Reich*. Kiel: Arndt Verlag, 2000.

Stoves, Rolf. *Die Gepanzerten und Motorizierten Deutschen Grossverbände 1935–1945*. Friedberg: Podzun Pallas Verlag, 1986.

Strik-Strikfeldt, Wilfried. *Against Stalin and Hitler. Memoir of the Russian Liberation Movement 1941–1945*. New York: John Day Co., 1973.

Tec, Nechama. *The Bielski Partisans*. Oxford: Oxford University Press, 1993.

Tessin, Georg. *Verbände und Truppen der deutschen Wehrmacht und Waffen SS, 1939–1945*. Osnabrück: Biblio Verlag, 1975–2002, 18 vols.

Tessin, Georg, with Neufeldt, H.J. and Huck, J. *Zur Geschichte der Ordnungspolizei, 1936–1945*. Koblenz: Bundesarchiv, 1956.

Tessin, Georg, Kannapin, Norbert and Meyer, Brün. *Waffen-SS und Ordnungspolizei im Kriegseinsatz 1939–1945*. Biblio Verlag: Osnabruck, 2000.

Thomas, Nigel et al. *Partisan Warfare 1941–45*. London: Reed International Books Ltd, 1983.

Thomas, Nigel and Caballero Jurado, Carlos. *Wehrmacht Auxiliary Forces*. London: Osprey Publishing, 1992.

Thorwald, Juergen. *The Illusion: Soviet Soldiers in Hitler's Armies*. Harcourt Brace Jovanovich, 1975.

Thurston, Robert W. and Bonwetsch, Bernd (eds). *The People's War: Responses to World War II in the Soviet Union*. New York: University of Illinois Press: Urbana, 2000.

Tieke, Wilhelm. *Das Ende Zwischen Oder Und Elbe: Der Kampf Um Berlin 1945*. Stuttgart: Motorbuch Verlag, 1994.

Tolstoy, Nikolai. *The Secret Betrayal 1944–1947*. New York: Charles Scribner's Sons, 1977.

Tys-Krokhmaliuk, Yuriy. *UPA Warfare in Ukraine: The Ukrainian Insurgent Army*. New York: Vantage Press, 1972.

Ullrich, Sebastian. *Der Weimar-Komplex. Das Scheitern der ersten deutschen Demokratie und die politische Kultur der frühen Bundesrepublik 1945–1959*. Göttingen: Wallstein Verlag, 2009.

Vakar, Nicholas P. *Belarusia: The Making of a Nation: A Case Study*. Cambridge: Harvard University Press, 1956.

Vizetelly, Frank H. (ed.) *Funk and Wagnall's New Standard Encyclopedia of Universal Knowledge*. New York: Funk & Wagnall's Company, 1931. Vol. 25.

Wegner, Bernd. *The Waffen-SS: Organization, Ideology and Function*. Oxford: Basil Blackwell, 1990.

Werbizky, George G. *Ostarbeiters: Belarusian, Russian and Ukrainian Forced Laborers in Nazi Germany – World War II*. Endwell: Self Published, 2002.

Westermann, Edward B. *Hitler's Police Battalions: Enforcing Racial War in the East*. Lawrence: University Press of Kansas.

Westwood, David. *The Waffen SS: Higher formations, Divisions, Brigades 1939–1945*. Derbyshire: Privately Published, n.d.

Wette, Wolfram. *The Wehrmacht: History, Myth, Reality*. Cambridge: Harvard University Press, 2007.

Wicziok, Wilhelm. *Die Armee Der Gerichteten. Zur besonderen Verwendung – Bewaehrungsbataillon 500*. Essen: Heitz & Hoeffkes Verlag, 1992.

Wilhelm, Hans-Heinrich. *Die Einsatzgruppe A: der Sicherheitspolizei und des SD 1941/42*. Frankfurt am Main: Peter Lang Verlag GmbH, 1996.

Witte, Hans Joachim and Peter Offermann. *Die Boeselagerschen Reiter: Das Kavallerie-Regiment Mitte die aus ihm hervorgegangene 3. Kavallerie-Brigade/Division*. München: Schild Verlag, 1998.

Witter, Robert E. *Chain Dogs: The German Army Military Police of World War II*. Missoula: Pictorial Histories Publishing Co., 1994.

Yelton, David K. *Hitler's Volkssturm: The Nazi Militia and the Fall of Germany, 1944–1945*. Lawrence: University Press of Kansas, 2002.

Yerger, Mark C. *Riding East. The SS Cavalry Brigade in Poland and Russia 1939–1942*. Atglen: Schiffer Publishers, 1996.

Yerger, Mark C. *Allgemeine SS*. Atglen: Schiffer Military Publishing, 1997.

Yerger, Mark C. *Waffen SS Commanders: Augsberger to Kreutz*. Atglen: Schiffer Military Publishing, 1997.

Yerger, Mark C. *Waffen SS Commanders: Krüger to Zimmermann*. Atglen: Schiffer Military Publishing, 1999.

Zaloga, Steven. *Bagration 1944: The Destruction of Army Group Centre*. London: Osprey Military, 1996.

Zawodny, J.K. *Nothing But Honor: The Story of the Warsaw Uprising, 1944*. Hoover Institution Press, 1978.

Ziemke, Earl F. and Bauer, Magna E. *Moscow to Stalingrad: Decision in the East*. Washington DC: Centre of Military History, US Army, 1987.

Index

Persons

German Formations

Anti-Partisan Operational Codenames

Nazi Organizations

Police Formations and Commands

SS Formations and Commands

SS Murder Commandos

Secret Field Police Units (GFP)

Wehrmacht Units and Commands

Other Eastern Formations

Baltic Volunteer Formations – Lithuanian

Baltic Volunteer Formations – Estonians

Baltic Volunteer Formations – Latvians

Belarusian Collaborationist Formations

Ukrainian Volunteer Formations

Special Russian Volunteer Brigades

Axis Allied Units

Russian Formations

Russian Army

Partisan Formations